Building Synergy for High-Impact Educational Initiat

First-Year Seminars and Learning Communities

EDITORS
Lauren Chism Schmidt
Janine Graziano

Cite as:

Chism Schmidt, L., & Graziano, J. (Eds.). (2016). *Building synergy for high-impact educational initiatives: First-year seminars and learning communities*. Columbia, SC: University of South Carolina, National Resource Center for The First-Year Experience & Students in Transition.

ISBN: 978-1-889271-98-9

Published by:
National Resource Center for The First-Year Experience® and Students in Transition
University of South Carolina
1728 College Street, Columbia, SC 29208
www.sc.edu/fye

Production Staff for the National Resource Center:
Project Manager: Tracy L. Skipper, Assistant Director for Publications
Design and Production: Allison Minsk, Graphic Artist
External Reviewers: Juan Huerta, Director University Core Curriculum
Programs, Texas A&M University – Corpus Christi
Emily Lardner, Director, Washington Center for the
Improvement of Undergraduate Education
Karen L. Weathermon, Director, Learning
Communities/Freshman Focus, Washington
State University

Library of Congress Cataloging-in-Publication Data

Names: Schmidt, Lauren Chism, editor. | Graziano, Janine, editor. |
National Resource Center for the First-Year Experience & Students in Transition
  (University of South Carolina)
Title: Building synergy for high-impact educational initiatives : first-year seminars and learning
communities / edited by Lauren Chism Schmidt and Janine Graziano, editors.
Description: Columbia, SC : National Resource Center for the First-Year
  Experience & Students in Transition, 2016. | Includes index.
Identifiers: LCCN 2015025072 | ISBN 9781889271989
Subjects: LCSH: College teaching--Methodology. | College freshmen. |
  Seminars. | Professional learning communities. | College
  teaching--Methodology--Case studies. | College freshmen--Case studies. |
  Seminars--Case studies. | Professional learning communities--Case studies.
Classification: LCC LB2331 .B793 2016 | DDC 378.1/25--dc23
LC record available at http://lccn.loc.gov/2015025072

About the Publishers

National Resource Center for The First-Year Experience and Students in Transition

The National Resource Center for The First-Year Experience and Students in Transition was born out of the success of University of South Carolina's much-honored University 101 course and a series of annual conferences focused on the freshman year experience. The momentum created by the educators attending these early conferences paved the way for the development of the National Resource Center, which was established at the University of South Carolina in 1986. As the National Resource Center broadened its focus to include other significant student transitions in higher education, it underwent several name changes, adopting the National Resource Center for The First-Year Experience and Students in Transition in 1998.

Today, the Center collaborates with its institutional partner, University 101 Programs, in pursuit of its mission to advance and support efforts to improve student learning and transitions into and through higher education. We achieve this mission by providing opportunities for the exchange of practical and scholarly information as well as the discussion of trends and issues in our field through convening conferences and other professional development events such as institutes, workshops, and online learning opportunities; publishing scholarly practice books, research reports, a peer-reviewed journal, electronic newsletters, and guides; generating, supporting, and disseminating research and scholarship; hosting visiting scholars; and maintaining several online channels for resource sharing and communication, including a dynamic website, listservs, and social media outlets.

The National Resource Center serves as the trusted expert, internationally recognized leader, and clearinghouse for scholarship, policy, and best practice for all postsecondary student transitions.

Institutional Home

The National Resource Center is located at the University of South Carolina's (UofSC) flagship campus in Columbia. Chartered in 1801, the

University's mission is twofold: (a) to establish and maintain excellence in its student population, faculty, academic programs, living and learning environment, technological infrastructure, library resources, research and scholarship, public and private support, and endowment; and (b) to enhance the industrial, economic, and cultural potential of the state. UofSC offers 324 degree programs through its 14 degree-granting colleges and schools. Students have been awarded more than $16.7 million for national scholarships and fellowships since 1994. In fiscal year 2013, faculty generated $220 million in funding for research, outreach and training programs. UofSC is one of only 63 public universities listed by the Carnegie Foundation in the highest tier of research institutions in the United States.

Washington Center for Improving Undergraduate Education

The Washington Center for Improving Undergraduate Education, a public service center of The Evergreen State College, is a statewide resource for two- and four-year higher education institutions with a national reach and a sustained record of educational reform.

We focus on

- helping campus teams develop sustainable, high-quality learning community programs that engage and support learners at critical points in their educational pathways;

- collaborating with campuses to insure that their learning community programs are in sync with other campus reform efforts and student success initiatives;

- providing high-quality, professional development workshops focused on effective teaching, on campuses and at state and national gatherings;

- working with statewide and regional consortia to provide curriculum planning retreats aimed at strengthening classroom and institutional practices;

- collaborating with other professional organizations to provide technical assistance and coaching for national educational reform projects; and

- expanding connections between campuses and communities through projects like Curriculum for the Bioregion.

As the National Resource Center for Learning Communities, the Washington Center organizes the National Summer Institute on Learning Communities; publishes *Learning Community Research and Practice*, a biannual, open-access peer-reviewed electronic journal; supports the development of statewide and regional learning community networks; offers an online integrative learning library; and hosts the learning community directory and the LEARNCOM listserv.

Contents

Tables and Figures ix
Foreword xi
Tracy L. Skipper

Introduction...xv
Janine Graziano and Lauren Chism Schmidt

Part I: Rationale for and Implementation of Combined Programs

Chapter 1.. 3
The Case for Connecting First-Year Seminars and Learning Communities
Ashley Finley and George D. Kuh

Chapter 2.. 19
National Practices for Combining First-Year Seminars and Learning Communities
Jean M. Henscheid, Tracy L. Skipper, and Dallin G. Young

Chapter 3.. 41
Administering Combined First-Year Seminar and Learning Community Programs
Nia Haydel and Liya Escalera

Chapter 4.. 61
Teaching in Combined Programs
Lisa Dresdner and Ruthanna Spiers

Chapter 5.. 83
What Should We Be Assessing and Why?
Michele J. Hansen and Maureen A. Pettitt

Part II: Contexts for Implementation: Models From Two- and Four-Year Institutions

Case Study 1 .... **105**
Inviting the Mother Tongue and a First-Year Seminar to Promote Success Among Spanish-Speaking ESL Students
Bronx Community College

Case Study 2 .... **115**
The Metro College Success Program: Redesigning the First Two Years of College
City College of San Francisco and San Francisco State University

Case Study 3 .... **127**
The Targeted Learning Community: A Comprehensive Approach to Promoting the Success of First-Year Students in General Chemistry
Kennesaw State University

Case Study 4 .... **139**
Common Courses: A Developing Linked Coursework Perspective
The University of South Carolina

Case Study 5 .... **151**
Need a Little TLC? Incorporating First-Year Seminars in Themed Learning Communities
Northern Illinois University

Case Study 6 .... **159**
Writing Across the Curriculum Through Community Engagement: Exploring the Foster Care System in a Thematic Living and Learning Community
Cabrini College

Case Study 7 .... **171**
Advancement via Individual Determination (AVID)
Mt. Hood Community College

Conclusion **179**
Lauren Chism Schmidt and Janine Graziano

Index **185**

About the Contributors **205**

Tables and Figures

Tables

Table 1.1   Effects of Participating in High-Impact Activities on Student Engagement 5

Table 1.2   Effects of Participating in High-Impact Activities on Deep/Integrative Learning and Gains 6

Table 2.1   Connection of Seminar to LC by Seminar Type 24

Table 2.2   LC Features by Seminar Type 25

Table C1.1   Comparative Outcomes for First-Time, First-Year ESL 03 Students 110

Table C3.1   Comparison of Pre- and Post-MSLQ Scores 133

Table C3.2   Student Feedback to Focus-Group Questions 134

Table C4.1   Common Courses Student Survey Responses, Fall 2012 Cohort 145

Table C4.2   EBI First-Year Initiative Survey Responses (Common Courses Versus Randomized Sample of All U101 Sections) 147

Table C4.3   Independent Samples t-Test for Academic Performance Differences for A&S Course Sections 147

Table C5.1   EBI Map-Works Factors and Associated Questions 154

Table C5.2   Students' Map-Works Factors by Program Type 155

Table C5.3   Students' GPA and Retention by Program Type 156

Table C7.1   Pre- and Post-Survey Comparison for AVID LC Students, Fall 2012 – Winter 2013 176

Figures

Figure 2.1   LC Characteristics When Co-enrollment in Some or All Courses Present 25

Figure 2.2   Role of FYS in LC Based on Open-Ended Responses to the 2012-2013 NSFYS 26

Figure 2.3   Characteristics of HIPs Shared by LCs and FYSs.................................. 35

Figure 4.1   Cycle of Disengaged Teaching and Learning 64

Figure 4.2   Taxonomy of Significant Learning.. 74

Figure 4.3   The Interactive Nature of Significant Learning..................................... 74

Figure C2.1   Transfer Preparedness of Metro Versus Non-Metro Students, City
              College Metro Academy of Health, 2010 and 2011 Cohorts....... 120

Figure C2.2   San Francisco State University Metro Persistence Rates as
              Compared to All Non-Metro First-Time, Full-Time First-Year
              Students 120

Figure C2.3   San Francisco State University Metro Academies of Health and
              Child Development Four-Year Graduation Rates as Compared
              All Non-Metro First-Time, Full-Time First-Year Students and
              Non-Metro Historically Underrepresented First-Year Students,
              2010 Cohort 121

Figure C2.4   Cost Comparison of Metro Versus Non-Metro Students 122

Figure C3.1   Letter Grade Distribution Among First-Year Students Enrolled in
              TLC as Compared to All Other First-Year Students Enrolled in
              General Chemistry I 132

Figure C4.1   Alignment Across Common Courses, Goals, and Assessment
              Methods 143

Figure C5.1   Map-Works Risk Factors for Withdrawal by Program
              Participation 157

Figure C7.1   First-Year Course Sequence Featuring LC and Stand-Alone Course
              Tracks 173

Figure C7.2   Retention of Developmental Reading and Writing Students in
              AVID LC Versus Stand-Alone Courses, Winter 2013 – Winter
              2015... 175

Figure C7.3   Average Pass Rates for Developmental Coursework, AVID LC
              Versus Stand-Alone Courses, Spring 2013................................ 176

Foreword

Tracy L. Skipper

First-year seminars and learning communities have followed a similar historical trajectory, tracing their origins to the late 19th and early 20th centuries and their initial prominence to calls for educational reform in the 1980s. The first courses designed to address the transition issues of new college students were offered around the turn of the 20th century at Boston University, the University of Michigan, and Oberlin College (Hunter & Linder, 2005). As colleges began to enroll an increasingly diverse and unevenly prepared population in the late 1970s and early 1980s, they sought ways to ensure students remained enrolled and succeeded. First-year seminars provided an ideal vehicle for meeting these goals.

While first-year seminars evolved from a desire to make sure new students were fit for the university, learning communities emerged from a different ethos, seeking to make sure the university was fit for the student. Current learning community models emerged in the 1980s and 1990s but trace their origins to educational reforms efforts of the 1920s and the 1960s focusing on the integration of classroom learning and real-world experiences and the social nature of learning (Goodsell Love, 1999). Like first-year seminars, learning communities helped students succeed academically and remain enrolled, yet they also responded to the educational crisis of the 1980s by making learning more relevant, offering opportunities to synthesize a fragmented curriculum, and actively engaging students in the construction of knowledge.

More recently, the recognition of first-year seminars and learning communities as high-impact educational practices—that is, educationally effective initiatives linked to increased student engagement and retention—has led to a renewed interest in these structures. Moreover, there is evidence the parallel trajectories of learning communities and first-year seminars are intersecting and merging on many campuses.

A 2012 study of student success practices at four-year institutions (Barefoot, Griffin, & Koch) found that 87% of respondents provided some type of transition seminar for their students. Of those, 96% offered a first-year seminar. Learning communities are less common—just over half of the institutions responding include these among their curricular initiatives—but most of them (90%)

provided these opportunities to first-year students. Of those offering first-year learning communities, 58% reported that a seminar was one of the courses in the learning community. It is not surprising that institutions choose to embed first-year seminars in learning communities given that the reported goals for these two initiatives bear striking resemblances to one another. Both are invested in helping students make connections to faculty and other students, improving academic performance, and increasing persistence and graduation (Barefoot et. al, 2012).

A more recent study examining student success initiatives in two-year colleges (Koch, Griffin, & Barefoot, 2014) suggested a strong, if somewhat smaller, presence for such practices at these institutions. Of those responding, 80% offered a first-year seminar and 23.3% a learning community. For institutions providing a learning community, the first-year seminar was reported as an embedded course by 33% of respondents.

This book is designed to explore the merger of these two high-impact practices. In particular, it is designed to offer some insight into how institutions connect them and the impact of those combined structures on student learning and success. In this regard, the volume is an important contribution to the high-impact practice literature. Yet, much work remains. We assume that the merger of first-year seminars and learning communities would have a synergistic effect for students, but this has not been born out consistently in the literature. Moreover, the results have not always been positive. We need additional research to determine what works, for which students, and why.

Answering such questions is complicated by the wide variation existing in learning communities and first-year seminars. For example, Visher and colleagues (2012) identified four components of learning communities (i.e., course linkages and student cohorts, faculty collaboration, curricular integration, and student support) that ranged along a continuum from basic to advanced. At a minimum, their model suggests a dozen different possibilities for learning community structures. Similarly, research by the National Resource Center for The First-Year Experience and Students in Transition over the past 25 years suggests that first-year seminars are not of a single type; rather, a seminar may fit any one of five basic definitions or a hybrid containing elements of one or more of those five. That same line of inquiry suggests that campuses frequently offer more than one type of seminar to their first-year students. Such diversity points to the challenge of mounting multi-institutional studies examining the impact of combined first-year seminar and learning community programs and may explain why such studies have been rare up to this point.

Given the diversity of these programs and the seemingly endless possibilities for combining them, well-designed single-institution studies may seem the best way forward in the short term. The present volume offers examples of assessed institutional initiatives. While the outcomes described may be limited by institutional context and program design, they do provide insight into how we might gauge the effectiveness of these interventions and what we could expect on our own campuses.

One other limitation of institutional studies to date—and of much research on first-year seminars and learning communities in general—is that they have tended to look at a narrow range of outcomes, especially those connected to academic performance and retention. The literature advocating for the inclusion of high-impact practices in the curriculum cites a range of other potential outcomes, including knowledge of human cultures and the physical and natural world, intellectual and practical skills, personal and social responsibility, and integrative and applied learning (Schneider, 2008). The cases provided here offer examples of how institutions are moving beyond traditional student success metrics to explore a broader range of outcomes.

As noted at the outset, learning communities and first-year seminars have followed similar trajectories—sometimes set on parallel tracks and other times intersecting for the benefit of the college students they are designed to serve. Similarly, the National Resource Center for The First-Year Experience and Students in Transition and the Washington Center for Improving Undergraduate Education have operated for many years on parallel but complementary tracks. Each organization has sought to provide resources, professional development opportunities, and support to educators engaged in the work of facilitating student learning and success. We are pleased to be able to come together around two educational practices—first-year seminars and learning communities, respectively—that have been a central focus of our efforts for many years. We hope this collaboration provides readers with the practical strategies necessary to create successful mergers of first-year seminars and learning communities on their own campuses. As always, we welcome your feedback on this volume.

References

Barefoot, B. O., Griffin, B. Q., & Koch, A. K. (2012). *Enhancing student success and retention throughout undergraduate education: A national survey*. Brevard, NC: John N. Gardner Institute for Excellence in Undergraduate Education.

Goodsell Love, A. (1999). What are learning communities? In J. H. Levine (Ed.), *Learning communities: New structures, new partnerships for learning* (Monograph No. 26, pp. 1-8). Columbia, SC: University of South Carolina, National Resource Center for The First-Year Experience and Students in Transition.

Hunter, M. S., & Linder, C. W. (2005). First-year seminars. In M. L. Upcraft, J. N. Gardner, & B. O. Barefoot (Eds.), *Challenging and supporting the first-year student: A handbook for improving the first year of college* (pp. 275-291). San Francisco, CA: Jossey-Bass.

Koch, S. S., Griffin, B. Q., & Barefoot, B. O. (2014). *National Survey of Student Success Initiatives at Two-Year Colleges.* Brevard, NC: John N. Gardner Institute for Excellence in Undergraduate Education.

Schneider, C. G. (2008). Liberal education and high-impact practices: Making excellence—once and for all—inclusive. In G. D. Kuh, *High-impact educational practices: What they are, who has access to them, and why they matter* (pp. 1-8). Washington, DC: Association of American Colleges and Universities.

Visher, M. G., Weiss, M. J., Weissman, E., Rudd, T., & Wathington, H. D. (2012). *The effects of learning communities for students in developmental education: A synthesis of findings from six community colleges.* New York, NY: National Center for Postsecondary Research, Teachers College, Columbia University.

Introduction

Janine Graziano and Lauren Chism Schmidt

Over the years, a number of interventions aimed at increasing student engagement and performance have been implemented in higher education. Some of these, labeled *high-impact practices* (HIPs), when done well, have led to documented evidence of student success. Two approaches that have been identified as HIPs—first-year seminars and learning communities—are often brought together into what we refer to here as *first-year seminar/learning community* (FYS/LC) programs. In this book, authors from both two- and four-year colleges and universities across the country explore the rationale for offering these combined programs, make suggestions for successfully implementing and supporting them, and provide snapshots of a variety of existing FYS/LC structures. Before examining programs that offer first-year seminars and learning communities *together,* each of these practices is considered separately.

What Are First-Year Seminars and Learning Communities?

First-year seminars have been recognized as "the most commonly implemented curricular invention designed specifically for first-year students" (Upcraft, Gardner, Barefoot, & Associates, 2005, p. 56), and, according to the 2012-2013 National Survey of First-Year Seminars (Young & Hopp, 2014), 89.7% of institutions reported having such a course. Similarly, the majority of colleges and universities report having learning community programs (Barefoot, 2002). Given the popularity of both first-year seminars and learning communities, it is not surprising that there is a great deal of variety in how these programs are conceptualized, structured, and implemented. As a result, the terms *learning community* and *first-year seminar* have each been used to refer to wide range of program types.

For example, Love (1999) noted an "explosion in the use of the term 'learning community'" (p. 1), and, as of this writing, a simple Google search produces more than 1.6 million results, including uses in K-12 and higher education, the corporate and nonprofit sectors, and elsewhere. The disparity among these groups suggests the wide range of programs that are referred to as learning communities.

Likewise, first-year seminars are defined in a number of ways. Greenfield, Keup, and Gardner (2013) noted that variety exists not only among institutions, but also on individual campuses, which often offer more than one type of seminar. In fact, at Indiana University-Purdue University Indianapolis (IUPUI), "variation among individual sections is expected and even encouraged" (IUPUI, 2010, p. 3). Seminars may be offered in an online, hybrid, or face-to-face format; they may focus on themes, professional disciplines, or career exploration; and within any of the seminar designs, the activities and assignments may differ.

Given the variety that exists among programs referred to as either first-year seminars or learning communities, for the sake of clarity and ease of discussion, both terms, as they apply to this volume, are defined below. In restricting the definitions of these terms, however, we recognize that we are excluding a number of very effective programs that may be referred to as learning communities or first-year seminars, but which are not described here because they do not fit the definitions that follow.

As defined within this book, learning communities (LCs) enroll cohorts of students in purposefully linked courses designed to promote connections between and across disciplines and beyond the classroom. The inclusion of more than one course creates the opportunity for integration of content across disciplines; therefore, this definition presupposes that students are co-enrolled in at least two courses. LCs have been targeted toward a diverse group of students including those at various points in their college careers, belonging to a particular population (e.g., ESL, honors, or sharing a common residence), in certain academic majors (e.g., biology, math), or in career programs (e.g., nursing, criminal justice), among others. While structures and instructional teams vary by institutional context (e.g., may include a residential experience, peer mentoring, tutoring, discussion groups, and a variety of other features), LCs generally are aimed at (a) fostering close connections between and among students, faculty, and staff as active participants in the learning process and (b) providing students with an integrative learning experience. In this way, they go beyond simple block scheduling of courses. Further, while LCs may be referred to as *linked courses, clusters,* or *cohort models,* these terms lack the connotation of intentional integration central to true LCs. In fact, Lardner and Malnarich (2008) argued that, "learning-community work *done well* [emphasis added] … requires a skillful balancing of two moves: one structural, the other pedagogical and cross-disciplinary. When a campus gets it right, enriched integrative learning is the result" (p. 29). And, as discussed below, the focus on integration is not only the hallmark of LCs done well; it is also a main impetus for implementing them.

A seminar, by definition, is a small discussion-based course in which students and their instructors exchange ideas and information. In this volume, a first-year seminar (FYS) is defined as a course designed to "assist students in their academic and social development and in their transition to college. In most cases, there is a strong emphasis on creating community in the classroom" (Hunter & Linder, 2005, pp. 275-276), giving them something in common with LCs. Work by the National Resource Center for The First-Year Experience and Students in Transition (Greenfield et al., 2013; Young & Hopp, 2014) has identified six types of first-year seminars:

1. **Extended orientation seminar** (sometimes called freshman orientation, college survival, college transition or student success course) where content often includes introduction to campus resources, time management, academic and career planning, learning strategies, and an introduction to student development issues;

2. **Academic seminar with uniform content across sections** may be interdisciplinary or theme-oriented, or part of a general education requirement where some attention is given to academic skills components, such as critical thinking and expository writing;

3. **Academic seminar with variable content across sections** is similar to that described in (2) above, but where topics, typically connected to the faculty member's area of interest or expertise, differ from section to section;

4. **Preprofessional or discipline-linked seminar** designed to prepare students for the demands of the major or discipline and the profession and generally taught within professional schools or specific disciplines, such as engineering, health sciences, business, or education;

5. **Basic study-skills seminar** offered for academically underprepared students and focused on basic academic skills, such as grammar, note taking, and reading texts; and

6. **Hybrid seminar**, which has elements of two or more types of seminars.

Regardless of type, however, FYSs *done well* foster academic engagement; supportive relationships with peers, faculty, and staff; and campus involvement. In other words, they are a holistic initiative helping new students make the transition to college.

The positive impact of seminars on first-year retention and graduation rates has been well documented (see Pascarella & Terenzini, 2005, for an overview of research on first-year seminars). Similarly, participants in learning communities often demonstrate higher retention rates and grade point averages than their peers who did not participate (Baker & Pomerantz, 2000-2001; Johnson, 2000-2001; Shapiro & Levine, 1999; Taylor, Moore, MacGregor, & Lindblad, 2003; Tinto, 2003). Given the success of FYSs and LCs individually, a number of institutions have chosen to bring these two practices together in combined FYS/LC programs. For the most part, combining FYSs and LCs means embedding seminars into LCs. According to the 2012-2013 National Survey of First-Year Seminars, approximately one third of institutions offering a FYS connect it to an LC; this is true at both two-year (32.8%) and four-year (38.1%) institutions (Young & Hopp, 2014). The proportion of respondents reporting an FYS/LC structure has doubled over the last decade and continues to rise (Young & Hopp, 2014).

Why FYS/LC Combined Programs?

Why are so many institutions choosing to embed FYSs into LCs? The reasons range from increasing success *while* students are in college to increasing their success *beyond college*. The transformational effect these programs often have on campus culture provides additional impetus. Given the positive effects of participation in LCs, it makes sense to have them available to students in their very first semester—when they are also offered FYSs. In this way, the kind of integrative learning experiences and sense of belonging fostered in LCs can set the tone for a student's entire college career—encouraging students to make connections among all their courses and situate themselves in the college community. Also, the variety of FYS types noted above suggests a number of possibilities for connecting these to other courses in LCs. For example, in a FYS that focuses on skills, content from the linked course(s) can provide the context in which skills can be embedded and practiced; an academic FYS can focus on a theme relevant to the course cluster while a preprofessional seminar can offer students opportunities to apply theoretical and practical concepts to professional tasks when paired with courses required for the program and/or general education prerequisites. In addition, it can be cost-effective to combine programs, especially in times of economic downturn. Resources that might need to be duplicated in two separate programs can often be shared in combined programs, such as student advisement and professional development opportunities. Finally, students can be expected to reap increased benefits from combined programs; Kuh (2008) reported cumulative benefits when students participate in more than one HIP.

On our own campuses, we have seen the positive effects of combined programs. At Kingsborough Community College, the social policy research group, MDRC, randomly assigned 1,500 students to one of the Opening Doors FYS/LCs or to a control group. Six years of follow-up data show a 4.6 percentage point impact of FYS/LC participation on graduation rates, representing a 15% increase in degrees earned. The program also had a positive impact on total credits earned, student enrollment, and credit accumulation (Weiss, Mayer, Cullinan, Ratledge, Sommo, & Diamond, 2014). Similarly, at IUPUI, findings suggest that participation in a FYS/LC contributes to academic success. When compared to students who participate in first-year seminars, learning communities, or no special curricular program, students in FYS/LCs had higher first-year grade point averages and persistence rates, even when considering student background characteristics (Hansen & Schmidt, 2015).

But colleges are not only interested in how well students do *while* they are in college, they are also invested in how well students are prepared for life *after* college, especially when disciplinary boundaries have eroded. "Technology and globalization have transformed knowledge and practices in all the disciplines, professions, and arts... we are awash in information in all areas of life, ... and 'flexibility' and 'mobility' are the watchwords of the new economy" (Huber & Hutchings, 2005, p. 2). At such a time, drawing from multiple knowledge bases, perspectives, and experiences is necessary in order to fully participate and thrive as educated citizens. Based on input from both educators and employers, The National Leadership Council for Liberal Education and America's Promise (LEAP), in *College Learning for the New Global Century* (AAC&U, 2007), made recommendations regarding the kind of essential learning outcomes needed by today's graduates. Key among these learning outcomes was integrative learning as "demonstrated through the application of knowledge, skills, and responsibilities to new settings and complex problems" (p. 12). As a result, there has been a call, throughout higher education, for an emphasis on educating students to think in a more intentionally integrative way.

In *A Statement on Integrative Learning*, the Association of American Colleges and Universities (AAC&U) and the Carnegie Foundation for the Advancement of Teaching (2004) noted that integrative learning "comes in many varieties: connecting skills and knowledge from multiple sources and experiences; applying theory to practice in various settings; utilizing diverse and even contradictory points of view; and, understanding issues and positions contextually" (para. 2). They identified integrative learning experiences as those which often occur as students address real-world problems that require a broad knowledge base and multiple modes of inquiry and that benefit from diverse perspectives. Such problems challenge the notion that a single solution is sufficient to resolve them.

Yet, in their statement, AAC&U and the Carnegie Foundation pointed out that cultivating this type of learning is one of the greatest challenges of higher education. Institutional structures, disciplinary divisions, hierarchies, and battles for resources stifle collaborative efforts and turn departments into silos. Antiquated methods of teaching linger, treating students as potential repositories of information—a role that often encourages student passivity—rather than active participants in the construction of knowledge.

FYSs and LCs directly support the aim of integrative learning and thinking; further, both do so by emphasizing community. In learning communities, cohorts naturally provide opportunities for building relationships with peers and instructors. FYSs, similarly, encourage students to forge academic and social connections by helping them situate themselves in the larger learning environment. But bringing these programs together means addressing the barriers noted above. It requires working across divisions—opening the door to the kind of cross-campus collaboration that often sparks a shift in institutional culture. This collaboration, if effective, not only supports the success of FYS/LC programs but also can serve as the impetus for institutional transformation. That is, as silos are dismantled and collaboration becomes the norm, how an institution "does business" (e.g., establishes goals, sets priorities, manages resources, assesses progress) becomes more inclusive. As a result, offering these two HIPs together in combined FYS/LC programs provides the institution with the opportunity to transform campus culture while helping students not only to see connections *in the world* but also to connect themselves *to the world*.

Implementing FYS/LC Programs

The positive effects of HIPs depend upon them being done well—so what does it mean to do FYSs and LCs well *together*? The aim of this book is to answer this question, and, to that end, it is organized into two parts. In Part I, contributing authors from a variety of institutional settings discuss core issues surrounding the implementation of combined FYS/LC programs. These concerns include providing a rationale for such programs, choosing from among a wide range of program models, making decisions regarding program administration, considering pedagogical implications, and assessing program outcomes. In Part II, seven FYS/LC case studies present an array of program models in a variety of settings. Cases range from an integrative general education program in the rural cornfields of DeKalb, Illinois, to a social justice program thriving in an urban community college system in San Francisco, to a science metacognition program in suburban Atlanta.

Part I: Rationale and Implementation of Combined Programs

Combining FYSs and LCs seems a natural pairing as LCs can help entering students find their place and make a connection to the college or university, and provide a context in which students can apply traditional FYS topics, such as studying, note taking, and test-taking skills. But is there evidence that there are benefits to bringing these two HIPs together in a combined program? In Chapter 1, Ashley Finley and George D. Kuh argue that there is. They begin by tracing how FYSs and LCs came to be considered HIPs, exploring empirical evidence of the positive impacts that each of these practices has been shown to have on outcomes such as engagement, persistence, and grade point averages. The authors then go on to explore findings in regards to participation in multiple HIPs. Finley and Kuh draw attention to the need to ensure the features that contributed to the programs' designation as high impact are consistently maintained. Jean Henscheid, Tracy Skipper, and Dallin Young explore this last point in Chapter 2 where they consider the various roles seminars can play in LCs. They begin by acknowledging that the ways of embedding FYSs in LCs are as varied as the needs of the students these programs serve. They discuss the range of roles seminars can play in LCs—including serving as sites for activities where material and concepts from other courses in the link can be integrated, applied, and practiced—and how course goals, assignments, activities, assessment, and faculty roles vary with different models for embedding seminars in LCs. Ultimately, however, it is up to individual institutions to decide which model best fits their needs. To that end, the authors comment on the advantages and disadvantages of various models, as well as the issues to consider when choosing a model for implementation.

In Chapter 3, Nia Haydel and Liya Escalera address the nuts and bolts of implementing and sustaining FYS/LC programs. What structures and funding must be in place, what new collaborations must be forged, and what practical adjustments must be made to the way a college does business for FYS/LC programs to work? Changes that are made to support these programs often have a wide-ranging impact on an institution, transforming the culture in the process. Implementing FYS/LC programs requires reexamining an array of services, processes, and policies, including course scheduling and requirements, recruitment, orientation, advisement, and registration. And, since the benefits of program participation are not always immediately apparent, it is often necessary to offer incentives. Of course, getting programs up and running is one task, sustaining them is another, so Haydel and Escalera also suggest strategies for keeping programs viable.

Good teaching stands at the heart of FYSs and LCs done well. In Chapter 4, Lisa Dresdner and Ruthanna Spiers discuss the process of shifting teaching practices to focus on integrative learning. They encourage educators to disrupt the cycle of disengaged teaching and learning in order to create opportunities for significant learning experiences, and offer practical strategies on how faculty can collaborate to synthesize content across disciplines and design integrative assignments.

While Chapters 1 through 4 focus on how to design, implement, and support FYS/LC programs, in Chapter 5, Michele Hansen and Maureen Pettitt explore how we can discover whether or not these programs are successful—information that is crucial in helping to document the importance of such programs in fulfilling an institution's mission to support student success. They begin by discussing traditional approaches to researching and assessing FYSs and LCs, noting their limitations, followed by suggestions for alternative directions, including evaluating more varied outcomes at multiple levels and employing more rigorous research designs. However, echoing Finley and Kuh in Chapter 1, they recognize the need for new assessment techniques to investigate the possible synergistic effects when students participate in multiple HIPs simultaneously.

Part II: Contexts for Implementation: Models From Two- and Four-Year Institutions

With the flexibility inherent in both LCs and FYSs, it is difficult to provide a holistic picture of what combined FYS/LC programs look like in action. To be effective, the programs must be contextualized in the unique characteristics of each institution and cater to the dynamic student populations they are designed to serve. Accordingly, this publication intentionally includes examples from diverse institutions across the country: two- and four-year (and even a program uniting two-and four-year institutions); public and private; urban, suburban, and rural; institutions serving predominately majority or historically underrepresented students; and institutions with as few as 1,300 to as many as 32,000 undergraduate students. The variety extends beyond the programs and into an array of assessment methods employed to measure program outcomes. Examples include quantitative analyses investigating cost-effectiveness, exam scores, grade point average, persistence, graduation rates, pre- and post-surveys, qualitative interviews, analyses of meta-reflection papers, and open-ended survey responses. Collectively, the cases provide a comprehensive picture of the diversity, flexibility, and value of combined FYS/LC programs, alongside examples for measuring outcomes and improving future practice.

Bronx Community College provides an intimate look at how combined FYS/LC programs can serve nonnative English speakers as they explore the cultural context of learning in U.S. higher education. Metro Academies of City College of San Francisco and San Francisco State University offer a glimpse into measuring the cost-effectiveness of combined programs, which is paramount when institutions have increasingly limited resources and are asked to demonstrate return on investment. Kennesaw State University explores metacognition in students enrolled in a combined program including chemistry, which provides a nice contrast to the residentially based FYS/LC offered through the Common Courses program at the University of South Carolina. Northern Illinois University describes how MAP-Works data shed light on students' experiences in combined programs, while Cabrini College shares rubrics used to investigate direct measures of learning in social justice writing assignments. Finally, Mt. Hood Community College details a comprehensive program for students in developmental courses connected to various themes.

Conclusion

Just as teaching in FYS/LC programs defies the usual institutional culture of working in isolation, writing for this publication required authors to work in concert. The more than 30 authors contributing to this volume modeled the collaboration and partnerships essential to successful FYS/LC programs. Co-authors from distinctly different institutional backgrounds worked incredibly hard to join forces in crafting chapters combining research and practice. We thank all of the contributors for sharing their experiences, observations, and reflections, and invite readers to draw from these as they plan, implement, or further develop FYS/LCs at their institutions.

References

The Association of American Colleges and Universities (AAC&U). (2007). *College learning for the new global century.* Washington, DC: Author. Retrieved from http://www.aacu.org/sites/default/files/files/LEAP/GlobalCentury_final.pdf

The Association of American Colleges and Universities and the Carnegie Foundation for the Advancement of Teaching. (2004, March). *A statement on integrative learning.* Retrieved from the Gallery of Teaching and Learning website: http://gallery.carnegiefoundation.org/ilp/uploads/ilp_statement.pdf

Baker, S., & Pomerantz, N. (2000-2001). Impact of learning communities on retention at a metropolitan university. *Journal of College Student Retention: Research, Theory & Practice, 2,* 115–126.

Barefoot, B. O. (2002). *Second National Survey of First-Year Academic Programs.* Brevard, NC: Policy Center on the First Year of College. Retrieved from http://www.firstyear.org/uploads/File/2002_2nd_Nat_Survey_Responses_ALL.pdf

Greenfield, G. M., & Keup, J. R., & Gardner, J. N. (2013). *Developing and sustaining successful first-year programs: A guide for practitioners.* San Francisco, CA: Jossey-Bass.

Hansen, M. J., & Schmidt, L. (2015, April 10). *The synergy of and readiness for high-impact practices during the first year of college.* Manuscript submitted for publication.

Huber, M. T., & Hutchings, P. (2005). *Integrative learning: Mapping the terrain.* Washington, DC: Association of American Colleges and Universities.

Hunter, M. S., & Linder, C. W. (2005). First-year seminars. In M. L. Upcraft, J. N. Gardner, B. O. Barefoot, & Associates, *Challenging and supporting the first-year student: A handbook for improving the first year of college* (pp. 275-291). San Francisco, CA: Jossey-Bass.

Indiana University-Purdue University Indianapolis (IUPUI). (2010). *A template for first-year seminars.* Retrieved from http://resources.uc.iupui.edu/LinkClick.aspx?fileticket=FBV4bBWZwDE%3D&tabid=882&mid=8083

Johnson, J. L. (2000-2001). Learning communities and special efforts in the retention of university students: What works, what doesn't, and is the return worth the investment? *Journal of College Student Retention, 2*(3), 219-38.

Kuh, G. D. (2008). *High impact educational practices: What they are, who has access to them, and why they matter.* Washington, DC: Association of American Colleges and Universities.

Lardner, E., & Malnarich, G. (2008). A new era in learning-community work: Why the pedagogy of intentional integration matters. *Change, 40,* 30-37.

Love, A. G. (1999). What are learning communities? In J. H. Levine (Ed.), *Learning communities: New structures, new partnerships for learning* (Monograph No. 26, pp. 1-8). Columbia, SC: University of South Carolina, National Resource Center for The First-Year Experience & Students in Transition.

Pascarella, E. T., & Terenzini, P. T. (2005). *How college affects students: A third decade of research, Vol. 2*. San Francisco, CA: Jossey-Bass.

Shapiro, N. S., & Levine, J. (Eds.). (1999). *Creating learning communities: A practical guide to winning support, organizing for change, and implementing programs*. San Francisco, CA: Jossey-Bass.

Taylor, K., Moore, W. S., MacGregor, J., & Lindblad, J. (2003). *Learning community research and assessment: What we know now* (National Learning Communities Project Monograph Series). Olympia, WA: The Evergreen State College, Washington Center for Improving the Quality of Undergraduate Education, in cooperation with the American Association for Higher Education.

Tinto, V. (2003). Learning better together: The impact of learning communities on student success. In *Promoting student success in college* (Higher Education Monograph Series, 2003-1, pp. 1-8). Syracuse, NY: School of Education, Syracuse University.

Upcraft, M. L., Gardner, J. N, Barefoot, B. O., & Associates. (2005). *Challenging and supporting the first-year student: A handbook for improving the first year of college*. San Francisco, CA: Jossey-Bass.

Weiss, M. J., Mayer, A., Cullinan, D., Ratledge, A., Sommo, C., & Diamond, J. (2014). *A random assignment evaluation of learning communities at Kingsborough Community College: Seven years later*. New York, NY: MDRC.

Young, D. G., & Hopp, J. M. (2014). *2012-2013 National Survey of First-Year Seminars: Exploring high-impact practices in the first college year* (Research Reports on College Transitions, No. 4). Columbia, SC: University of South Carolina, National Resource Center for The First-Year Experience & Students in Transition.

Part I
Rationale for and Implementation of Combined Programs

Chapter 1
The Case for Connecting First-Year Seminars and Learning Communities

Ashley Finley and George D. Kuh

Of the many efforts to improve undergraduate education introduced during the last quarter century, few have been as well received and promising as first-year seminars and learning communities. Each of these programmatic interventions is associated with such desirable short- and long-term student outcomes as satisfaction, engagement in educationally purposeful activities, and persistence, among others. This trifecta of student performance indicators led the Association of American Colleges and Universities (AAC&U) to include first-year seminars and learning communities on its list of 10 *high-impact practices* (Kuh, 2008).

What is a high-impact practice (HIP)? What is it about first-year seminars and learning communities that warrants each being designated as one? And, equally important, do students who take a first-year seminar that is part of a learning community benefit more than their counterparts who experience one or the other but not both?

In this chapter we address these questions, drawing on our own research and on related literature. First, we review the short history of HIPs, including how they were identified, their distinguishing features, and the empirical research that documents their noteworthy effects. We then briefly review different types of first-year seminars and learning community structures and discuss why certain formats are more likely to qualify as high-impact practices. We also examine some of the existing research regarding the synergistic advantages of integrating a first-year seminar into a learning community to promote student engagement and success. And finally, we close with some observations about the importance of implementation quality to ensure that first-year seminars and learning communities have the intended positive effects on students.

A Brief History of High-Impact Practices

One of the five clusters of effective educational practices originally used to report results from the National Survey of Student Engagement (NSSE) is Enriching Educational Experiences. This set of items (sometimes called a benchmark) was the last to be named, primarily because its nine components had not previously been grouped either conceptually or empirically into a single scale. However, the design team that helped create the NSSE questionnaire in 1998 was convinced that the individual activities and experiences that made up the Enriching Educational Experiences cluster were too important *not* to be represented on the survey (Kuh, 2008). The research supporting the value of certain educationally enriching activities, such as service-learning and experiences with diversity, was substantial, growing, and almost uniformly positive. At the same time, even though the anecdotal evidence was favorable, there was not as much empirical support for the benefits of other educationally enriching activities, including student-faculty research, internships, and study abroad.

It was this uneven empirical support for the activities making up the Educationally Enriching Experiences cluster that led George Kuh in 2005 to ask the NSSE analyst team at the Indiana University Center for Postsecondary Research to take a closer look at the relationships between the Educationally Enriching Experiences cluster and other NSSE items, including self-reported outcomes as well as grades and persistence. The data for the latter two variables were collected under the auspices of the Connecting the Dots study, which involved an analysis of 11,420 individual student ACT/SAT score reports, transcripts, and financial aid records from 18 baccalaureate-granting colleges and universities, including four historically Black institutions and three Hispanic-serving institutions (Kuh, Cruce, Shoup, Kinzie, & Gonyea, 2008; Kuh, Kinzie, Cruce, Shoup, & Gonyea, 2007).

In his 2008 AAC&U monograph, Kuh summarized what the NSSE analysts discovered. Four additional AAC&U publications have appeared since, examining different facets of high-impact practices. Brownell and Swaner (2009) reviewed the literature documenting the positive effects of participating in one of five HIPs: first-year seminars, learning communities, service-learning, student-faculty research, and study abroad. Kuh and O'Donnell (2013) discussed what is needed to enhance the implementation quality of HIPs and to bring them to scale so that larger numbers of students at more institutions will benefit. Finley and McNair (2013) reported the findings from their research that illustrates the unusually positive effects of participation for students from underserved groups. Finally, Wellman and Brusi (2013) offered insights and suggestions for evaluating the return on investing in and scaling selected HIPs in terms of persistence and other student success proxies.

The main story line running through all these publications is that students who participate in, for example, either a learning community or service-learning course in the first college year are more engaged in the educationally purposeful activities represented in the four other NSSE clusters (Table 1.1). The likely reasons for this pattern of findings are a function of the kinds of student behaviors and interactions that are characteristic of a HIP. When done well (a point about which we will say more later), a HIP typically demands more time on task by students, induces more student-faculty interaction, generates more opportunities for feedback from both faculty and peers, and more frequently puts students in situations where they have to transfer and apply what they are learning. When faculty or internship or field supervisors ask students to systematically reflect on and distill meaning from these experiences and connect them to other aspects of their education and life, these activities become even more meaningful.

Table 1.1
Effects of Participating in High-Impact Activities on Student Engagement

	Level of academic challenge	Active and collaborative learning	Student-faculty interaction	Supportive campus environment
First-year students				
Learning communities	++	+++	+++	++
Service-learning	++	+++	+++	++
Seniors				
Study abroad	++	++	++	+
Student-faculty research	+++	+++	+++	++
Internship	++	+++	+++	++
Service-learning	++	+++	+++	++
Culminating experience	++	++	+++	++

$+ p < .001$. $++ p < .001$ & Unstd $B > .10$. $+++ p < .001$ & Unstd $B > .30$.

These features of a HIP explain in large part why students report more frequently using deep learning behaviors, such as integrating and applying information from different courses to practical problems, discussing ideas with faculty members and peers, and making judgments about the value of information (Table 1.2). Students who have participated in a HIP also report making greater gains in general education outcomes, personal and social development, and practical competence. These same patterns of differences substantially favoring first-year students who have experienced a high-impact practice hold for seniors, and have been corroborated every year since 2007 in NSSE annual reports (e.g., NSSE, n.d.).

Table 1.2

Effects of Participating in High-Impact Activities on Deep/Integrative Learning and Gains

	Deep learning	General gains	Personal gains	Practical gains
First-year students				
Learning communities	+++	++	++	++
Service-learning	+++	++	+++	++
Seniors				
Study abroad	++	+	++	
Student-faculty research	+++	++	++	++
Internship	++	++	++	++
Service-learning	+++	++	+++	++
Culminating experience	++	++	++	++

+ $p < .001$. ++ $p < .001$ & Unstd $B > .10$. +++ $p < .001$ & Unstd $B > .30$.

These findings are both statistically significant and have unusually large effect sizes, which represent the magnitude of the statistically significant differences between those who have been in a high-impact practice and those who have not. In Tables 1.1 and 1.2, the + signs represent effect sizes. The more + signs associated with an outcome, the greater the effect size. The overwhelmingly positive pattern of large effect size differences suggests that the impact of these experiences is likely manifested in students in observable and personally meaningful ways. Perhaps the most concrete example is data from California State University, Northridge showing that students who participate in one or more HIPs are more likely to persist and graduate (Kuh & O'Donnell, 2013), and findings reported by Finley and McNair (2013) indicating higher perceived learning gains with greater participation in HIPs. Moreover, the positive relationships between HIP involvement and desired outcomes generally hold for all students, background characteristics notwithstanding. In fact, the students who are not as well prepared academically (as indicated by precollege achievement test scores, such as ACT or SAT) or are from underserved backgrounds appear to benefit more than their better prepared peers, which is a form of compensatory effect (Cruce, Wolniak, Seifert, & Pascarella, 2006; Finley & McNair, 2013; Kuh, 2008; Pascarella & Terenzini, 2005). We will say more about some of these benefits later.

First-Year Seminars and Learning Communities as High-Impact Practices

As mentioned earlier, first-year seminars and learning communities are among the most commonly offered and, thus, highly subscribed HIPs. Sometimes a stand-alone first-year seminar by itself is what the institution considers to be its *first-year experience.* In other instances, the first-year seminar is integrated into a learning community or is a component of a campuswide effort to enhance the first year of college. Before we explore the rationale for integrating these two curricular practices, we examine the educational effectiveness of each individually.

First-Year Seminars

The exhorted value of the first-year seminar dates back centuries, probably to ancient Greece (Keup, 2012). However, the rationale, structure, and intended outcomes have evolved over time from a narrow focus on imparting knowledge and indirectly socializing newcomers to the academic ethos to intentional efforts to teach typically traditional-age first-year students "how to do college" in a psychosocially supportive context. For example, small classes taught in tutorial format were a staple at colleges in the Colonial era. A discussion–oriented course taught by a faculty member using the Socratic approach with a small number of first-year students (e.g., 15-20) was a central component of the undergraduate curricular reform ineffectively championed by Robert Maynard Hutchins when he was president of the University of Chicago in the 1930s. Even into the 1960s, many colleges continued to organize the first-year curriculum in a manner that featured at least one small required class taught by full-time faculty, which was usually part of the general education component of the baccalaureate degree, such as a literature, history, or social science offering.

As undergraduate enrollments swelled through the 1970s, universities traded the small required first-year class(es) for large enrollment lecture-oriented sections, which made class discussion difficult if not impossible. Moreover, for all practical purposes, this trend also allowed first-year students to be anonymous, even among other students in the same class, exacerbating the sense that "I am on my own here." Anonymity—though students may say they prefer it—is the enemy of connecting in personally meaningful and satisfying ways with peers and faculty or learning how to successfully manage academic challenges and navigate the institutional culture.

These factors, along with the reports that an unacceptably large number of students were leaving college prematurely, inspired the University of South Carolina, under the leadership of John N. Gardner, to create University 101, an orientation-to-college course that was the central organizational component of what became The First-Year Experience (FYE) movement. More than 40 years later, over 95% of campuses report having something akin to a first-year seminar (Barefoot, Griffin, & Koch, 2012).

What is generically called a first-year seminar can take different forms, even on the same campus. At some institutions, the first-year seminar is required of all students; at others the course is optional. Some seminars are offered pass-fail; others may be graded. The number of credits assigned to the seminar also varies from one campus to another. Most seminars are one-semester offerings, but some continue through the entire first year. The backgrounds of instructors vary, with seminars being led by faculty teaching academic content related to their primary disciplinary affiliation on some campuses and by student affairs or library personnel on others. Sometimes instructors teach the first-year seminar as part of their regular teaching load, but occasionally instructors receive additional compensation for doing so.

The goals of the seminar—often multiple—also vary. According to a recent survey of more than 800 institutions with first-year seminars (Young & Hopp, 2014), the most commonly cited goals of seminars included helping students develop a connection with the institution (44.9%), providing an orientation to campus resources and services (37.8%), and developing academic skills (36.3%). About one third of respondents (31.8%) reported that service-learning or community service activity is part of the first-year seminar.

All this is to say that there is considerable variation in the activities and student experiences that constitute a first-year seminar. This makes it difficult to determine which effects can be attributed to which first-year seminar format or structural elements. Even so, there is considerable research showing the positive effects of participating in a first-year seminar, much of it gathered by staff at the University of South Carolina's National Resource Center for The First-Year Experience and Students in Transition.

Learning Communities

Just as the first-year seminar can take different structural forms, so it is with learning communities. And the understanding of what constitutes a learning community also has evolved over time. Thus, there are some similar challenges to teasing out the key features of learning communities that make them high impact.

Decades ago, many institutions considered the entire campus to be a learning community, implying that an ethic of belonging, shared intellectual pursuits, and coherence of purpose characterized the curriculum and cocurriculum. Even today, one can find such language in the catalogues of small colleges. As institutions have grown in size, it has become physically unsustainable for all students to know one another or study the same material at the same time. Yet, at certain institutions—most notably large public universities, such as the University of Oregon and University of Washington—efforts were made to reproduce many of the more educationally effective attributes of the small college through structural interventions designed to have similar effects. Central to this conception of the contemporary learning community is the notion that students in the critical transition period between high school and college or some other life experience (e.g., military, employment) and university study can benefit from connecting in meaningful ways with peers engaged in similar intellectual pursuits.

The most common feature of these efforts is assigning students to block-scheduled courses linked by a common theme often pertaining to a social issue or contemporary topic (Brownell & Swaner, 2010); that is, the same small groups of students (e.g., 18-22) are co-enrolled in the same sections of two or three classes, such as a writing class and introduction to psychology, or some other combination. For example, the Themed Learning Community (TLC) implemented successfully since 2003 at Indiana University-Purdue University Indianapolis (IUPUI) is made up of three or four courses (one of which is a first-year seminar) in which 25 or fewer students are co-enrolled. The instructional team consists of three to five faculty members, an academic advisor, a librarian, and a peer mentor. Such a design provides students with common intellectual material and allows them to come to know one another in an academic setting, making it easier for them to study together and help one another manage common problems and challenges. On average, the first-to-second-year persistence rates of students in a TLC at IUPUI are between 2 and 9% higher than their peers who do not have such an experience (IUPUI, 2011b). Also, the first-year grades of TLC participants in a given year tend to be on average .1 to .2 points higher (IUPUI, 2011a).

In some instances, institutions provide incentives for faculty who teach the courses that make up the learning community with the expectation that they will collaborate on the design of assignments and other experiences so that students will have to synthesize and integrate material from the different courses. An upper-division undergraduate peer preceptor or mentor is sometimes part of the instructional team, as in the IUPUI example. Some residential campuses, such as the University of Missouri, link housing assignments to the blocked courses to create a Freshman Interest Group, wherein students taking the same courses also live in close proximity. This structural feature—sometimes including a peer preceptor who lives in the same residence and organizes out-of-class activities— helps facilitate peer interaction outside the classroom.

Even though learning communities take different forms, NSSE data show that students in learning communities—defined as the same group of students taking two or three classes together—spend on average 20% more time per week preparing for class. As Tables 1.1 and 1.2 show, such students are more engaged overall in their learning and benefit more than their peers who do not have such an experience.

According to the Washington Center for the Improvement of Under-graduate Education at The Evergreen State College, learning communities are morphing into a new stage, which it calls *new era learning communities*, focused on fostering greater levels of learning. What was originally introduced as a curricular reform focused on content is now cast more broadly and incorporates an emphasis on helping students learn about the campus culture as well as how to learn and thrive in college (Lardner & Malnarich, 2008).

Is Two Better Than One? The Synergistic Payoff of Linking HIPs

The varied and effective forms of both first-year seminars and learning communities help explain their popularity. Too often, however, these programs function independently of one another, almost as if they are parallel, rather than connected, student experiences. This can contribute to feelings of *initiative fatigue* on the part of involved faculty and staff members—the sense of being overwhelmed because they are expending time and effort beyond their regular duties by implementing what may appear to be programs and services that are not mission relevant or strategic priorities (Kuh & Hutchings, 2015). One way to ameliorate initiative fatigue is to make plain how programs, such as learning communities and first-year seminars, are related and contribute to institutional goals like improved persistence and graduation rates and higher levels of integrative learning, among other student outcomes. Perhaps even more important, embedding a first-year seminar in a learning community may have the happy prospect of accentuating the positive effects of each.

We do know something about the benefit of students' cumulative participation over time in HIPs. Finley and McNair (2013) found that students reported persistently greater gains in desired learning outcomes and more frequent participation in deep learning activities when engaging in multiple HIPs. The highest perceived gains were associated with participating in five to six HIPs over the course of the college career. Moreover, these perceived gains were reported by different groups of students, including transfer, first-generation, underrepresented minority, and traditionally advantaged students.

As noted earlier, California State University-Northridge found that participation in multiple HIPs was linked to higher graduation rates, with a compensatory boost in graduation rates for Latino students. In fact, although HIPs participation translated into higher graduation rates for both White and Latino students, when Latinos participated in five to six of these experiences, they graduated at a higher rate than their White counterparts (Kuh & O'Donnell, 2013).

What the above research does not clarify is the degree to which the effect on student outcomes is amplified when students participate in two HIPS, such as a first-year seminar and a learning community, simultaneously. There is, however, evidence to suggest that weaving together two HIPs into the same experience may indeed be more powerful than either one is alone.

The Case for Integrating First-Year Seminars and Learning Communities

The 2012-2013 National Survey of First-Year Seminars found that more than "90% of survey respondents reported intentionally connecting at least one high-impact practice (HIP) to their first-year seminar (National Resource Center, 2013, p. 3). For most of the nearly 800 campuses responding to this question, the majority enhanced first-year seminars by using collaborative assignments. Approximately one half of campuses responding to the survey reported including diversity and global learning experiences into first-year seminars, while a third reported including service-learning experiences. A third of campuses in the sample indicated that first-year seminars were connected with learning communities (National Resource Center, 2013).

In their instructive review of the research on five HIPs (i.e. first-year seminars, learning communities, service-learning, undergraduate research, capstone courses and projects), Brownell and Swaner (2010) briefly discussed the potential of incorporating multiple HIPs into the same activity, particularly first-year seminars and learning communities. Their review of the literature indicated that "connecting the first-year seminar with a learning community was associated with better outcomes for students" (p. 41). Among these improved outcomes were greater student engagement, both inside and outside of the classroom; more frequent substantive interactions with peers and faculty; intellectual growth; and personal development in terms of improved study skills, time management skills, and an enhanced sense of well-being.

Combining first-year seminars and learning communities has also been associated with improvement in certain institutional outcomes, such as persistence (Hanover Research 2011; Tampke & Durodoye, 2013). Additionally, integration of HIPs need not stop at only two experiences. For example, Brownell and Swaner (2010) suggested that adding service-learning to the first-year seminar linked to a learning community may yield even greater positive effects. Service-learning "focuses students on real, unscripted problems, and issues; and it broadens students' thinking about what it means to be part of a community, expanding that concept beyond the campus"(p.43).

Additional research about the effects of linking first-year seminars and learning communities will likely produce additional valuable insights into how student and institutional outcomes are affected by the pairing of HIPS. At the same time, as we emphasize later, calling something a high-impact practice does not necessarily make it so. Intentional design and careful attention must be paid to the ways in which these practices are implemented to ensure that the label high impact also means high *quality*.

The Case for Quality

The reality on many campuses is that faculty often commit themselves to lead a HIP without a clear understanding of what exactly makes the experience high impact or a plan for ensuring that the features meet a standard for quality. Too often, important questions are not raised, such as, What types of activities maximize engagement in first-year seminars? How does the *community* aspect of a learning community get translated into actual practice or reflective assignments? and In what ways should performance expectations or feedback be elevated to challenge students in appropriate ways?

Kuh (2008) offered an important observation about why students who participate in certain educational programs or practices tend to benefit in unusually positive ways: "There is growing evidence that—*when done well*—[emphasis added] some programs and activities appear to engage participants at levels that elevate their performances across multiple engagement and desired-outcomes measures" (p. 14). It is not enough to offer a first-year seminar or a learning community or a service-learning course. Institutions must also ensure that the qualities of what makes a learning experience high impact are also intact; these qualities (Kuh & O'Donnell 2013, p. 8)[1] include the following:

- *Expectations set at appropriately high levels*. Students feel challenged and assignments are constructed accordingly.

- *Significant investment of time and effort*. Students are expected to engage skills frequently and persistently throughout the experience.

- *Interactions with faculty and peers*. High levels of discussion and collaborative problem solving are present among students themselves and in concert with faculty.

- *Experiences with diversity*. Students are exposed to differing viewpoints, ways of knowing, and life experiences.

- *Frequent and constructive feedback*. Students receive consistent feedback from instructors focused on improvement and student development.

- *Periodic and structured opportunities for reflection and integration*. Critical reflection assignments are a regular part of the experience, perhaps connected with an electronic portfolio.

- *Relevance through real-world applications*. Students have the opportunity to connect learning to life experiences or current social contexts.

- *Public demonstration of competence*. Students make public presentations to their peers, such as a capstone poster presentation or participation in a colloquium event.

These quality dimensions represent common markers of what makes an experience high impact. The expectation is that when students participate in HIPs, they are also more likely to engage in the behaviors or activities mentioned above, such as interacting with peers or applying learning to real-life contexts, than in other types of learning experiences. As many faculty who have implemented a HIP (particularly on the first try) can attest, simply calling something a learning community or a first-year seminar does not necessarily make it high impact. Rather, it is the intentional, perhaps even serendipitous, inclusion of the quality dimensions that help differentiate the experience from others and move it toward something transformative for the student. Nevertheless, a full understanding of the weight or significance of these qualities remains an unknown aspect of the efficacy of HIPs. We do not know, for example, if high levels of interaction are

---

[1] Some of these qualities are also addressed in Kuh (2008).

more beneficial than students demonstrating competence publicly. We similarly do not know whether particular characteristics of quality may be more salient for particular types of practices. Future research might illuminate, for instance, whether engagement with diversity is critical for first-year seminars but is less so for learning communities.

The answers to these and related questions have yet to be teased out through research and campus practice. Until then, an intentional, unrelenting focus on quality is needed to increase the likelihood that students will, indeed, benefit in the ways that the research on HIPs promises.

Conclusion

Bass (2012) pointed to a fundamental gap between how educators have come to understand what best promotes learning inside and outside the classroom and the structures (better interpreted as confines) of the system that have been created to educate students: "Our understanding of learning has expanded at a rate that has far outpaced our conceptions of teaching" (p. 23). Perhaps the best example is the growing critique of the credit hour or seat time as a measure of learning to understand the tension between what educators know about actual cognitive development and the imperiousness of bureaucratic structures.[2] HIPs are effective because each practice, *when done well*, encourages students to engage deeply, communally, and reflectively throughout the duration of the activity. As Bass contends,

> One key source of disruption in higher education is coming not from the outside but from our own practices, from the growing body of experiential modes of learning, moving from margin to center, and proving to be critical and powerful in the overall quality and meaning of the undergraduate experience. (p. 24)

Taking Bass's assertion seriously also means challenging ourselves to infuse what we know into what we do, and then take it to a scale so that not just the privileged or curious few students find these practices but that they are accessible, even *required*, for all students. Doing this involves the will and leadership to move HIPs from boutique campus programs often at the periphery of institutions to

---

[2] See, for example, the argument presented by Laitinen (2012) in an education policy paper from the New America Foundation.

the center of the curriculum (i.e., infused within general education curricula). The more we know about the efficacy and implementation of HIPs, the more we can explore how best to implement and integrate these practices at a scale in which the majority of students, not just the lucky ones, can participate.

We do not yet know enough about the best ways to combine HIPs into a single, integrated experience. Even so, the emerging evidence suggests campuses would do well to look carefully and strategically at the possibility of doing so. At the national level, there is strong evidence that students' cumulative participation in HIPs over time results in higher levels of perceived learning, learning gains, and graduation rates. Research from single campus, multicampus, and national studies strongly suggests that certain HIPs, particularly first-year seminars and learning communities, may be even more beneficial when well integrated.

Sadly, the reality is that at present most students do not participate in even one high-impact practice, let alone experience two or more simultaneously (Kuh, 2008; Finley & McNair 2013). And even when students do engage in a HIP, they may have little understanding of what the experience means or why it is beneficial. As one focus group student commented in a recent national study of HIPs, "I have teachers that take us out of the building. I don't know what it's called. It's called something here. [Faculty] take you out of the building, and you go learn about like the vegetable gardens...there's a lot of professors here that teach differently." [3] As campus leaders build transformative learning experiences— whether singularly or in combination—this quote is a good reminder of the need to be as intentional about communicating the purpose of those experiences to students as we are about processes of implementation and securing budgets.

There is much to be excited about as the research and campus models involving HIPs continue to evolve. The possibilities for linking first-year seminars and learning communities and building synergy among high-impact learning experiences are especially promising. But to truly learn all we can about these experiences, we must take seriously the following points. First, we must make sure that all students have access to these experiences, particularly students from underserved populations. Too often these practices are the opportunity of a select or willing minority on campuses. Second, we must challenge ourselves to implement HIPs with an eye toward the dimensions of quality identified earlier in this chapter. The full promise of the depth of these practices is gained through supporting the quality of their implementation. Finally, we must be rigorous in

---

[3] The research was funded by TG Philanthropy Program and produced the report, *Assessing Underserved Students' Engagement in High-Impact Practices* (Finley & McNair, 2013).

capturing the efficacy of these practices through thoughtful assessment. The ability to learn more about the transformative potential of HIPs lies in our diligence to fully understand the experiences that are already taking place.

References

Barefoot, B. A., Griffin, B. Q., & Koch, A. K. (2012). *Enhancing student success and retention throughout undergraduate education: A national survey.* Brevard, NC: John N. Gardner Institute for Excellence in Undergraduate Education. Retrieved from http://www.jngi.org/wordpress/wpontent/uploads/2012/04/JNGInational_survey_web.pdf

Bass, R. (2012, March/April). Disrupting ourselves: The problem of learning in higher education. *Educause Review,* 23-33.

Brownell, J. E., & Swaner, L. E. (2010). *Five high-impact practices: Research on learning outcomes, completion, and quality.* Washington, DC: Association of American Colleges & Universities.

Cruce, T. M., Wolniak, G. C., Seifert, T. A., & Pascarella, E. T. (2006). Impacts of good practices on cognitive development, learning orientations, and graduate degree plans during the first year of college. *Journal of College Student Development, 47*(4), 365-383.

Finley, A., & McNair, T. (2013). *Assessing underserved students' engagement in high-impact practices.* Washington, DC: Association of American Colleges & Universities.

Hanover Research. (2011). *Improving student retention and graduation rates.* Washington, DC: Author.

Keup, J. (2012, March). *Demonstrating the impact of first-year seminars on student outcomes.* Paper presented at the American College Personnel Association 2012 Annual Convention, Louisville, KY.

Kuh, G. D. (2008). *High-impact educational practices: What they are, who has access to them, and why they matter.* Washington, DC: Association of American Colleges & Universities.

Kuh, G. D., Cruce, T. M., Shoup, R., Kinzie, J., & Gonyea, R. M. (2008). Unmasking the effects of student engagement on college grades and persistence. *Journal of Higher Education, 79,* 540-563.

Kuh, G. D. & Hutchings, P. (2015). Assessment and initiative fatigue: Keeping the focus on learning. In G. D. Kuh, S. O. Ikenberry, N. Jankowski, T. R. Cain, P. T. Ewell, P. Hutchings, & J. Kinzie, *Using evidence of student learning to improve higher education* (pp. 183-200). San Francisco, CA: Jossey-Bass.

Kuh, G. D., Kinzie, J., Cruce, T., Shoup, R., & Gonyea, R .M. (2007, January). *Connecting the dots: Multifaceted analyses of the relationships between student engagement results from the NSSE and the institutional policies and conditions that foster student success* (Final report to Lumina Foundation for Education). Bloomington, IN: Indiana University Center for Postsecondary Research. Retrieved from http://nsse.iub.edu/pdf/Connecting_the_Dots_Report. pdf

Kuh, G. D., & O'Donnell, K. (2013). *Ensuring quality and taking high-impact practices to scale.* Washington, DC: Association of American Colleges & Universities.

Indiana University-Purdue University Indianapolis (IUPUI). (2011a). *Are the TLCs making a difference: GPA.* Retrieved from University College Themed Learning Communities website: http://tlc.iupui.edu/TLCPrograms/ AretheTLCsMakingaDifferenceGPA.aspx

Indiana University-Purdue University Indianapolis (IUPUI). (2011b). *Are the TLCs making a difference: Retention.* Retrieved from University College Themed Learning Communities website: http://tlc.iupui.edu/ TLCPrograms/AretheTLCsMakingaDifferenceRetention.aspx

Laitinen, A. (2012, September). *Cracking the credit hour* (Education Policy Paper). Washington, DC: New American Foundation. Retrieved from https://static. newamerica.org/attachments/2334-cracking-the-credit-hour/Cracking_ the_Credit_Hour_Sept5_0.ab0048b12824428cba568ca359017ba9.pdf

Lardner, E., & Malnarich, G. (2008). A new era in learning-community work: Why the pedagogy of intentional integration matters. *Change, 40,* 30-37.

National Resource Center for The First-Year Experience & Students in Transition. (2013). *National Survey of First-Year Seminars: Executive summary 2012-2013.* Retrieved from http://www.sc.edu/fye/research/surveys/ survey_instruments/pdf/Executive_Summaries_2013_National_ Survey_FirstYearSeminars.pdf

National Survey of Student Engagement (NSSE). (n.d.). *NSSE findings: Annual results 2013.* Retrieved from http://nsse.indiana.edu/NSSE_2013_ Results/

Pascarella, E. T., & Terenzini, P. T. (2005). *How college affects students: A third decade of research.* San Francisco, CA: Jossey-Bass.

Tampke, D., & Durodoye, R. (2013). Improving academic success for undecid-ed students: A first-year seminar/learning community approach. *Learning Communities Research and Practice, 1*(2), Article 3. Retrieved from http:// washingtoncenter.evergreen.edu/cgi/viewcontent.cgi?article=1028&con-text=lcrpjournal

Wellman, J., & Brusi, R. (2013). *Investing in success: Cost-effective strategies to increase student success.* Washington, DC: Association of American Colleges & Universities.

Young, D. G., & Hopp, J. M. (2014). *2012-2013 National Survey of First-Year Seminars: Exploring high-impact practices in the first college year* (Research Reports on College Transitions, No. 4). Columbia, SC: University of South Carolina, National Resource Center for The First-Year Experience & Students in Transition.

Chapter 2
National Practices for Combining First-Year Seminars and Learning Communities

Jean M. Henscheid, Tracy L. Skipper, and Dallin G. Young

Modern learning community advocates, beginning with Gabelnick, MacGregor, Matthews, and Smith (1990), maintain that these structures are at their best when they feature tight content and process integration among two or more courses in which students are co-enrolled and, ideally, with participating students' cocurricular experiences. This gold standard for learning communities extends across types, including those linked with first-year seminars. These tight linkages are the source of some of the greatest gains for participating students, faculty, staff, and institutions (Lardner & Malnarich, 2008). This chapter examines data from a national survey of first-year seminars, a portion of which looked at the connection between the seminar and other high-impact practices, including learning communities. While data from this survey suggest that programs on many campuses may be designed somewhat short of the ideal described above, examples close to the ideal can be found at nearly every type of institution. Lardner and Malnarich (2008) even suggested that tighter integration across learning community components may be gaining momentum.

This chapter reviews quantitative and qualitative findings from the 2012-2013 administration of the National Survey of First-Year Seminars (NSFYS, Young & Hopp, 2014), providing insight into how learning communities are structured and the role the seminar plays within them. Nine primary roles for the seminar within first-year learning communities are described and illustrated with examples drawn from survey responses and other learning community research initiatives. The chapter concludes with a recommendation for maximizing the impact of learning communities linked with first-year seminars and suggestions for future research, program evaluation, and assessment.

The National Survey of First-Year Seminars

The National Resource Center for The First-Year Experience and Students in Transition has administered a national survey every three years for the last quarter century to explore the nature and prevalence of first-year seminars in American higher education. The survey first began asking about the inclusion of first-year seminars in learning communities in 1994, when the percentage of respondents reporting a seminar embedded in a learning community was 17.2% (Barefoot & Fidler, 1996). In the 2012-2013 administration, 276 individuals each representing a single institution (or 36.8% of all respondents who completed the entire survey about first-year seminars) indicated that their institutions embed seminars in learning communities (Young & Hopp, 2014). This is roughly the same percentage (35.7%) of respondents who indicated in the 2009 national survey that their campuses make such a link (Padgett & Keup, 2011).

The 2012-2013 NSFYS included a series of questions about the connection between seminars and learning communities. If respondents indicated that the seminar was connected to a learning community, they were invited to answer two additional questions. The first asked them to identify the characteristics of the first-year learning community and the second asked them to *describe the role the learning community plays in the first-year seminar.*

2012-2013 NSFYS Definitions

First-year seminars. The same typology for first-year seminars that has been used in the National Survey of First-Year Seminars since 1991 was also used in the 2012-2013 administration. Each survey respondent was asked to identify all types of seminars available to students on their campus and the one type that served the highest percentage of students. The selection of seminar types, as noted in the introduction, included (a) extended orientation, (b) academic with common content, (c) academic with variable content, (d) preprofessional or discipline linked, (e) basic study skills, and (f) hybrid (Young & Hopp, 2014). Survey questions related to course goals, structure, instruction, and administration—including the connection of the seminar to a first-year learning community—were answered with respect to the seminar type serving the highest percentage of students on a given campus.

Learning communities. Respondents were asked to identify whether the first-year seminar was connected to a learning community, defined as "linking a cohort of students in the first-year seminar to one or more courses or to a common set of theme-based experiences" (Young & Hopp, 2014, p. 44) and indicate the defining characteristics of that linkage. The definition of learning communities and the characteristics used for the survey were derived from several extant learning community typologies (Gabelnick et al., 1990; Inkelas & Longerbeam, 2008; Lenning & Ebbers, 1999; Love & Tokuno, 1999; MacGregor, Smith, Matthews, & Gabelnick, 1997; Shapiro & Levine, 1999; Smith, MacGregor, Matthews, Gabelnick, & Associates, 2004; Snider & Venable, 2000; Stassen,

2003). As such, the definition is much broader than the one offered in 2007 by the Association of American Colleges and Universities (AAC&U), which guides this volume and confines the term learning community to students enrolling in two or more linked courses that "encourage integration of learning across courses … involve students with 'big questions' that matter beyond the classroom … [and encourage] students [to] work closely with one another and with their professors" (p. 53).

To gain greater insight into the nature of first-year learning communities, survey respondents also described the characteristics of the learning community of which the seminar is a part:

- Students are co-enrolled in the first-year seminar and one or more other course, but not all courses in the students' schedules.

- Students are co-enrolled in the first-year seminar and all other courses in the students' schedules.

- Course content is intentionally coordinated by the instructors of the first-year seminar and other linked courses.

- Course content in the first-year seminar and other linked courses is connected by a common intellectual theme.

- Students in the first-year seminar participate in a common set of theme-based experiences outside of the course, such as discussion groups, a speaker series, or other educational programs.

- The learning community includes a residential component (i.e., a living-learning community). (Young & Hopp, 2014)

The Role of First-Year Seminars in Learning Communities

Over the past 15 years, the National Resource Center and the Washington Center for Improving the Quality of Undergraduate Education have sought to clarify how first-year seminars and learning communities work together. In 2000, a textual analysis of some 100 syllabi and program descriptions revealed nine non-mutually exclusive models for embedding first-year seminars within learning communities (Henscheid, 2000). Three additional types were later added by then National Learning Communities Project Codirector Jean MacGregor (personal communication, February 14, 2003). Since that time, conversations with first-year seminar and learning community instructors and administrators, content of presentations at National Resource Center conferences, and feedback from respondents to the NSFYS have helped refine the list. The resulting nine possible roles served as a set of a priori themes for coding the open-ended responses to the 2012-2013 NSFYS describing the role of the first-year seminar in the learning community. Of the 276 participants reporting an FYS/LC structure, open-ended responses from 252 participants were analyzed. Their responses were coded in the following ways:

1. ***Sharing common readings, assignments, and projects.*** This code was assigned if the respondent specified which readings, assignments, and/ or projects were features of the FYS/LC.

2. ***Pulling together concepts from other courses.*** This code was assigned to responses that more vaguely referred to a theme components of the FYS/LC shared.

3. ***Serving as a place to process concepts from other courses and focus on metacognition, or learning about learning itself.*** This code referred to the first-year seminar as a "learning lab" or "site for reflection" within the learning community.

4. ***Serving as a place for faculty members from other courses in the link to visit and discuss connections.*** This code referred to visits to the first-year seminar or another course from faculty members teaching in the FYS/ LC.

5. ***Serving as a place to explicitly connect personal and/or social concepts with concepts learned in linked course(s).*** This code was assigned when respondents indicated that the first-year seminar and/or any outside-of-class experience included explicit reference to connections between social and academic concepts.

6. ***Serving as a place to discuss skills, behaviors, and dispositions important to achievement in linked course(s).*** Assignment of this code was restricted to responses that specified which skills, behaviors, and/or dispositions required for success in other learning community courses were addressed in the first-year seminar.

7. ***Serving as a site for community building.*** This code was assigned if the respondent identified cohesion among students in a subpopulation and/ or facilitation of a student's sense of belonging as goals of the FYS/LC. Subpopulations included students in developmental education courses, honors students, scholars of color, students assigned to one residence hall, and other small groups within the larger campus community.

8. *Serving as a site for career exploration related to learning community themes and topics.* Responses assigned this code identified the FYS/LC as targeted to students in the same academic degree program (or to premajors). FYS/LCs described explicitly as career focused were also coded this way.

9. *Serving as a site for service-learning connected to learning community themes and topics.* This code was assigned when service experiences were described as part of the FYS/LC.

The Structure of FYS/LCs on American College Campuses

The discussion of the findings on learning community structures from the 2012-2013 NSFYS is divided into two parts. The first part offers an overview of what the quantitative survey data reveal about the primary features of FYS/LCs on American college campuses. In the second part, the analysis of the open-ended responses related to the role of the first-year seminar in the learning communities program provides additional insight into which aspects of the program are most salient for respondents, adding depth to our understanding of FYS/LC structures. This discussion is illustrated by descriptions of FYS/LC models drawn from survey responses and institutional websites. The first author identified additional program models over the course of the Pew Charitable Trusts-funded National Learning Communities Project (from 2000 to 2006) and from the Washington Center, the major national clearinghouse for learning communities. Institutional examples drawn from these sources are parenthetically identified as *NLCP/Washington Center.*

FYS/LC Prevalence and Structures

As noted above, slightly more than one third of respondents to the 2012-2013 NSFYS reported connecting the seminar to a learning community. This configuration was seen more frequently among four-year (38.1%) than two-year respondents (32.8%) and significantly more likely among public (42.5%) than private institutions (30.1%). FYS/LC structures are also reported much more frequently at large institutions than small ones—51.8% of respondents from institutions of 4,000 or more first-year students identify this configuration as part of their first-year offerings compared to 27.7% for institutions with fewer than 500 entering students (Young, & Hopp, 2014). Finally, the connection of seminars to learning communities is fairly evenly distributed across seminar type (Table 2.1). While a slightly higher proportion of preprofessional seminars and a lower percentage of seminars identified as *other* acknowledge a connection to a learning community, these differences did not rise to statistical significance.

Table 2.1
Connection of Seminar to LC by Seminar Type

Seminar type	LC connection %	No LC connection %
Extended orientation (EO)	36.9	73.1
Academic uniform content (AUC)	38.9	61.1
Academic variable content (AVC)	37.7	62.3
Preprofessional/discipline-linked (PRE)	44.8	55.2
Basic study skills (BSS)	32.1	67.9
Hybrid	32.7	67.3
Other	14.3	85.7

The definition of learning community present in the 2012-2013 NSFYS was broader than that used elsewhere in the literature, yet the survey findings suggest that the FYS/LC models described were largely consistent with the understanding of a learning community as primarily a linkage of two or more courses. That is, nearly three quarters of the respondents (73.8%) reporting on learning communities in the survey identified co-enrollment in a seminar and at least one other course as a characteristic of the FYS/LC model. An additional 9.1% noted having co-enrollment in the seminar and all other courses (Young & Hopp, 2014). When combined, 80.7% of respondents reported linking the seminar to one or more other courses. Less than 12% of those indicating they had a learning community (11.9%) identified theme-based experiences outside the course or a residential component exclusively as the defining characteristic of the FYS/LC model. Moreover, many of the respondents who identified co-enrollment as a feature of the learning community also named one or more other characteristics as being present (Figure 2.1). For example, 40% of respondents who indicated that the FYS/LC model included co-enrollment also suggested that the content was coordinated across the courses in the LC. Common themes, cocurricular experiences, or residential components were also frequently noted characteristics of co-enrollment models. The presence of multiple features in FYS/LC structures suggest that many of the programs described by survey respondents may approach the ideal discussed in the chapter introduction.

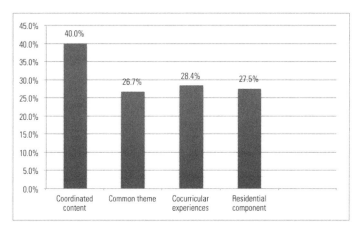

Figure 2.1. LC characteristics when co-enrollment in some or all courses present.

The characteristics of FYS/LC models reported do not vary significantly by seminar type with two exceptions (Table 2.2). Students were more likely to be co-enrolled in extended orientation and hybrid seminars and at least one other course than in other seminar types. A residential component was more likely to be part of a FYS/LC model when the seminar was academic variable content or preprofessional or discipline-linked. While interesting, these two trends should be interpreted with caution given low cell counts in several of the comparisons.

Table 2.2
LC Features by Seminar Type

	EO ($n = 106$)	AUC ($n = 56$)	AVC ($n = 55$)	PRE ($n = 13$)	BSS ($n = 9$)	Hybrid ($n = 35$)	Other ($n = 1$)
Some co-enrollment*	82.1%	62.5%	65.5%	69.2%	77.8%	82.9%	0.0%
Full co-enrollment	8.5%	8.9%	10.9%	15.4%	0.0%	5.7%	100.0%
Coordinated content	34.9%	33.9%	30.9%	38.5%	33.3%	40.0%	0.0%
Common theme	23.6%	32.1%	25.5%	15.4%	33.3%	25.7%	0.0%
Cocurricular experiences	27.4%	41.1%	32.7%	46.2%	22.2%	40.0%	0.0%
Residential component*	28.3%	21.4%	45.5%	46.2%	0.0%	31.4%	0.0%

Note. EO = extended orientation, AUC = academic with uniform content, AVC = academic with variable content, PRE = preprofessional or discipline-linked, BSS = basic study skills.
* $p < .05$.

Primary Role of Seminar in Learning Community

The analysis of open-ended data drew on roles for seminars in learning communities established in the literature. Figure 2.2 offers an overview of the presence of these themes in 2012-2013 NSFYS responses. A relatively low presence of a theme should not be interpreted as a lack of this role for the seminar. For example, only 7% of open-ended responses described shared assignments as a role of the seminar in the learning community. Yet, 34.5% of survey respondents indicated that intentional coordination of content was a feature of the FYS/LC. As such, open-ended responses related to shared assignments provide insight into what coordinated content may look like rather than its relative presence or absence in the seminar.

The rest of the section describes a range of possible roles for the seminar drawing on survey responses and other institutional examples. They are organized from most to least prominence in the open-ended responses.

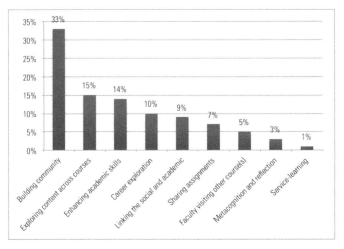

Figure 2.2. Role of FYS in LC based on open-ended responses to the 2012-2013 NSFYS (*n* = 252).

Building community. The most salient role for the seminar in LC structures among NSFYS respondents was building a sense of community among students and, often, among students, faculty, and staff. More than a third (33%) of respondents indicated that this was a main function of the FYS/LC. Research also suggests this may be an important feature of FYS/LC initiatives. A study of 174 developmental education learning communities offered to nearly 7,000 students at six community colleges (Visher, Weiss, Weissman, Rudd, & Wathington,

2012) confirmed earlier findings (MacGregor, 1991; Nownes & Stebleton, 2010; Tinto & Goodsell-Love, 1993) that students identify socioemotional support as an important benefit of participation in these programs. One student involved in FYS/LCs at Valencia College (n.d.-b.), a public, two-year institution in Orlando, Florida describes this support:

> Being in the R.E.A.C.H. (Recognize Each Academic Challenge Head-on) program is a very good experience. I love the fact that we all got the opportunity to meet new people and actually form good relationships. I also enjoy the way we can all relate to one another.

The sense that community building is a priority for the Valencia program spills over to faculty. "I think working with the colleagues has been wonderful because we stay in contact, coordinate our game plan" (Valencia College, n.d.-a.). A four-year public institution, Worcester State University (Massachusetts), has built its liberal arts and sciences curriculum (LASC) around learning communities with variable levels of connections between courses, including the first-year seminar. The thread running along the continuum of FYS/LC options is mutual support through the creation of small communities of learners.

Exploring concepts across courses. Fifteen percent of respondents described opportunities to discuss academic concepts introduced across linked courses as a role of the seminar in the LC. Exploring shared intellectual concepts through multiple lenses is a hallmark of the Themed Learning Communities (TLCs) at Indiana University-Purdue University of Indianapolis (IUPUI). This program engages

> students, faculty, librarians, advisors, and others in a community of learners that explore interdisciplinary connections both in and out of the classroom. Students are encouraged to explore relationships among different academic disciplines and develop a comprehensive perspective on higher education. Through the use of thematically linked curricula, service-learning, and cocurricular experiences, TLCs provide enriching learning experiences that foster interdisciplinary understanding. TLC faculty have developed creative strategies to integrate their assignments across disciplines and with co-curricular events. (IUPUI, n.d.)

Lindsey Wilson College, a four-year private institution in Columbia, Kentucky, offers a wide variety of learning communities involving student co-enrollment in two or more courses by academic major or other shared interests. The first-year seminars in these LCs serve as the site for students to actively engage around the community's theme through readings, discussions, and service activities. Students in the college's nursing learning community, for example, complete a service project at a health care facility, take a field trip to a different facility, and read articles about nursing in the first-year seminar.

Each of Worcester State University's FYS/LCs is built around essential learning outcomes adopted from the AAC&U's LEAP (Liberal Education and America's Promise) initiative. These shared outcomes are the key concepts that cut across all aspects of the FYS/LCs and include preparing students to be lifelong learners; engaged citizens; and to meet the daily challenges of work and life in an increasingly complex, rapidly changing global environment.

Enhancing skills, behaviors, and dispositions important to academic achievement. Fourteen percent of respondents described the seminar as a site for students to build skills, learn behaviors, and adopt dispositions important to succeeding in the linked and in all other courses. At Eastern New Mexico University (ENMU, n.d.) in Portales, all first-year students with fewer than 30 earned college credits are required to enroll in the Eastern Learning Community program, groups of 20-25 students taking two or more academic courses, including the first-year seminar, and exploring a common theme. The first-year seminar addresses learning skills, such as time management, note taking, active reading, test taking, oral presentations, library skills, computer use, and other topics deemed essential to academic success.

Career exploration. Ten percent of respondents to the FYS/LC question on the national survey described the role of the seminar as linking career exploration to learning community themes and topics. Delaware Technical Community College (NLCP/Washington Center), with campuses at four locations, offers a wide variety of career-focused FYS/LCs from a beer-brewing option for business majors to one entitled Adventures in Agriculture. One student publically praised the FYS/LC on the institution's website:

> The learning community was interesting because we ran weather simu-
> lations on our computer model to determine ways the school could save
> on energy costs. The work we did is identical to what we could be doing
> in the real world as a career. (Delaware Technical Community College,
> n.d.)

Students who are undecided about an academic major at Texas State University in San Marcos are invited to enroll in the Career Exploration Learning Community. A sample fall 2014 course schedule for participants included a university seminar and courses in communications and English. The same cohort of students enrolled in history, English, psychology, and political science in the spring 2015 term. Each member of the learning community worked with a peer mentor and career counselor, lived in the same residence hall with other participants, and took part in several career exploration activities outside the class (Texas State University, n.d.)

University of Nevada, Reno (NLCP/Washington Center) offers a similar FYS/LC for its undecided students. This program is open to all first-year students who are either undecided about their major or are in a major not included in another of the nine learning communities offered on campus. Members of this community enroll in math and English courses with other residents living on their residence hall floor and in Academic and Career Exploration (ACE 100), a first-year seminar (University of Nevada, Reno, n.d.).

Linking the social with the academic. Nine percent of respondents to the NSFYS described connecting the personal and social with the academic as goals of their FYS/LC. For example, the Explore, Discover, Decide Living-Learning Community at Slippery Rock University (NLCP/Washington Center), a four-year public institution in Pennsylvania, co-enrolls a group of students in three courses, including the First-Year Studies (FYRST) seminar, and assigns them to the same residence hall. Students who participate in this community engage in out-of-class activities that enhance their academic program and commit to exploring their personal strengths as they relate to the theme of the FYS/LC (Slippery Rock University, n.d.).

Sharing readings, assignments, and projects. While more than one third of NSFYS respondents reported coordinating content across courses, just 7% of the open-ended responses offered details about how sharing across courses works. Strategies offered in open-ended responses included joint field trips and readings, and shared classroom spaces. Other illustrations may also be found at the Washington Center's (n.d.) Integrative Learning Library, which offers links to fully integrated assignments. One assignment that is a part of a FYS/LC at Cerritos College (California) is the Konstructing Kafka: Radio Theater Project developed by Roger Ernest and David Young (NLCP/Washington Center). The link is between an introduction to college composition and a success in college and career course (the FYS). Chandler-Gilbert Community College (Chandler, Arizona) instructors Heather Horn and Vanessa Sandoval collaborated to design Perception and Communication in Meet the Parents, an assignment across developmental writing and college guidance (the FYS). The Pan African Learning Community at Sacramento State University (NLCP/Washington

Center) was designed by Tina Jordan, Boatomo Mosupyoe, Toni Tinker, and Jerry L. Blake and integrates assignments across a first-year seminar, introduction to Pan African studies, a basic writing course, and an FYS group tutorial.

Enthusiasm for exploring ideas through interdisciplinary lenses and completing assignments across courses have long been identified by students as a positive outcome of their experiences in learning communities. In their 1990 volume, Gabelnick et al. quoted a student involved in a community college coordinated studies program:

> At first, I thought we were studying English, economics, environmental science, and math in a balanced approach. I have come to realize that we have been using English and math to study the dynamics of economics and ecology. In other words, we have been attempting to use two languages to understand the interaction between a social and a biological science. (pp. 70-71)

Faculty members visit other linked classes. Respondents to the 2012-2013 NSFYS offer little insight into the extent to which faculty participate in courses across the LC. Just 5% described this occurring on their campuses. Two private universities in California offer examples of how it can be done. At the University of San Diego (NLCP/Washington Center), preceptors in FYS/LCs are full-time faculty members who teach linked, general education, first-year seminars and serve as their students' academic advisors and primary mentors, guiding students toward a high level of intellectual inquiry and, more practically, helping them complete course registration and academic program planning. Students who live both off and on the campus are invited to participate in a Living Learning Community (LLC) with commuting students taking part in just the curricular component. One student expressed her gratitude in a typical way: "Being in an LLC enabled me to have a personal connection with my professor, a chance I wouldn't have had if I had gone to a bigger university" (University of San Diego, n.d.).

On the University of La Verne campus 30 miles outside Los Angeles, faculty members team teach two courses in the FLEX program and students are co-enrolled in a third, smaller writing seminar. As an instructional team, faculty members are in each other's classes, collaborate on designing integrated curriculum and cocurricular experiences, and are committed to engaging with students in academically purposeful activities outside of class.

Metacognition and reflection. The seminar as a site for processing concepts related to the theme of the LC or to reflect on learning in general was described by 3% of survey respondents. Yet, this type of learning is implicit in several themes discussed elsewhere including those that help students make links between the personal, social, and academic; career-focused programs as described above; and those that emphasize service-learning. Illinois College, a small, residential liberal arts college in Jacksonville, offers a FYS/LC that combines the seminar, other courses, and a service component. Instructors build in reflective writing, particularly as it relates to completion of the service project and interdisciplinary themes. Kennesaw State University outside of Atlanta offers a FYS/LC that supports first-year science students enrolled in a general chemistry course. The program pairs a first-year seminar with the science course to increase the likelihood of student success in beginning chemistry; prevent early attrition among science majors; and increase student metacognition, which was identified as an important component of problem solving in the chemistry course and of critical thinking necessary for success in a science major (see the case in Part II of this volume for more information).

The career/academic major exploration FYS/LC is one type of program that lends itself to supporting student metacognition. These programs focus on linking learning in the curriculum and the cocurriculum with an individual's evolving sense of self and life purpose. One such program at Inver Hills Community College (NLCP/Washington Center), located in the southeastern suburbs of Minneapolis–St. Paul, linked a beginning writing course with a career exploration seminar. In their report of this experience, instructors Nicholas Nownes and Michael Stebleton (2010) concluded that this pairing resulted in students writing far more and more deeply in the linked writing course than in a nonlinked section taught by the same instructor. Reflective writing assignments allowed students to examine how learning and personal values converged with future career options.

Service-learning and FYS/LCs. Nearly one third (31.8%) of respondents to the 2012-2013 NSFYS reported that they embedded service-learning in first-year seminars (Young & Hopp, 2014). In fact, institutions that reported linking the first-year seminar to a learning community were significantly more likely to also include service-learning in the seminar (44.2%) than those reporting no learning community connection (24.6%, $p < .01$). While these data suggest the possibility of tight connections among these three high-impact practices, the extent to which service becomes an organizing theme for FYS/LC models is unclear. Just 1% of the open-ended responses described service-learning in connection to the FYS/LC.[4]

Despite limited evidence from the 2012-2013 NSFYS, examples of FYS/LCs integrating service-learning are available across institution types. Colorado Northwestern Community College (NLCP/Washington Center) in Rangely offers the Vision Learning Community where students enroll in several linked courses for a full two years. The first semester includes a 14-credit course block comprised of a first-year seminar, beginning English composition, introduction to sociology, outdoor leadership, and general college biology. Past service-learning projects completed by FYS/LC students at this institution have included a Wilderness Survival Planning Project, a Nutrition Awareness Project, the Northwest Colorado Wild Horse Project, Assisted Living Activities Project, and a Sea Turtle Rescue Project. Students, including the one quoted below, offer generally positive reviews of the VLC experience:

> In our group we not only discuss what we will do, we actually put these ideas in motion to help better the community. During the meetings we all put in thought for our projects. It is never a one man job, everyone is involved somehow. And through these projects we not only better the community, but ourselves as well. (Colorado Northwestern Community College, n.d.)

The Colorado Northwestern experience exemplifies an approach for connecting service-learning with learning communities advocated by Oates and Leavitt (2003) who asserted that combining learning communities and service-learning makes sense because of features common to both high-impact practices, such as (a) active-learning environments, (b) community building, and (c) opportunities to apply theory to practice beyond the classroom. Oates and Leavitt (2013) drew upon experiences from New Century College (NCC) at George Mason University (GMU, Fairfax, Virginia), which houses the Cornerstones Program for new students (NLCP/Washington Center).

---

[4] The low number of responses in this category may be an artifact of the location of questions related to FYS/LC below those about service-learning. Respondents may have decided that they had already answered questions about service-learning in a previous section and considered offering additional information redundant. Other efforts to understand how high-impact practices combine would need to account for this potential problem. One recommendation in this regard is offered in this chapter's conclusion.

Participating students, who may go on to graduate from NCC's Integrated Studies program, complete 24 credits in learning communities and 12 to 24 experiential learning credits. Some of those credits are completed as part of seminars emphasizing service-learning. These courses "offer students, faculty, and community partners an opportunity to work together to integrate and apply knowledge to address community needs. Learning goals, action strategies, and assignments [are] developed collaboratively" (GMU, n.d., para. 2). Students involved in another FYS/LC, the Leadership and Community Engagement Living-Learning Community, live together in the same residence hall and enroll as a group in a one-credit seminar both fall and spring that emphasizes learning through service. Most recently students in this FYS/LC completed a service trip to Assateague Island to restore dunes, participated in an AIDS walk, took part in and facilitated reflection at a hunger banquet, and created blankets for animals in shelters and children in transitional housing.

A report from the Higher Education Research Institute (Astin, Vogelgesang, Ikeda, & Yee, 2000) established that service participation by students shows significant positive effects on 11 outcome measures, including academic performance, values clarification, self-efficacy, leadership, choice of a service career, and plans to participate in service after college. Some 80% of the 22,000 students surveyed reported they believed their service made a difference and that they were learning from the experience. This GMU student's comment is typical of others who participate in service-learning connected to a learning community:

> Service-learning has helped me understand, in a more in-depth manner, what happens to [people with AIDS] throughout the process of the virus. I truly believe in learning by doing. It enhances what I have learned by helping others to understand more thoroughly. I was able to use what I learned in class to help educate people. (Oates & Leavitt, 2003, p. 25).

Combining First-Year Seminars and Learning Communities

As combined high-impact practices, first-year seminars and learning communities can be designed to have a bidirectional effect on each other, or the components of each may have very little impact on how the others are delivered. The seminar and other features of the LC may also take turns serving as the driver in the linkage. At other times, the components may be designed together to share responsibility for linkages. The latter approach is seen, for example, at the University of La Verne, a four-year private institution in California's Los Angeles County. This institution requires every student to participate in the La Verne Experience, a four-year program that University President Devorah Lieberman described as integrating "academic curricular, co-curricular activities, and civic and community engagement with the university's values and traditions" (Lieberman, 2014, p. 52). During the first year of the La Verne Experience, incoming students participate in a FLEX (First-Year La Verne Experience) learning community involving student cohort enrollment in two discipline-based courses and a writing course, which serves as the first-year academic seminar. Disciplinary courses are taught by faculty members who have collaborated to ensure that course links are made around the students' shared interests and that cocurricular experiences, including community service, are designed to complement what occurs in the courses. In the writing course, students reflect on the connections between the two disciplinary courses and on community engagement activities that require application of theory to practice. FLEX is an example of a FYS/LC intentionally crafted to allow the components to work together. In this case, one component would be offered in a wholly different way without the presence of its counterpart.

FLEX also embodies four characteristics that past research indicates are common to many first-year seminars and learning communities (Henscheid, 2004; Johnson, 2013; Pascarella & Terenzini, 2005; Smith et al., 2004). These shared characteristics (Figure 2.3) are among eight listed in Chapter 1 and identified by Kuh (2008) and Kuh and O'Donnell (2013) as features of high-impact practices: (a) time-on-task (Chickering, & Gamson, 1987), (b) engagement (Kuh, 2008), (c) self-authorship (Baxter Magolda, 2008), and (d) deep learning (Tagg, 2003). Labels applied to these four characteristics may differ from campus to campus and program to program, but they are implicit in Kuh's list (2008). The overlap of these characteristics suggests a distinct opportunity for designing high-quality FYS/LCs around shared features.

Lardner and Malnarich (2008) reported that campuses applying to participate in the National Summer Institute on Learning Communities are increasingly indicating that they are interested in learning communities as an avenue for positively impacting how students learn. However, as they and others (MacGregor, 1991; Nownes, & Stebleton, 2010; Visher et al., 2012) noted, designing learning-focused learning communities, including those with first-year seminars, continues to elude most campuses. The continued resistance (intended or not) of the academy to create integrated learning experiences in FYS/LCs has prompted the Washington Center to call for a new era of learning communities emphasizing faculty collaboration around the following core strategy:

Notice what needs work, pay attention to research, try out new ways of working in the company of supportive peers, share insights, refine, and revise. If this approach to faculty development is tied to questions raised by using [an integrative learning] heuristic, developing a pedagogical plan, and looking at student work, it will surely have an impact, not just on learning communities but on the pursuit of our collective aim: a high-quality education for every student. (Lardner & Malnarich, 2008, p. 37)

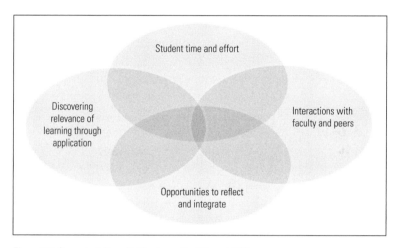

Figure 2.3. Characteristics of HIPs shared by LCs and FYSs.

Recommendations and Conclusion

The answer to Finley and Kuh's question in Chapter 1 about what the *best* practices are for embedding first-year seminars in learning communities is most likely "it depends on the campus." Campus-based studies may, therefore, be the first place to start looking for an answer. A study of six community colleges authored by Visher and colleagues (2012) offered methodological guidance for designing empirical studies and evaluations on programs at both two- and four-year institutions. Researchers and program evaluators are also invited to review methods and findings from the studies done at the University of North Texas (Tampke & Durodoye, 2013), Kennesaw State University (Smith, Goldfine, & Windham, 2009 and in this volume), Appalachian State University (Friedman, & Alexander, 2007), Indiana University-Purdue University of Indianapolis (Chism, Baker, Hansen, & Williams, 2008), and from the University of California Los Angeles' Higher Education Research Institute (Keup, 2006).

The FYS/LC as a hybrid, high-impact educational experience also deserves a clear definition of its own that is consistently used in institutional practice and in scholarship. Continued testing and refinement of a definition may also allow scholars and practitioners to devise a reliable and valid instrument for collecting national and local data for research and program evaluation purposes. Methods for better understanding the FYS/LC combination should also vary. Visher and colleagues (2012) pointed out that determining the quality of learning communities is not a primary role of quantitative techniques. They recommend formal observations of teaching and learning and collection of qualitative data from students, faculty, and other program participants. Similar advice, specifically related to FYS/LCs, was offered by Greenfield, Keup, and Gardner (2013) and in the chapter in this volume on assessment of FYS/LC structures.

Final Thoughts

The publication of this volume and the work of Oates and Leavitt (2003) on combining service-learning and learning communities take us a few steps closer to understanding how, and how well, high-impact practices are combined. As imperfect as it is to tease out who does what and when in these hybrid approaches, the effort is worth it if educators can more clearly see what is, is not, and should be happening to improve students' learning and increase their opportunities for success. It is the hope of most educational researchers that better understanding leads to improved practice.

References

The Association of American Colleges and Universities. (2007). *College learning for the new global century.* Washington, DC: Author. Retrieved from http://www.aacu.org/sites/default/files/files/LEAP/GlobalCentury_final.pdf

Astin, A. W., Vogelgesang, L. J., Ikeda, E. K., & Yee, J. A. (2000). *How service-learning affects students.* Los Angeles, CA: Higher Education Research Institute, University of California Los Angeles.

Barefoot, B. O., & Fidler, P. P. (1996). *The 1994 National Survey of Freshmen Seminar Programs: Continuing innovations in the collegiate curriculum* (Monograph No. 20). Columbia, SC: University of South Carolina, National Resource Center for The Freshmen Year Experience and Students in Transition.

Baxter Magolda, M. B. (2008). Three elements of self-authorship. *Journal of College Student Development, 49*(4), 269-284.

Chickering, A. W., & Gamson, Z. F. (1987, March). Seven principles for good practice. *AAHE Bulletin, 39*(7), 3–7.

Chism, L. P., Baker, S. S., Hansen, M. J., & Williams, G. (2008). Implementation of first-year seminars, the summer academy bridge program, and themed learning communities. *Metropolitan Universities, 19*(2), 8-17.

Colorado Northwestern Community College. (n.d.). *Vision learning community student-testimonials.* Retrieved from http://www.cncc.edu/cms/content/vision-learning-community-student-testimonials

Delaware Technical Community College. (n.d.). *Learning community testimonials* [Jake Biggs]. Retrieved from https://www.dtcc.edu/academics/learning-options/learning-communities

Eastern New Mexico University (ENMU). (n.d.). *Learning communities.* Retrieved from http://www.enmu.edu/future-students/freshmen/communities.shtml

Friedman, D. B., & Alexander, J. S. (2007). Investigating a first-year seminar as an anchor course in learning communities. *Journal of The First-Year Experience & Students in Transition, 19*(1), 63-74.

Gabelnick, F., MacGregor, J., Matthews, R. S., & Smith, B. L. (1990). *Learning communities: Creating connections among students, faculty, and disciplines* (New Directions for Teaching and Learning No. 41). San Francisco, CA: Jossey-Bass.

George Mason University (GMU). (n.d.). *NCLC 394: Service-learning experience.* Retrieved from http://ncc.gmu.edu/courses/1377

Greenfield, G. M., Keup, J. R., & Gardner, J. N. (2013). *Developing and sustaining successful first-year programs: A guide for practitioners.* San Francisco, CA: Jossey-Bass.

Henscheid, J. M. (2000). *Responses to 1997 National Survey of First-Year Seminar Programs* [Unpublished raw data]. Columbia, SC: University of South Carolina, National Resource Center for The First-Year Experience & Students in Transition.

Henscheid, J. M. (2004). First-year seminars in learning communities: Two reforms intersect. In J. M. Henscheid (Ed.), *Integrating the first-year experience: The role of learning communities in first-year seminars* (Monograph No. 39, pp. 1-8). Columbia, SC: University of South Carolina, National Resource Center for The First-Year Experience & Students in Transition.

Indiana University-Purdue University Indianapolis (IUPUI). (n.d.). *Themed learning communities.* Retrieved from http://uc.iupui.edu/StudentServices/ThemedLearningCommunities.aspx

Inkelas, K. K., & Longerbeam, S. D. (2008). Working toward a comprehensive typology of living-learning communities. In G. Luna & J. Gahagan (Eds.), *Learning initiatives in the residential setting* (Monograph No. 48, pp. 29-41). Columbia, SC: University of South Carolina, National Resource Center for The First-Year Experience & Students in Transition.

Johnson, K. E. (2013). Learning communities and the completion agenda. *Learning Communities Research and Practice, 1*(3), Article 3. Retrieved from http://washingtoncenter.evergreen.edu/lcrpjournal/vol1/iss3/3

Keup, J. R. (2006). The impact of curricular interventions on intended second year re-enrollment. *Journal of College Student Retention: Research, Theory & Practice, 7*(1-2), 61-89.

Kuh, G. D. (2008). *High-impact educational practices: What they are, who has access to them, and why they matter.* Washington, DC: Association of American Colleges & Universities.

Kuh, G. D., & O'Donnell, K. (2013). *Ensuring quality & taking high-impact practices to scale.* Washington, DC: Association of American Colleges and Universities.

Lardner, E., & Malnarich, G. (2008). A new era in learning-community work: Why the pedagogy of intentional integration matters. *Change, 40*(4), 30-37.

Lenning, O. T., & Ebbers, L. H. (1999). *The powerful potential of learning communities: Improving education for the future* (ASHE-ERIC Higher Education Report No. 26.6). Washington, DC: The George Washington University, Graduate School of Education and Human Development.

Lieberman, D. (2014). The La Verne experience: A common core for undergraduate and graduate students, *Liberal Education, 100*(1), 52-57.

Love, A. G., & Tokuno, K. A. (1999). Learning community models. In J. H. Levine (Ed.), *Learning communities: New structures, new partnerships for learning* (Monograph No. 26, pp. 9–18). Columbia, SC: University of South Carolina, National Resource Center for The First-Year Experience & Students in Transition.

MacGregor, J. (1991). What differences do learning communities make? *Washington Center News, 6*(1), 4-9.

MacGregor, J., Smith, B. L., Matthews, R. S., & Gabelnick, F. (1997, March). *Learning community models.* Paper presented at the National Conference on Higher Education, American Association of Higher Education, Washington, D.C.

Nownes, N., & Stebleton, M. J. (2010). Reflective writing and life-career planning: Extending the learning in a learning community model. *Teaching English in the Two-Year College, 38*(2), 118-131.

Oates, K. K., & Leavitt, L. H. (2003). *Service-learning and learning communities: Tools for integration and assessment.* Washington DC: Association of American Colleges & Universities.

Padgett, R. D., & Keup, J. R. (2011). *2009 National Survey of First-Year Seminars: Ongoing efforts to support students in transition* (Research Reports on College Transitions No. 2). Columbia, SC: University of South Carolina, National Resource Center for The First-Year Experience & Students in Transition.

Pascarella, E. T., & Terenzini, P. T. (2005). *How college affects students: A third decade of research.* San Francisco, CA: Jossey-Bass.

Shapiro, N. S., & Levine, J. H. (1999). *Creating learning communities: A practical guide to winning support, organizing for change, and implementing programs.* San Francisco, CA: Jossey-Bass.

Slippery Rock University. (n.d.). *Living learning communities.* Retrieved from http://www.sru.edu/life-at-sru/housing/living-learning-communities

Smith, B. L., MacGregor, J., Matthews, R. S., Gabelnick, F., & Associates. (2004). *Learning communities: Reforming undergraduate education.* San Francisco, CA: Jossey-Bass.

Smith, D. N., Goldfine, R., & Windham, M. (2009). Comparing student learning outcomes in an independent section of a first-year seminar to a first-year seminar embedded in a learning community. *Journal of The First-Year Experience & Students in Transition, 21*(2), 47-63.

Snider, K. J. G., & Venable, A. M. (May, 2000). *Assessing learning community effectiveness: A multi-campus approach.* Presentation given at the 2000 Association for Institutional Research Annual Forum, Cincinnati, OH.

Stassen, M. L. A. (2003). Student outcomes: The impact of varying living-learning community models. *Research in Higher Education, 44*(5), 581-613.

Tagg, J. (2003). *The learning paradigm college.* Bolton, MA: Anker.

Tampke, D. R., & Durodoye, R. (2013). Improving academic success for undecided students: A first-year seminar/learning community approach. *Learning Communities Research and Practice, 1*(2), Article 3. Retrieved from http://washingtoncenter.evergreen.edu/lcrpjournal/vol1/iss2/3

Texas State University. (n.d.). *Current living-learning communities.* Retrieved from http://www.reslife.txstate.edu/llc/Current.html

Tinto, V., & Goodsell-Love, A. (1993). Building community. *Liberal Education, 79*(4), 16-21.

University of Nevada, Reno. (n.d.). *Nine living learning communities.* Retrieved from http://www.unr.edu/housing/on-campus-housing/living-learning-communities/llc-nine-communities

University of San Diego. (n.d.). *Living learning communities* [Video Comment]. Retrieved from http://www.sandiego.edu/cas/llc/

Valencia College (n.d.-a). *LinC: Learning in community.* Retrieved from http://valenciacollege.edu/linc/

Valencia College (n.d.-b). *Start college strong with REACH.* Retrieved from http://valenciacollege.edu/REACH/Quotes-from-REACH-Students.cfm

Visher, M. G., Weiss, M. J., Weissman, E., Rudd, T., & Wathington, H. (2012). *The effects of learning communities for students in developmental education: A synthesis of findings from six community colleges.* New York, NY: MDRC.

Washington Center for the Improvement of Undergraduate Education. (n.d.). *Integrative learning library.* Retrieved from http://www.evergreen.edu/washingtoncenter/intlearning/index.html

Young, D. G., & Hopp, J. M. (2014). *2012-2013 National Survey of First-Year Seminars: Exploring high-impact practices in the first college year* (Research Reports on College Transitions No. 4). Columbia, SC: University of South Carolina, National Resource Center for The First-Year Experience & Students in Transition.

Chapter 3
Administering Combined First-Year Seminar and Learning Community Programs

Nia Haydel and Liya Escalera

Traditionally, the structure of higher education has been fragmented; knowledge and research have been divided into departments, and student affairs and academic affairs have been viewed as distinct institutional functions. First-year seminar and learning community (FYS/LC) initiatives dismantle such boundaries, intersecting with multiple administrative and academic areas within the institution. They also require a commitment to forging deep partnerships between and among work areas if they are to be effective. Administering a FYS/LC program can be challenging due to the level of integration required, but addressing these challenges serves to deepen the inherent value of both first-year seminars and learning communities. Combined programs force institutions to confront barriers to student success, examine issues of access and equity, and collaborate across work areas to develop creative and innovative solutions to these challenges. Because this work often involves rethinking and reworking existing policies, procedures, and practices, when FYS/LC programs are successfully implemented, the result is a stronger, more learner-centered organization. The result is often transformational. Not only are student learning and engagement enhanced but faculty and staff also become more effective practitioners as they form deeper connections with their colleagues and delve further into the study of teaching, learning, and student development.

Institutions that decide to implement combined FYS/LC programs may do so with one, both, or neither individual initiative initially in place. Once implemented, continued attention and ongoing assessment is necessary to sustain FYS/LC programs and, if desired, to grow them (Laufgraben & Shapiro, 2004). This chapter addresses areas to consider in the implementation and expansion of successful FYS/LC programs: (a) aligning the initiative with the college mission, (b) identifying the target population, (c) allocating resources and identifying funding, (d) locating the program within the organizational structure, (e) engaging all stakeholders, and (f) supporting professional development. Strategies for assessment are explored in Chapter 5.

Environmental Scanning

Many campuses engage in environmental scanning as the first stage in developing a new or scaling an existing initiative. Environmental scanning is the process of assessing the current conditions and needs that influence an organization's operations and decision-making processes (Albright, 2004). An environmental scan "enables decision makers both to understand the external environment and the interconnectedness of its various sectors and to translate this understanding" into action (Morrison, 1992, p. 1). Scanning processes that bring multiple perspectives together can be used to strengthen faculty and staff investment in FYS/LC programs and to increase commitment to resolving issues identified in the scan. Knitting environmental scanning into the college's assessment process also helps move FYS/LC initiatives from the periphery of the institution to the center. This is especially important in times of financial crisis; it is much simpler to trim programs from the budget when they exist on the margins. On the other hand, a program that is fully integrated into the fabric of the institution is more likely to survive a financial downturn.

Many campuses appoint steering committees or task forces when launching new initiatives or redesigning existing ones. The steering committee can play a key role in the environmental scan but only if the traditional approach to these work groups is rethought. Committees are usually focused on the logistics related to responsibilities and tasks associated with the pending project. In other words, individuals participating in a committee generally focus on the *what* instead of the *why* of a project—those philosophical underpinnings that serve as the foundation for the creation of the new initiative (Gano-Phillips & Barnett, 2008). Addressing the *why* when implementing or scaling FYS/LC programs demands meaningful collaboration across the campus that is guided by a committee or advisory board rather than dictated by a leadership team. One way to engage the rest of the campus in addressing the *why* of the project, is to use quantitative and qualitative data on student success to begin an honest dialog about the unmet needs and obstacles faced by students, faculty, and staff (Gano-Phillips & Barnett, 2008). Drawing on this feedback and connecting it directly to the outcomes and objectives of a FYS/LC program illustrates that it can be a vehicle for addressing institutional issues about which stakeholders on campus and in the community care.

The first step of the steering committee is to design an overall plan that will allow all necessary stakeholders to fully participate in the process. This may involve surveying or interviewing stakeholders, facilitating stakeholder focus groups, reviewing relevant online and print materials—or any combination thereof—in order to identify the stakeholder roles and objectives and clarify overall goals. In this way, individuals and departments articulate what they value as it relates to the implementation or scaling of the FYS/LC program, how they intend to exemplify those values throughout the program, and why those values are critical to its overall success. After the group solidifies the goals and objectives of the FYS/LC program, the next phase of the environmental scanning process is to evaluate the existing structural components that interface with the FYS/LC initiative to identify potential gaps in support and ways to bridge those gaps.

Environmental scanning considers FYS/LC structures within the framework of the organization and campus culture and explores the following key questions:

- How does an FYS/LC program align with the institution's mission and strategic plan?

- Who is the target population for the FYS/LC program?

- Does the college or institution have the necessary resources to support a successful FYS/LC program?

- Does the campus culture support or challenge program implementation or scaling?

- Where is the best place to locate the program?

Mission and Program Alignment

Creating a shared vision is a necessary first step in successfully implementing FYS/LC initiatives. In their 2005 study, Ferrari and Velcoff found that employees' commitment to an institution could be attributed to their perceptions of the institution's ability to execute its mission through the programs and services offered. This suggests that whether the institution delivers on the promises of their mission influences overall support of initiatives. Similar to the process of curricular mapping, a critical component of mission alignment is incorporating a process that matches specific program goals and learning outcomes with the institution's mission while simultaneously fostering an environment that encourages collegiality and collaboration (Uchiyama & Radin, 2009).

Along with the shared vision of the program, learning outcomes central to the FYS/LC initiative should be widely agreed upon and clearly articulated. Then, following the backwards design process of Wiggins and McTighe (2005), components central to all FYS/LCs can be determined. Many institutions include language about the development of critical thinking among their graduates in their mission statements. FYS/LC programs that emphasize integrative thinking align with and support this aspect of institutional mission. Moreover, when assignments encouraging the synthesis of content across disciplines are a part of each FYS/LC offering, there is even tighter alignment between these initiatives and institutional mission. Similarly, institutions often seek to promote engaged citizenship among their students. Again, this is an area where alignment can be achieved. When civic engagement is an outcome, experiences, such as service-learning, would be a required component of all FYS/LCs courses. A note of caution—it can be tempting for administrators to view the curriculum of a FYS/LC program as a vehicle to solve every problem facing new student success and to house every stray initiative for new students on campus. Thus, the core objectives and learning outcomes of an FYS/LC initiative can easily get lost if clear parameters guiding the curriculum are not in place.

Two main curricular questions must be addressed and periodically revisited in FYS/LC programs: Which courses will be linked for each FYS/LC? and Which learning outcomes and components will be shared by every FYS/LC? These course configurations must address the needs of the student population. For example, do FYS/LC models address general education, major, and/or graduation requirements? Would they respect college policies and prerequisites, or would they require exceptions? To adequately address these concerns, the model should return to the fundamental questions related to program priorities and the established processes for resolving varying perspectives.

Identifying a Target Population

The initial phase of environmental scanning is an opportunity to bring faculty and staff from across the campus together to review institutional data on student success and to determine where student achievement gaps, areas of curricular misalignment, or other institutional challenges exists that may serve as the focus of the combined initiative. In the current climate of higher education— marked by reduced resources and questions raised regarding the value and cost-effectiveness of higher education (Long, 2006), and subsequent calls for increased scrutiny and accountability— institutions can no longer concentrate their efforts merely on the recruitment and enrollment of large cohorts of students without clearly articulated plans for moving students through the higher education pipeline. For example, in reviewing persistence data, an institution may note that male students are retained or successfully complete courses in the first year at lower rates than females. In this case, faculty and staff will want to consider how the program design will draw on institutional knowledge, literature, and research to support the needs of male students. Similarly, an institution may find that the number of students declaring STEM majors is waning. Faculty and staff could then consider how a combined program might introduce new students to STEM fields while providing them with skills they will need to be successful in these majors. Ideally this phase of the environmental scan serves to create a shared vision where designers and implementers at all levels agree upon who will be served by the program; which institutional challenges will be addressed; and, based on these factors, the overarching goals.

Allocating Resources

The benefits of FYS/LC structures, as documented elsewhere in this volume, may prompt institutions to consider developing or expanding such an initiative. The initial exploration often requires an examination of the way institutional resources are currently allocated and how resources might be reallocated to support the creation or expansion of FYS/LC initiatives. The actual cost of an FYS/LC program depends greatly on its design and how well the institution is positioned to support that design. Some institutions may find that FYS/LC programs are low-cost, if there is an existing infrastructure that can support a combined program. In this case, the design may depend upon redefining and perhaps shifting current roles instead of creating costly new positions and structures. Other institutions may find that the current infrastructure cannot support the needs of a combined program, and implementation or scale may require a significant investment of resources in the form of additional faculty or staff, stipends and/or course releases for faculty, funding for professional development, the acquisition of physical space, and/or new technologies. Similarly, some programs may incorporate experiential or service-learning components that require additional funding for such activities. Once the costs are identified and the budget developed, it is necessary to engage in conversations related to funding sources, potential resource reallocation, and overall fiscal management of the program. Tinto (1999) and Lardner and Malnarich (2008) recommended beginning by experimenting with carefully focused pilots that target specific goals. In small pilots, logistical and financial concerns are easily managed, and administrators gain insight into the challenges of successful implementation, scalability, and sustainability.

Leveraging grant funding can be a great way to pilot a program. However, two questions must be addressed. First, do the objectives of the grant align with the objectives of the FYS/LC initiative? If grant funding is tied to priorities that conflict with program goals, administrators run the risk of allowing funding to steer the direction of the initiative, instead of grounding it in the shared vision and learning outcomes that have been established. Second, how will the program be institutionalized when the grant period ends? Will a certain percentage of the overall cost be shifted to the institutional budget each year, or will particular components become institutionalized and funded over time? A clear plan for weaning the program off grant funding and into the institutional budget needs to be delineated to ensure that it outlives the grant.

Focusing on sustainability from the design phase illustrates a commitment to the long-term program goals. This strategy requires making clear connections between carefully delineated objectives, action items, and resources. Creating goals that are realistic and identifying attainable benchmarks and outcomes contribute to institutional support for both the implementation of the program and its continuance once it is established.

Campus Culture

Campus culture can be difficult to identify as it often operates as a set of covert processes that manifest in the form of "hidden agendas, blind spots, organizational politics, the elephant in the room, secret hopes and wishes, tacit assumptions and unconscious dynamics" (Marshak, 2006, p. xi). Yet, it can sink a FYS/LC initiative. For this reason, the environmental scan is critical for effectively framing the program for particular constituents and confronting potential barriers to progress.

Depending upon the existing culture of a campus, the successful implementation of a FYS/LC program may require a cultural shift in how the institution approaches teaching and learning. It can be useful to draw on literature and research on organizational change theories to navigate and shift campus culture. Such theories provide frameworks that can be used to better understand how the institution's culture impacts the way the institution operates. Organizational theory related to collaborative leadership (Austin & Baldwin, 1991; Ansell & Gash, 2008; Bess & Dee, 2008; Gray, 2008; Kezar & Lester, 2009) and interdisciplinary education (Casey, 1994; Feller, 2002; Smith & McCann, 2001) is particularly applicable to FYS/LC administration.

Williams, Berger, and McClendon (2005) maintained that "campus leaders must pay attention to formal structures that can act as either barriers or conduits to educational transformation … if transformation is to be successful, senior administrators must examine and be willing to reengineer existing institutional hierarchies and resource allocations" (p. 13). Addressing campus culture directly through formal structures, such as committee appointments, academic programming, tenure and promotion decisions, budget processes, and policy creation, sends a message to faculty and staff that the institution backs the culture shift necessary to support the FYS/LC initiative. Often the change process and institutional transformation are bidirectional; change is necessary in order to implement an FYS/LC program, but the program, itself, and the process through which it is developed also result in meaningful change of the institution.

Locating the Program

Since FYS/LC initiatives are interdisciplinary and may not be housed in a single academic department, a number of questions arise about where they are to be located in the organizational structure. Deciding on the optimal location for the FYS/LC program on campus requires thoughtful consideration of the underlying philosophical principles and operational priorities shaping it. The location of the FYS/LC program within the organization may have broad implications for its priorities, thus identifying the program's objectives should be considered when conducting the environmental scan and assessing the campus culture.

An example of how location can influence priorities can be observed through the different expectations associated with a program supported through enrollment management, student affairs, or academic affairs. In an enrollment management division, the primary goal of activities may be matriculation, persistence, and graduation. Within student affairs, student engagement, academic support, and institutional policies and procedures may be greatly valued. Academic affairs administrators may emphasize student learning outcomes, assessment, and pedagogy. One can imagine how the perspectives listed above may influence the design and delivery of an FYS/LC initiative. Conflicting perspectives may cause disagreement as to the program's purpose if stakeholders on campus have not come to a consensus on its objectives and priorities.

Engaging Stakeholders

The process of developing FYS/LC structures that withstand the politics and tensions of institutional culture requires practices that afford all stakeholders opportunities to contribute to and engage in the implementation or scale of the FYS/LC initiative. However, faculty, staff, and student participation in planning and development does not necessarily generate ownership over a program. To achieve this, the contributions of all stakeholders must be valued when difficult decisions are made. Meaningful collaboration across the campus can be challenging given the busy schedules of students, faculty, and staff; the rapid pace of the academic year; and the deeply ingrained silos between work areas. However, a lack of collaboration can be costly. Failure to engage faculty may result in mistrust of an initiative perceived as being imposed by the administration. Similarly, student affairs staff may become frustrated if they attribute low faculty involvement to a lack of interest in supporting student success. Failure on the part of enrollment professionals and the registrar may result in a program design that is not compatible with admission and registration policies and practices. If students' voices have not been heard in the planning process, the FYS/LCs may not meet their needs.

Faculty

Faculty play a pivotal role in the success of any academic program, and this is particularly true in FYS/LC initiatives. Their influence is related to the role they play in the institution and the complex power dynamics between faculty, staff, and administrators in the overall campus culture. Consequently, the mechanisms and structures through which faculty are engaged and invited to participate in combined programs will have a profound effect on campuswide support for such initiatives. FYS/LC programs must be faculty-driven since their participation is essential in designing and delivering curriculum, assessing outcomes, aligning FYS/LCs with academic programs of study and degree requirements, and adopting effective pedagogies and practices. Therefore, faculty should be integrated into the conception, planning, and design of FYS/LC structures from the beginning. Involving them in the early stages of development creates a pipeline of faculty who are knowledgeable and enthusiastic about the initiative because they created it. Moreover, faculty ownership of the FYS/LC program signals to the campus community that its goals align with faculty values, legitimizing its place in the life of the institution.

Before delving more deeply into the role of the faculty, engaging in a brief discussion as to who makes up the faculty in combined programs is useful. Current research (Kezar, 2012) indicates that the vast majority of undergraduate students, particularly first-year students, are taught by part-time faculty with varying degrees of experience, institutional knowledge, and commitment to campuswide initiatives. According to the 2012-2013 National Survey of First-Year Seminars (Young & Hopp, 2014), FYSs are taught by a wide range of instructors, including full- and part-time faculty, academic counselors, academic support and student affairs professionals, and graduate students. This complicates the staffing of FYS/LC initiatives, as many institutions are grappling with the role that adjuncts and student affairs professionals should and can have in academic programs and how best to integrate them into the fabric of the institution.

Since most campuses cannot run combined programs on a large scale without relying to some degree on a contingent instructor pool, administrators must consider how they will involve these instructors in design and delivery, as their understanding of program goals and their support is essential. Kezar (2012) cautioned that integrating non-tenure-track faculty and part-time faculty into campuswide initiatives is challenging given the reality that they often teach on multiple campuses, carry heavy teaching loads, and may juggle careers outside higher education. Yet, excluding these instructors comes at a high price, as research documents a correlation between the marginalization of part-time and non-tenure-track faculty and lower levels of engagement, retention, and completion in the courses they teach (Kezar 2012). There are numerous models for integrating part-time and non-tenure-track faculty into FYS/LC programs ranging from requiring professional development seminars for part-time faculty, to including part-time and non-tenure-track faculty in college decision-making and governance processes, to establishing faculty mentoring initiatives (Burnstad, Hayes, Hoss, & West, 2007).

FYS/LC program success depends upon participation by faculty and other instructors who are ideologically aligned with both FYS and LC pedagogy and practice, and who will become champions of the FYS/LC initiative. Once faculty champions are established, recruitment can happen at the grassroots level within academic departments. Faculty-to-faculty recruitment tends to be more successful in identifying those who are a good fit for FYS/LC programs than recruitment by administrators or program coordinators who are not faculty and may be less aware of an individual's teaching philosophy or academic priorities (Visher, Schneider, Wathington, & Collado, 2010).

Since teaching in FYS/LCs presents unique challenges, it is important to make clear to instructors the scope of the work expected and the ways in which they will be compensated before involvement in the FYS/LC program begins. In this way, instructors can make informed decisions regarding their participation. At Kingsborough Community College, these expectations have been outlined in a faculty-developed Learning Community Agreement (Visher et al., 2010). Compensation may take the form of a stipend, course release, or graduate assistant support; however, in lean fiscal times, compensation may take other forms, such as letters of recognition that positively impact tenure and promotion decisions. Regardless of the compensation structure, sustaining an FYS/LC program over time requires that faculty participants are recognized and in some way rewarded for the work and collaboration inherent in teaching an FYS/LC.

In addition to compensation, administrators must research existing policies regarding faculty course loads, especially in unionized environments. For example, if FYS/LC instructors team teach courses, how many credits of the FYS/LC will count towards each faculty member's regular course load? Or, if faculty members from academic departments teach an FYS, will they receive a course reduction in their home department? If so, who will staff these courses? Will the institution need to hire additional part-time faculty to cover them? Moreover, do current policies regulate whether and how student affairs professionals can be compensated for teaching FYSs, particularly if they do so during their regular work hours?

Student Affairs Professionals

Blake (2007) argued that given the changing demographics of the student population and increased attention to educational outcomes and graduation rates, student affairs professionals are playing an increasingly critical role in student engagement, retention, and learning. This evolving role requires a paradigm shift in the way student affairs professionals are viewed on campus and how they are integrated into activities, such as curriculum design and development, that have been traditionally considered under the purview of academic affairs. The extent to which student affairs and academic support professionals are integrated into FYS/LC programs varies, however. If they are fully vested partners, their duties will inevitably shift from an emphasis on administrative support to a more active classroom role (Smith & Williams, 2007), which means working with faculty to integrate student development outcomes into the curriculum, participating in classroom activities periodically throughout the semester, and teaching or coteaching FYSs. The collaborative nature of FYS/LC programs provides an opportunity for all types of instructors to come together for meaningful partnerships around teaching and learning. As Smith and Williams (2007) noted, FYS/LC programs are a

> venue where faculty and student affairs educators can collaborate, coor-
> dinate, and ultimately create new common ground for learning … These
> programs often represent a move toward more holistic notions of student
> learning that take advantage of learning opportunities both in and out of
> class while forging new possibilities for students' and teachers' roles and
> relationships. (p. 1)

Student affairs staff are essential both in integrating FYS/LC initiatives into the advisement, enrollment, and orientation process for new students and in integrating student development outcomes into FYS/LC curriculum. For example, at Bunker Hill Community College, Success Coach Advisors play an essential role in the FYS/LC integrated support services model. The advisors are responsible for orientation and registration of new students, and they help new students enroll in FYS/LC offerings that match their interests. However, they also spend significant time working with faculty in the FYS/LC course development phase to integrate and contextualize student development outcomes, such as career and educational planning, into thematic FYS/LC course curricula. Similarly, at Dillard University, the student affairs staff serve as instructors for the FYS courses and assist with the implementation of all academic interventions coordinated through the Early Alert Program, which targets students who are in danger of failing the courses in the LC. The goals of these collaborations are to develop integrative activities and assignments that satisfy the learning outcomes of each course in the FYS/LC as well as meeting the college's student development outcomes for new students.

Academic Support Partners

A partner who is integral to the success of FYS/LC programs is the registrar or scheduler. FYS/LC initiatives require complex coordination of courses, management of enrollment capacities, and consideration of corequisite and prerequisite requirements and classroom availability. In order to support the creation of learning environments that will meet the needs of students enrolled in an FYS/LC program, the involvement of the individual who is often responsible for these components is essential.

In addition to the registrar, coordination with department chairs, deans, faculty, and staff who oversee the course scheduling process for individual departments is also essential. Deep knowledge of how different academic departments schedule courses and assign faculty and how these practices intersect with institutional deadlines and procedures is required to design a scheduling method that will work for the FYS/LC model. In initial pilots, it may seem easier to bypass campuswide course scheduling and registration processes and slip FYS/LC components into the empty spaces and peripheries of the schedule. However, working with academic departments from the outset to establish scheduling practices that support FYS/LC programs will make scaling pilots easier. FYS/LC programs, regardless of their size, often require planning and organization well ahead of the typical institutional cycle, so that when the regular scheduling cycle begins, deans, department chairs, and other key players are aware of the needs of the FYS/LC program and its effect on classroom space and faculty assignments.

The impact of FYS/LCs on the registration process can range from minor policy adjustments to a complete restructuring of registration functions (Smith & Williams, 2007). On some campuses, incoming first-year students register through academic advisors, who can explain FYS/LC requirements and encourage students to enroll in them. As such, these academic support professionals must be included in the FYS/LC planning process and updated on program developments as they are often the primary information source for students. On other campuses, entering students may register themselves online. In such cases, the registrar must input restrictions or rules in registration software that will enable co-requisites and/or reserve FYS/LC program courses for target populations. The importance of the logistics related to course scheduling must not be overlooked because an oversight could result in a less-than successful execution of the program.

Student Partners

As noted earlier, the inclusion of students in the planning, implementation, and scaling processes of the FYS/LC is essential; however, consideration must also be given to the ways in which students will be incentivized to participate in these experiences. As an FYS/LC program grows, it may become included in major or graduation requirements, but this is often not the case in the pilot phase. During this phase, it can be helpful to draw students' attention to the benefits of participating in FYS/LCs, which often include priority registration or a convenient schedule of courses running at prime times, greater opportunity to connect with full-time faculty in their program of study, acceleration of developmental coursework, a cohort model, designated academic advisors or coaches, and peer mentoring and other integrated supports. Although the goal would be for the students to recognize the benefits of participation, the reality is that students often need to be able to clearly identify tangible advantages for them to support such initiatives.

The preceding discussion demonstrates the complexity of FYS/LC administration. FYS/LC administrators must investigate current policies and procedures, identify those that may be in conflict with the best interests of the program, and collaborate with faculty and staff to brainstorm and advocate for policy revisions that will accommodate the overarching needs of the institution, the FYS/LC initiative, and the individuals who support them.

Professional Development

Professional development is critical to the design, development, implementation, and continuous improvement of FYS/LC programs, as it is often a primary mechanism to recruit, train, and sustain involvement of faculty and staff in learning communities. Colleges that embed professional development on their campuses as a continuous and iterative cycle, deepen faculty engagement in teaching and learning. Through the process of collaborative professional development, participants share, identify gaps in, and construct new knowledge (Muhammad & Beyah, 2011). As Thoonen, Sleegers, Oort, Peetsma, and Geijsel (2011) described, "engagement in professional learning activities, in particular experimentation and reflection, is a powerful predictor for teaching practices" (p. 1).

Learning communities differ from traditional academic courses in their emphasis on collaborative teaching and student-centered learning (Gabelnick, MacGregor, Matthews, & Smith, 1990). Zhao and Kuh (2004) documented that participation in learning communities is positively correlated with student engagement, personal and social development, and overall satisfaction with the undergraduate college experience. Thus, it follows that replicating the social, collaborative, and learner-centered aspects of learning communities in professional development settings for faculty and staff will yield similar results in terms of faculty and staff engagement, development, and satisfaction.

Working effectively with first-year students in learning communities requires a set of competencies that are not necessarily intuitive and most likely not included in the knowledge base and skill set of instructors. Professional development can be a vehicle for assessing existing instructor knowledge of FYS/LC programs and goals, understanding of and commitment to the FYS/LC model, and identifying resources needed to be successful. The research and practice literature, including theories of student development and college transition, frameworks for student identity development, ways to use campus resources, first-year learning outcomes, learner-centered instruction, integrative curriculum, collaborative and problem-based learning, and interdisciplinary teaching and learning, is a useful starting point for helping those involved with FYS/LC work develop a common language and a strong foundation for teaching in these programs.

Given the heterogeneous composition of the faculty in FYS/LC programs, it is also important to consider ways in which training can be inclusive of novice and expert faculty from across the campus. Instituting a model that assumes everyone to be at the same baseline could undermine the involvement of experienced faculty who may find such an approach to be overly simplistic. However, if the training assumes too high a level of expertise, faculty who are new to FYS/LC programs may feel overwhelmed by the material presented. Another consideration is the expectation of faculty from different departments as to what exactly it means to engage in teaching scholarship. For example, Lueddeke (2003) found that business faculty were most interested in discovering new knowledge resources, computer science faculty were most interested in leveraging technology systems to monitor quickly changing external advancements, nursing faculty were most interested in innovative approaches to collaborative and case-based learning, and social science faculty were most interested in methodologies and theories related to the ways in which human development impacts learning.

FYS/LCs can be a rich setting, outside the hierarchies and politics of academic departments, where full-time faculty can mentor part-time faculty, part-time faculty can share their experiences teaching at multiple institutions or working in industries outside higher education, and academic support and student affairs professionals can contribute their knowledge of research and best practices in student development. The key is to create a professional development setting in which all program participants have something to learn and something to contribute. One such approach is inquiry-based professional development that inverts the traditional professional development model of workshop led by outside experts. The impact of inquiry-based professional development on improving classroom instruction is well documented (Biswalo, 2001; Loucks-Horsley & Matsumoto, 1999; Richardson, 2003; Thoonen et al., 2011; Wagner, 1998). An inquiry-based structure allows faculty and staff to become the experts as they coconstruct knowledge. Such approaches have four central characteristics: (a) faculty have significant control over the content and process of professional development; (b) issues of alignment among mission, curriculum, pedagogy, and assessment of learning are discussed; (c) activities draw on relevant data and research; and (d) a problem or issue is posed and serves as the focus of the activity (Richardson, 2003). Inquiry-based professional development experiences also serve as a normative process where faculty from various departments and student affairs professionals from different work areas can all collaborate toward shared goals.

For example, in a traditional professional development setting, a presenter might outline best practices for engaging first-year students who place into developmental English courses. However, in an inquiry-based model, faculty and staff would be invited to a session facilitated by national or local experts where a question is posed: How can we use learning communities to engage and support first-year students who place into developmental English? Participants would then be supplied with relevant local and national data and encouraged by the facilitator to brainstorm and create innovative solutions that bridge the research and data with their local experiences and contexts.

This faculty-driven process mirrors the kind of active, learner-centered instruction that is central to FYSs and LCs. It also avoids the common problem of disengagement that occurs when faculty perceive professional development as imposed on them by the administration. An additional benefit to this approach is that through the process, faculty and staff are identifying gaps in their knowledge about the subject at hand. They can then make requests and recommendations to FYS/LC program administrators for further areas of inquiry, which become the basis for the next round of professional development.

Graziano and Kahn (2013) pointed out that while initial professional development to support FYS/LC programs is common, it can be difficult for institutions to sustain ongoing efforts that result in meaningful collaboration, the promotion of reflective teaching, integrative thinking and learning, and respect for academic freedom. They recommend a cyclical model of professional development for faculty comprising three phases: (a) presemester development, (b) with-in semester development, and (c) postsemester development. In the presemester phase, faculty focus on curriculum design that supports integrative teaching and learning and embeds active-learning practices into course experiences and assignments. In this phase, faculty are also prompted to consider how they will manage team teaching if it is part of the FYS/LC design. Namely, they establish a team plan for how they will handle classroom management, academic policies, grading, and communication throughout the semester. The with-in semester phase focuses on reflection and communication and is designed to support faculty in navigating the day-to-day issues and concerns that arise as they deliver their learning community. The postsemester phase focuses on assessment of and reflection on the learning community, particularly in terms of faculty collaboration, student learning, and the degree to which integrative teaching and learning was achieved. Focusing on what worked and what did not work in the learning community feeds into another round of the cycle where lessons learned can shape presemester planning as the FYS/LC evolves.

Growth in national organizations that focus on the first-year experience and LCs have contributed to the research and practice literature on FYS/LC structures and to the availability of professional development opportunities. For example, the National Resource Center for The First-Year Experience and Students in Transition at the University of South Carolina sponsors the Annual

Conference on The First-Year Experience, which focuses on helping faculty, staff, and administrators plan, implement, and refine first-year experience programs. The conference features keynote addresses from higher education scholars, poster sessions, facilitated discussions, research on student transitions, current trends and issues in first-year programming. There are also many opportunities to send teams of faculty and staff for professional development events related to FYS/LCs. The Washington Center for the Improvement of Undergraduate Education hosts the National Summer Institute on Learning Communities annually at the Evergreen State College. The Institute draws on learning community research as well as practitioner knowledge to help teams of faculty and staff begin, refine, or scale learning community programs. It features presentations on learning community pedagogy and practice, hands-on workshops, and team planning time facilitated by resource faculty. Research and best practices on FYS/LCs for targeted populations may be found in more unlikely venues as well. The research in this area has become valued in that professional organizations outside the traditional genres are conducting extensive conversations related to the benefits of learning communities and seminars for their own work. For example, the National Collegiate Honors Council has featured FYS/LC programs as a way to foster community within the honor student population.

Such conferences offer opportunities to network with faculty who teach and brainstorm with administrators who manage FYS/LC programs, which can make research on best practices more concrete and meaningful. Networking with colleagues currently running FYS/LC initiatives or who are undergoing similar planning and implementation can be extremely beneficial to program designers in discovering *why* other campuses have adopted these efforts and *how* they approached the design, implementation, and assessment of those initiatives. Sending a team to visit a campus that has an existing FYS/LC program is equally beneficial as it allows stakeholders not only to talk with administrators, faculty, staff, and students but also to observe classes. Through these interactions comes the opportunity to be introspective about an institution's current practices while simultaneously considering the possibilities that exist outside the current local framework. However, it is important to note that while programs on other campuses may serve as models, it is essential that administrators, faculty, and staff collaborate on their own campus to customize the FYS/LC model to local contexts and to ensure that the program responds to local needs.

Conclusion

Shifting the culture of an institution is a monumental task, requiring buy-in from all levels of the institution. This involvement is usually the result of individuals working diligently to educate the community on how the proposed changes will create a shared benefit for the campus. FYS/LC initiatives deeply value campuswide collaboration for student success, and the administration of such programs should embody these values as well. Professor Judy Patton at the College of the Arts at Portland State University argued that the administration of FYS/LC programs should model learning community and first-year experience praxis—engagement, collaboration, diversity, and social justice. She encouraged institutions to "walk the talk:"

> If we are not working to change the faculty culture, it's unlikely the student culture will change. If we want students to take risks, use reflective practice, work in groups and so on, faculty members and others in teaching roles need to do the same. If we are validating the student voice, administrators need to validate the faculty voice, the staff voice—including the institution service staff. We need to work also on the social equality of higher education ... if we want to educate students for social justice. (quoted in MacGregor& Smith, 2005, p. 7)

Identifying and implementing intentional ways to engage all members of the campus community—faculty, staff, administration and students—ultimately creates a synergy similar to the learning paradigm described by Barr and Tagg (1995), where the teaching and learning environment extends beyond the classroom to encompass the entire campus. Teaching is not limited to faculty; all members of the educational community contribute to teaching, including the students. Learning is not limited to students; faculty and staff are engaged in a learning process as well. This dynamic of mutual responsibility for new student engagement and achievement is integral in ensuring that FYS/LC programs are not only successful, but are truly integrated into the fabric of the institution. As a result, FYS/LC structures can ultimately change the learning environment and student experience in a beneficial way.

References

Albright, K. S. (2004, May/June). Environmental scanning: Radar for success. *Information Management Journal,* 38-44.

Ansell, C., & Gash, A. (2008). Collaborative governance in theory and practice. *Journal of Public Administration Research and Theory, 18*(4), 543-571.

Austin, A. E., & Baldwin, R. G. (1991). *Faculty collaboration: Enhancing the quality of scholarship and teaching* (ASHE-ERIC Higher Education Report No. 7). Washington, DC: George Washington University.

Barr, R. B., & Tagg, J. (1995). From teaching to learning—A new paradigm for undergraduate education. *Change: The Magazine of Higher Learning, 27*(6), 12-26.

Bess, J. L., & Dee, J. R. (2008). *Understanding college and university organization: Theories of effective policy and practice: Vol. II. Dynamics of the system.* Sterling, VA: Stylus.

Biswalo, P. (2001). The systems approach as a catalyst for creating an effective learning environment. *Convergence, 34*(1), 53-66.

Blake, J. H. (2007). The crucial role of student affairs professionals in the learning process. *New Directions for Student Services, 117,* 65-72.

Burnstad, H., Hayes B., Hoss, C., & West, A. M. (2007). A consortium approach to supporting part-time faculty. In R. E. Lyons (Ed.), *Best practices for supporting adjunct faculty* (pp. 107-117). San Francisco, CA: Jossey-Bass/Anker.

Casey, B. A. (1994). The administration and governance of interdisciplinary programs. *New Directions for Teaching and Learning, 58,* 53-67.

Feller, I. (2002). New organizations, old cultures: strategy and implementation of interdisciplinary programs. *Research Evaluation, 11*(2), 109-116.

Ferrari, J. R., & Velcoff, J. (2005). *Measuring staff perceptions of university identity and activities: The mission and values inventory.* Paper presented at the Institute on College Student Values, Tallahassee, FL.

Gabelnick, F., MacGregor, J., Matthews, R. S., & Smith, B. L. (1990). *Learning communities: Creating connections among students, faculty, and disciplines* (New Directions for Teaching and Learning No. 41). San Francisco, CA: Jossey-Bass.

Gano-Phillips, S. & Barnett, R. (2008). Against all odds: Transforming institutional culture. *Liberal Education, 94*(2), 36-41. Retrieved from http://faculty.njcu.edu/fmoran/gscc/ganophillips.pdf

Gray, B. (2008). Enhancing transdisciplinary research through collaborative leadership. *American Journal of Preventive Medicine, 35*(2), S124-S132.

Graziano, J., & Kahn, G. (2013). Sustained faculty development in learning communities. *Learning Communities Research and Practice, 1*(2), Article 5.

Kezar, A. (2012). Spanning the great divide between tenure-track and non-tenure-track faculty. *Change: The Magazine of Higher Learning, 44*(6), 6-13.

Kezar, A. J., & Lester, J. (2009). *Organizing higher education for collaboration: A guide for campus leaders.* San Francisco, CA: Jossey-Bass.

Lardner, E., & Malnarich, G. (2008). A new era in learning-community work: Why the pedagogy of intentional integration matters. *Change: The Magazine of Higher Learning, 40*(4), 30-37.

Laufgraben, J. L., & Shapiro, N. S. (2004). *Sustaining and improving learning communities.* San Francisco, CA: Jossey-Bass.

Long, B. T. (2006, October). Using research to improve student success: What more could be done. *National Postsecondary Education Cooperative (NPEC).* Harvard University. Retrieved from https://nces.ed.gov/npec/pdf/resp_Long.pdf

Loucks-Horsley, S., & Matsumoto, C. (1999). Research on professional development for teachers of mathematics and science: The state of the scene. *School Science and Mathematics, 99*(5), 258-271.

Lueddeke, G. R. (2003). Professionalising teaching practice in higher education: A study of disciplinary variation and 'teaching-scholarship.' *Studies in Higher Education, 28*(2), 213-228.

Marshak, R. J. (2006). *Covert processes at work: Managing the five hidden dimensions of organizational change.* San Francisco, CA: Berrett-Koehler.

MacGregor, J., & Smith, B. L. (2005). Where are learning communities now? National leaders take stock. *About Campus, 10*(2), 2-8.

Morrison, J. L. (1992). Environmental scanning. In M. A. Whitley, J. D. Porter, & R. H. Fenske (Eds.), *A primer for institutional researchers* (pp. 86-99). Tallahassee, FL: The Association for Institutional Research.

Muhammad, E. A., & Beyah, L. (2011). *Effectiveness of an inquiry-based professional development program* (Doctoral dissertations, paper 72). Retrieved from http://ecommons.luc.edu/luc_diss/72

Richardson, V. (2003). The dilemmas of professional development. *Phi Delta Kappan, 84*(5), 401-407.

Smith, B. L., & McCann, J. (2001). *Reinventing ourselves: Interdisciplinary education, collaborative learning, and experimentation in higher education.* Bolton, MA: Anker.

Smith, B. L., & Williams, L. B. (2007). *Learning communities and student affairs: Partnering for powerful learning.* Olympia, WA: Washington Center for Improving the Quality of Undergraduate Education, Evergreen State College.

Thoonen, E. E., Sleegers, P. J., Oort, F. J., Peetsma, T. T., & Geijsel, F. P. (2011). How to improve teaching practices the role of teacher motivation, organizational factors, and leadership practices. *Educational Administration Quarterly, 47*(3), 496-536.

Tinto, V. (1999). Taking student success seriously: Rethinking the first year of college. *NACADA Journal, 19*(2), 5-9.

Uchiyama, K. P., & Radin, J. L. (2009). Curriculum mapping in higher education: A vehicle for collaboration. *Innovative Higher Education, 33*(4), 271-280.

Visher, M. G., Schneider, E., Wathington, H., & Collado, H. (2010). *Scaling up learning communities: The experience of six community colleges.* New York, NY: Teachers College, National Center for Postsecondary Research, Columbia University.

Wagner, T. (1998). Change as collaborative inquiry: A constructivist methodology for reinventing schools. *Phi Delta Kappan, 79*(7), 512.

Wiggins, G. P., & McTighe, J. (2005). *Understanding by design* (2nd ed). Alexandria, VA: ASCD.

Williams, D. A., Berger, J. B., & McClendon, S. (2005). *Towards a model of inclusive excellence and change in post-secondary institutions.* Washington, DC: Association of American Colleges and Universities.

Young, D. G., & Hopp, J. M. (2014). *2012-2013 National Survey of First-Year Seminars: Exploring high-impact practices in the first college year* (Research Reports on College Transitions No. 4). Columbia, SC: University of South Carolina, National Resource Center for The First-Year Experience & Students in Transition.

Zhao, C. M., & Kuh, G. D. (2004). Adding value: Learning communities and student engagement. *Research in Higher Education, 45*(2), 115-138.

Chapter 4
Teaching in Combined Programs
Lisa Dresdner and Ruthanna Spiers

The essential learning outcomes deemed necessary to succeed in the 21st century go well beyond the traditional discipline-based curriculum of our educational system. According to the American Association of Colleges and Universities (AAC&U, 2007), higher education institutions are being challenged to "recalibrate college learning to the needs of the new global century" and to identify skills that align with the "realities of our complex and volatile world" (p. vii). Central to these skills is the emphasis on a high level of integrative learning, which is, of course, at the heart of learning communities.

As the previous chapters have emphasized, learning communities (LCs) take a variety of forms across many different types of institutions, and when combined with first-year seminars (FYS), have the potential to become powerful and significant learning experiences. Teaching in the context of FYS/LCs, however, poses several unique challenges, three of which this chapter will focus on. First, faculty need to think differently about teaching and learning. Second, as a result of this new orientation, they need to modify their pedagogical methods. Finally, when the demands of the academic term pick up, instructors need to resist getting caught up in the chaos of the semester and stay the course with their revised habits of mind and teaching practices. That most students in FYS/LCs are traditional-aged, millennial students (Werth & Werth, 2011) further complicates these challenges. This chapter outlines approaches that will empower faculty to maximize the benefits of teaching in a FYS/LC, offers a framework for creating learning opportunities that reach beyond applied knowledge, and includes practical strategies and examples to help educators find realistic ways to maximize significant learning experiences for students.

Significant Learning Experiences

In a sense, the skills now considered most relevant to today's global society are a natural extension of the paradigm shift that refocused education from a model of instructional input (where teachers impart knowledge to students) to one of output (where students take greater responsibility for creating their own knowledge base). To be more specific, over the past two decades many faculty have rightly shifted their focus from teaching to the *production* of learning (Barr & Tagg, 1995), from being the clichéd "sage on the stage" to the "guide on the side" and facilitating students' learning through their own meaning-making efforts. Now that this shift is well underway, we are being challenged to take another step and ensure that the learning being produced is significant. If learning is defined as "the constant disruption of an old pattern, a breakthrough that substitutes something new for something old" (Davidson, 2011, p. 5), then *significant* learning experiences go one step further by offering students opportunities to create meaning out of this information and apply it to their lives. Fink (2013) emphasized that significant learning experiences, characterized by high energy and engagement, result in considerable changes in students that last well beyond the course itself and whose value students recognize in their personal, social, and work lives. Fink's tweaking deepens the focus on curricular design, in that the course moves from being oriented around content to centered on learning.

Thus, in contrast to the paradigm shift from instruction-centered to learner-centered (Barr & Tagg, 1995), which emphasizes pedagogical methodology, Fink's (2013) shift emphasized kinds of learning. Content is not abandoned by any means, and, in fact, by renaming content "foundational knowledge" (p. 43), Fink (2013) showed how it becomes the vehicle for achieving the other types of learning that are so essential to the 21st century, including integrative learning.

Integrative Learning

Integrative learning lies at the heart of FYS/LCs where the opportunity exists to collaborate and intentionally create educational experiences that cross curricular borders and enter real life. In their Statement on Integrative Learning, AAC&U (2004) explained that "integrative experiences often occur as learners address real-world problems, unscripted and sufficiently broad to require multiple areas of knowledge and multiple modes of inquiry, offering multiple solutions and benefiting from multiple perspectives" (p. 1). Later in this brief statement, the AAC&U emphasized the importance of intentionality in designing opportunities for students to make connections. The tension between an intentional but unscripted learning environment is precisely where FYS/LCs are located. This is where faculty delicately navigate between deliberate design of a curriculum (intentionality) while allowing for the natural dynamics inherent in learning and groups (unscripted) to give shape to the significant learning experience. Dunlap and Sult (2009) used an apt metaphor of a juggler to describe these instructors, who must be keenly aware of the multiple concepts and processes they simultaneously introduce while being firmly grounded in the present moment of the students' energies and needs. To accomplish this balancing act, faculty must remain flexible, adaptable, and responsive, which means that rather than concentrate only on what they think students *should* be doing, they need to heed what is *actually happening* with students in the learning environment. Only when instructors are able to let go of their notions of *shoulds* and be open to the realities of their classroom is significant learning able to take place.

Interrupting the Cycle of Disengaged Teaching and Learning

On the surface, creating opportunities for integrative learning and significant learning experiences appears to be simple. Unfortunately for many, it may also seem idealistic given the restraints of curriculum standards, limited time in the classroom, and the realities of daily life that limit collaboration outside one's work unit, especially when the focus is so often placed on course and departmental outcomes. The probability of accomplishing this seems to diminish even more when the challenges of teaching first-year students, whose busy, complex lives lead many to be disengaged in the learning process, is added to the list. These students are often underprepared when they get to college, frequently neglect to prepare for class (when they *do* attend), and their low test scores indicate how little information they retain. Additionally, today's students are not necessarily risk-takers; rather, they are plagued with an anxiety unknown to their predecessors, and their prove-it-to-me mentality leads to expectations that faculty should show them everything they need to know in an exciting way (Eisner, 2011; Montag, Camp, Weissman, Walmsley, & Snell, 2012). Concomitantly, faculty insist that they want their students to achieve higher standards of critical thinking, but many instructors have not kept pace with the pedagogical methods known to enhance deep learning. Even today, many faculty lecture as their primary method of instruction, introducing PowerPoint as their only concession to technology.

These traditional pedagogies, accompanied by faculty expectations that students be self-motivated learners who make connections on their own, result in a cycle of disengaged teaching and learning (Figure 4.1). Students initially attend class with some interest, but soon grow bored due to a lack of stimulation and obvious relevance to their lives. From there, they too easily fall into patterns of low class attendance and preparation. Likewise, faculty initially exhibit excitement for their courses, but are soon discouraged by apathetic student response, and then they retreat to conventional and familiar modes of teaching.

Figure 4.1. Cycle of disengaged teaching and learning.

The demands of the 21st century require a new kind of learning, and the combined programs of first-year seminars and learning communities are one answer to the question of how this might be achieved. But how are the challenges inherent in a FYS/LC solved? Instructors and students need to make a fundamental shift in their thinking and approach. Specifically, if the 3Rs, *Reading, wRiting,* and *'Rithmatic,* used to represent a quality education based on content, a revised understanding of the 3Rs based on practice is crucial. These 21st century 3Rs, *Risk-taking, Relevance,* and *Reflection,* offer a comprehensive strategy for disrupting the cycle of disengaged teaching and learning and create the opportunity for significant learning experiences. What this means for students and faculty is explored in more detail below.

R1: Risk-Taking

Our increasingly complex world, along with our new understandings of learning, suggests that we need new ways to view the teaching and learning dynamic. Graziano and Kahn (2013) underscored the synergy that exists between teaching and learning in their challenge to educators to view teaching as "a complex and relational process" just as we do learning (p. 7). The first *R–Risk-taking* responds to the challenge of rethinking teaching and learning. Faculty who teach in FYS/LCs are in a unique position to empower themselves and their students to take academic risks and enjoy deeper and more engaged learning. The nature of taking risks involves a willingness to make mistakes and to learn from them—the very thing educators try to teach students in any first-year seminar. Encouraging purposeful risk-taking is a way to develop intellectual curiosity, to foster exploration of self and the world, and to cultivate a community of learners.

Yet, first-year students are often averse to risk-taking. They are nascent learners, still developing their identities, and unsure of what they want out of school and life. FYS/LC programs provide a safe environment for students unused to taking academic risks if they offer a supportive foundation while challenging students to put a higher value on learning than on grades. However, the shift in focus from grades to learning is particularly difficult for the current generation of students. Their entire academic lives have been centered on standardized tests and pressure to achieve the highest possible GPA in high school. How then do educators help students uncover the relevance of what they are learning as it relates to their personal lives and teach them ways to engage more purposefully with the material? Learning community faculty can do this by creating safe opportunities for students to take risks by allowing rewrites, offering points for researching the correct answers to missed questions on exams, putting more focus on meeting clearly outlined criteria rather than judging students' opinions, or permitting students to drop a certain number of lower-stakes assignments at the end of the term. Other strategies include encouraging students to ask questions that have no single answer, inviting students to brainstorm the ways their learning connects to life outside school, and pausing midlesson to have students write questions or areas of confusion anonymously on notecards. Once the cards are gathered, the instructor can respond to the questions or have students answer them in small groups.

If getting students to embrace risk-taking is a challenge, then getting faculty to do so can be even more difficult. Many faculty face barriers that diminish their desires to take academic risks, and these include lack of recognition in tenure and promotion for this significant amount of work, limited support from administration or departmental leadership, and lack of professional development to assist them in their efforts (Fink, 2013; Gross, Whitbred, Skalski, & Lui, 2013). However, the importance for faculty to reach beyond their comfort zones and take risks on several levels cannot be emphasized enough. Not only will doing so model the kind of desired behavior for students to emulate but it might also re-energize the instructors themselves.

One of the risks faculty might take is to explore how their own immersion into specialized areas can hinder their adoption of broader perspectives. In other words, despite knowing that subject boundaries are largely constructed, faculty who rethink their approach and teach with a nod to the permeability of disciplines are better able to facilitate interdisciplinary and integrative learning by making meaning through connections. And, just as a FYS/LC can offer a supportive and safe environment for students to take risks, faculty can find reassurance by reaching out to other colleagues teaching in learning communities and serving as continuous sounding boards for each other. Often, the ability to make connections outside the discipline is simply a matter of practice and familiarity, so one way faculty can begin is to take advantage of informal conversations with colleagues and ask what disciplinary perspectives or content each might share. By identifying and sharing the connections they make with other faculty in a variety of disciplines, professors model integrative thinking for their students.

Taking risks and making changes is no small feat, and it is usually uncomfortable because it involves the new and unfamiliar. What adds to this discomfort is that when we learn, we do not simply build on old ideas; rather, we have to challenge our biases and fixed ways of thinking. Sometimes this unlearning involves structures and material systems, such as when migrating to a new course management system, or from a PC to a Mac. But other times, the unlearning occurs in the nexus of the cognitive and affective domains, such as that Aha! moment when beliefs or values that have long been considered a fundamental part of one's identity are challenged and new insights result. Unlearning involves breaking old habits of seeing, recognizing the filters that shape how and what we understand, and being open to seeing things differently (Davidson, 2011). It does not mean to empty the brain, but is, rather, part of a dialogical process that involves taking in new information, reacting to what we already know (prior knowledge), and organizing information into different patterns that yield new understanding. Students are encouraged to do this when they are asked to reflect on their high school experiences and then to consider how college is different, or to identify certain social behaviors and attitudes and then think about who or what dictates those norms. First-year college students are ripe for these kinds of challenges as they are embarking on a new stage in their lives.

Faculty and students participating in a FYS/LC are asked to unlearn the traditional methods of instruction to which they are accustomed: (a) disciplines presented in isolation from other courses and (b) learners operating as competitive individuals rather than cooperative members of a community. These strategies might seem frustrating or even insulting to faculty who are trapped in the cycle of disengaged teaching and learning where they put forth effort only to be met by unprepared, uninterested students. However, faculty are encouraged to reframe this reaction by focusing not on the students who fuel this cycle with their lack of interest and low effort but instead focusing on the students who are figuring out how to prioritize their efforts in all their classes to maximize their potential, are balancing school and work to support themselves, and were not adequately prepared for the transition to college and are doing their best to navigate it one day at a time.

R2: Relevance

When safe opportunities for risk-taking are created and some focus is removed from grades, the opportunity to increase relevance and, therefore, significant learning emerges. We live in a consumer culture, and students' view of education is no exception. Students want adequate return for their investment (ROI) of time and work. Again, this notion might understandably frustrate faculty who have dedicated their careers to becoming experts in their disciplines and to furthering this knowledge through research and teaching. But once more, faculty are challenged to reframe this reaction and instead meet students where they are. In other words, the way to help students realize an ROI is to increase the relevance of their learning. This can be accomplished in a number of ways: by (a) creating assignments that with only slight revisions can count for more than one course, (b) constructing learning opportunities that reinforce what is being taught in other courses, (c) allowing group or collaborative work that maximizes benefits of the community of learners, and (d) encouraging students to find connections between their learning and their lives outside the classroom. Through these strategies students gain increased value for their investment of time and effort, and faculty see greater effort being made in completing assignments, thereby breaking the cycle of disengaged teaching and learning.

When paired with any class, the FYS in all its myriad forms is an appropriate vehicle to facilitate change in the way students think—about a discipline, the curriculum, and their own investment in learning. Friedman and Alexander (2007) explained that since the FYS fosters peer relationships that serve as the foundation for study groups and often emphasizes other skills necessary for success in college, this course might be considered the prime means by which students "transfer learning strategies to other content-based classes" (p. 64). In fact, one of the most important dynamics that occurs in a FYS is the building of "an academic community in which students feel comfortable asking questions and seeking assistance" (p. 67), allowing FYS/LCs to efficiently create a conducive learning environment in a relatively short period of time offered by a semester.

A key factor to achieving a favorable learning environment in combined programs is that faculty must be intentional and clear with students about shared outcomes across courses, how they intend to achieve them, and how integrative assignments are relevant both to the FYS/LC and to students' lives. Friedman and Alexander (2007) suggested that at the beginning of the semester faculty include contact information on the syllabi for all instructors involved in the LC as well as a purpose statement about their goals for integration. In reality, of course, it is not always possible for all faculty to participate in a high level of integration. For example, a world history professor teaching a 200-student lecture class, 25 of whom are in a learning community, is clearly less able to attend specifically to those learning community students than a faculty member teaching a LC-specific section of the same course. Similarly, as more students enter college having earned general education credits through AP testing or dual enrollment, it is possible that not every student will be enrolled in all classes in the learning community. Faculty are encouraged to be creative by offering options that allow the LC students to participate in interdisciplinary and integrative assignments that use the FYS as the vehicle to reinforce content from other co-enrolled courses.

Changing approaches increases the opportunities to make learning relevant, even as they involve some risk. Beaulieu and Williams (2013) considered these risks "micro-strategies" or "small efforts, intentional in nature, that make a difference for a few students at a time" (p. 3). Their point is that change need not be radical to be meaningful. Possible micro-strategies include incorporating short, reflective, ungraded writing assignments that focus more on the discovery process than on grammar. Such assignments encourage students to take their focus off the formal aspects of writing and attend to meaning making instead. Low-stakes reflective writing assignments afford faculty the opportunity to find out what students are thinking and learning without spending time on grading. Asking students to explore a topic being studied in a co-enrolled course can further enhance relevance.

Additionally, faculty members can reinforce messages of other faculty in the combined program through course discussions and assignments. For example, the instructor of a math course paired with an FYS might ask students how what they are learning about time management or study skills is influencing their choices and behaviors in the math class, or, conversely, the students could analyze the relationship of time spent on homework versus test grades to reinforce similar skills that may be taught in a FYS. Similarly, when an FYS is paired with a different course, such as psychology, sociology, or history, faculty can focus on a shared disciplinary reading, concept, or relevant event and examine how it might be viewed from multiple perspectives. One of the central means to enhance relevance is to take the extra step of incorporating content or a skill learned in one course into the other course(s), which, even at a micro level, begins to break down the cycle of disengaged teaching and learning and opens the opportunity for significant learning.

R3: Reflection

The third main challenge identified at the beginning of this chapter is how easily faculty can become overwhelmed with the chaos of the semester and revert to old habits. If instructors, who have taken care to outline and organize their curriculum, begin to feel anxious by the consuming and competing needs of the profession, just imagine how new students must feel! That is why the response to this challenge is the third R—*Reflection*. Rather than simply ruminating or mulling over something, reflection is actively making connections in disciplined and deliberate ways. Yet, for reflection to have real value, it involves asking and answering two main questions: *Why these* connections? and *What* do these connections *mean*? (Huber, Hutchings, Gale, Miller, & Breen, 2007).

In her careful examination of John Dewey's philosophy of reflective thinking, Rodgers (2002) explained that reflection "is the bridge of meaning that connects one experience to the next [and] that gives direction and impetus to growth" (p. 850). Reflective practice requires intentionally moving away from the chaos of learning, deliberately pausing, and contemplating the relationship between past and present with an eye to the future. Effective reflective practice involves meaning making; entails systematic, rigorous, and disciplined practice; happens in a community; and requires attitudes that value personal and intellectual growth (Dewey, 1916/1944, cited in Rodgers, 2002, p. 850). Just as it is important for students to engage in reflection to deepen their learning, faculty, too, must take time to reflect on how their shared assignments are working; how they are infusing the FYS/LC with relevance; and, importantly, how their shared cohort of students is progressing.

Students do not usually come by reflective practice easily. Their typical epistemological perspective is that knowledge is concrete and faculty are authorities who know the truth and share it with students. As such, the need for reflection is eliminated (Baxter-Magolda & King, 2004). The goal of higher education is to move students further along the epistemological continuum toward the view that knowledge is created and recreated as each person reflects upon it with his or her own unique lens. Baxter Magolda and King (2004) referred to this process as self-authorship, suggesting that it actually goes against the core of what students experience in K-12 educational settings. That is, teaching to the test and teaching to create meaning are at odds with one another.

Using the metaphor of a tandem bicycle, Baxter Magolda and King (2004) suggested the student be in the front seat steering the bike while the teacher rides on the back, creating momentum and providing guidance when the student is lost. Students can be given opportunities to steer through reflective practice and timely, constructive feedback. The three questions that make up the most common reflective model are What? So what? and Now what? Offering a slightly different approach, Rodgers (2006) used five basic questions, emphasizing the unending nature of the learning process: (a) What are you learning? (b) How do you know you are learning it? (c) What is getting in the way of your learning? (d) What is helping your learning? and (e) How are you feeling? (p. 219). Students can also be asked to reflect on their reaction to what was learned in class that day or on how learning in one class connects to a co-enrolled class. A specific example might involve an English composition instructor teaching her students to write more descriptively: She could ask students to describe what it would feel like to live in the Nazi concentration camp they are studying in their history course, enhancing their skills in descriptive writing while also encouraging them to go beyond memorizing the information in their co-enrolled history course. Instead, such an assignment compels students to reflect on real people and the nature of their experiences, deepening their learning and making it more significant.

Other ways faculty can support students' reflective practice is to have them engage in reflective writing at the end of class and submit it before leaving. This activity gives instructors feedback on what students are learning so they might revise the next lesson. Faculty can also model reflective writing by sharing their own reflections (e.g., I've noticed/observed ... or I recognize we need to adjust ...), by providing anonymous examples from previous students, and by inviting peer mentors to be the first to post their reflective writings in online conversations. Online learning portals are valuable venues for student reflection, especially when faculty encourage students to read each other's writings and comment on them. Whether the feedback comes from peers or from faculty, it helps students begin to reflect more effectively and deepen their learning. Over time, students gain confidence and skill and become able to talk themselves through their questions. Eventually, the teacher is able to get off the bicycle, and the student rides on without him or her. The combined use of these 3Rs cannot be overstated: Reflection helps students become more comfortable taking risks because it is a low-stakes activity, and it helps create relevance in their learning by connecting course material to their lives.

Powerful Learning Communities

As noted so far, building an effective FYS/LC requires creating an environment and structure conducive to taking risks, engaging in the process of learning/unlearning/relearning to generate relevance, and practicing reflection. These 3Rs lead to what Lenning, Hill, Saunders, Solan, and Stokes (2013) referred to as powerful learning communities.

The power of a learning community emerges in large part from its intentional design, and many have outlined the essential features that lead to robust integrative learning (Fink, 2013; Gale, 2006; Huber, 2006; Hutchings, 2006; Lardner & Malnarich, 2008, 2009; Lenning et al., 2013). The necessary environmental qualities include safety and trust, openness, respect, responsiveness, collaboration, relevance, challenge, enjoyment, esprit de corps, and empowerment (Lenning et al., 2013). These characteristics have been summarized and synthesized into the following six components:

- *Intentionality.* Learning communities must be built upon a foundation of intentional growth and a shared vision, established by setting the tone at the beginning of the semester that communicates the importance of the relational aspects of the community.

- *Transparency.* Faculty must be transparent about expectations, purpose, and relevance of the LC experience to the students, and, importantly, garner consensus by all stakeholders. This transparency extends to establishing standards and practices that support the community and adhering to them (Lenning et al., 2013).

- *Open communication and respect.* Faculty must stress the importance of open communication and respect between *all* members (i.e., faculty and students, students and students, faculty and faculty) during class, outside class, and online. Diverse perspectives and questioning should be encouraged. Different online resources and apps, such as Groupme, can be valuable in providing opportunities for communication and creating shared vision faster, especially for a seminar that meets only once a week.

- *Safe environment.* The environment must offer a safe space to take risks with ideas, to try things that might seem out of the norm, and to think creatively. Sometimes, achieving this might be as simple as changing the location of the class. While distinctive meeting places foster a sense of belonging and ownership, Fink (2013) suggested moving to a different place periodically (even outside when weather permits) to help defend against stagnation and to facilitate changes in perspectives. When changes in location are not logistically possible, simply altering class routines or rearranging desks can have a similar effect by helping to avoid monotony and build greater community among the group.

- ***Common experiences.*** Student learning takes place both in and out of the classroom, and opportunities for FYS/LC students to participate as a group in events such as talks or performances that take place on or off campus allow for sustained connections. Institutional common-read initiatives, which are becoming much more prevalent, often generate a range of activities organized by both academic and student affairs. While faculty time limitations might curtail their own participation, peer mentors are excellent candidates to carry out this part of the community building. They are knowledgeable about different social events taking place on campus and can facilitate student participation. Additionally, faculty can use group assignments as a tool to get students to collaborate outside the classroom.

- ***Intellectual connections.*** Finally, intellectual connections are critical to creating a powerful FYS/LC. These connections should be transparent in class assignments and activities. A "hallmark of powerful LCs," Lenning et al. (2013) remind us, is to develop "proficiency in connecting and making meaning from what appears on the surface to be isolated experiences, facts, and topics" (p. 69). Connections can link high school and college experiences, in-class and out-of-class learning, theory to practice, and learning across disciplines (Klein, 2005).

The experience of being a member of a learning environment with these characteristics enhances students' potential to become what Costa and Kallick (2004) defined as self-directed learners who "exhibit the dispositions and habits of mind required to be self-managing, self-monitoring, and self-modifying" (p. 51). Self-managing learners are able to critically analyze a situation fully before finalizing conclusions and taking action, thus preparing to take risks. Self-monitoring learners are able to consider how their personal views influence their learning, hence engaging in the process of reflection. Finally, self-modifying learners are able to adjust their views as a result of new knowledge, thereby allowing for unlearning and relearning to occur and emphasizing relevance.

Teaching for Significant Learning Experiences

This chapter introduced the concept of the 3Rs as well as how practicing them helps break down the cycle of disengaged teaching and learning and, in so doing, creates significant learning experiences and powerful learning communities. In this section, strategies are suggested for modifying pedagogical methods to adapt to this new framework of instruction.

Bloom's (1956) taxonomy of educational objectives in the cognitive domain launched a new way of understanding learning and, a half century later, it is still widely used to guide instructional design and educational assessment. Yet, as integrative thinking gains prominence as an educational outcome, this taxonomy is no longer adequate to address the needs of teachers and learners. Fink's (2013) taxonomy of significant learning, developed with the fundamental understanding that learning involves change, serves as a valid successor to Bloom's taxonomy (Figure 4.2).

By abandoning a hierarchical structure, Fink (2013) highlighted the relational aspects of learning experiences and the ways instructors can help students make connections between what he called their "course file" and their "life file" (p. 7). As Fink observed, students tend to view their lives at school as being completely separate from their personal lives. Faculty may know that all aspects of our lives are inextricably intertwined, but students need to be taught to make the connections between what they see as their two (or more) different lives. Fink offered a dynamic visual to draw attention to the synergy inherent in the taxonomy of significant learning experiences, which emphasizes that the whole is greater than the sum of its parts and that achieving one kind of learning enhances other kinds of learning (Figure 4.3).

This image also speaks to what Bass (2012) referred to as the "porous boundaries" that exist between the classroom and life experience and that create "disruptive moments in teaching" (p.24). Bass here is referring to Christensen's (1997) concept of disruptive innovation, in which some kind of innovation takes root and eventually displaces and transforms the status quo. Bass explained that while our current educational system privileges a formal learning curriculum, that is, one that is content-based and course-specific, what is increasingly being recognized as having significant value is the informal learning that takes place on the margins in experiential, cocurricular activities, and the "participatory culture of the Internet" (p. 24). These cocurricular activities, many of which have been identified by Kuh (2008) as high-impact practices (HIPs), are the disruptive innovations in education, particularly in that their emphasis is less on *what* we

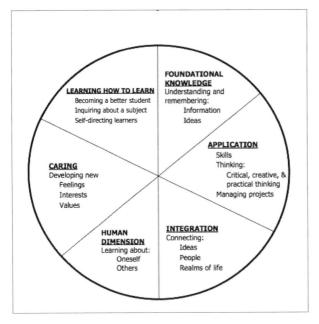

Figure 4.2. Taxonomy of significant learning. Adapted from *A Self-Directed Guide to Designing Courses for Significant Learning*, by L. D. Fink, 2014, p. 9. Copyright 2014 by L. D. Fink.

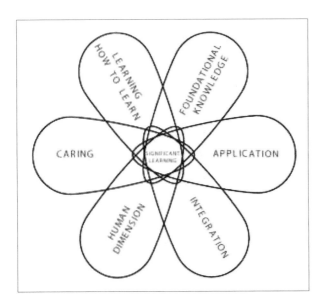

Figure 4.3. The interactive nature of significant learning. Adapted from *A Self-Directed Guide to Designing Courses for Significant Learning*, by L. D., 2014, p. 10. Copyright 2014 by L. D. Fink.

learn and more on *how* we learn (Brown & Adler, 2008, p. 18). We move from "learning about" to "learning to be" (Brown & Adler, 2008, p. 19), and this slight modification marks a shift toward teaching students to be integrative learners and multiplistic thinkers who will be valued in the workforce. Pedagogically, faculty can use integrative assignments to move into this updated approach to teaching.

Designing Integrative Assignments

Students need many opportunities across time and disciplines to practice integrative learning (Lardner & Malnarich, 2008, 2009; Huber et al., 2007). Lardner and Malnarich (2008, 2009) offered a heuristic for designing integrative and purposeful assignments that includes a common rubric, shared definition of success, regular meetings, and responsibility for addressing content from all courses in the FYS/LC. Research suggests that five primary qualities contribute to effective integrative pedagogies: (a) acknowledging the realities of a changing world (Huber et al., 2007); (b) cultivating a community approach to learning (Lenning et al. 2013); (c) embracing "intellectual dexterity" and commitment to welcoming dialogue and conflict (Huber et al., 2007); (d) incorporating regular and systematic reflective practice (Rodgers, 2006); and (e) demanding a flexible approach to assessment (Davidson, 2011).

How these qualities are achieved is up to the instructors teaching in the FYS/LC, but active-learning strategies, such as role playing, case studies, debate, small group learning, service-learning, and write-to-learn assignments, are among the most common. Any one or combination of these strategies can be an effective way to promote integrative learning in a FYS/LC. The following example draws from a FYS/LC where students are co-enrolled in a first-year seminar, English composition, and Introduction to Sociology. In sociology, the students are studying the bystander effect on domestic violence; in English composition, they are studying persuasive writing; and in the first-year seminar, they are focusing on building confidence for participation and presentations. Integrative assignments might be incorporated by having the students in the first-year seminar complete a low-stakes reflective writing assignment responding to a case study on the topic. Following this initial writing, they could be assigned a persuasive essay on the topic in English composition. After getting feedback on their essays, they would participate in a class debate on the topic in the first-year seminar, allowing them to understand multiple perspectives become more comfortable sharing their opinions and speaking up in class. The sociology and English faculty would be encouraged to attend and clear up any misunderstandings the students have on the content being focused on in their courses.

Faculty can also practice these strategies spontaneously when the occasion warrants. For example, if a class is clearly split in their perspectives about a topic, rather than discuss it as a whole class, they can be divided into groups that focus on a particular view, and an impromptu debate is quickly accomplished. The same situation might lend itself to a role-playing activity where students are assigned roles, given a limited amount of time to prepare, and then perform in small groups.

Integrative assignments take a variety of shapes and involve a range of faculty participation levels—not every FYS/LC instructor has the liberty to incorporate integrative assignments due to class size, non-FYS/LC students in the course, lack of time, or amount of content required. But even in the most loosely paired courses, faculty can facilitate integration by simply sharing their syllabus with the other FYS/LC faculty members and allowing them to use relevant topics for integrative assignments as time and energy allow. For example, when students are about to take their first exam in their co-enrolled class, the FYS instructor might address test taking to encourage them to start studying, or use materials and topics from the co-enrolled classes to demonstrate study skills at strategic times. Sharing syllabi and assignments might make an instructor feel vulnerable, but faculty can use it as on opportunity to model risk-taking for their students, approaching the task by adopting micro-strategies before moving on to larger changes.

Harnessing Technology for Integrative Assignments

If we agree that integrative learning is vital to student success, and we acknowledge the necessity of implementing occasions and strategies to ensure such learning can take place, we must also keep pace with emerging tools and practices to help us achieve these goals. When designing integrative assignments, faculty are encouraged to take advantage of the many multimodal tools available and ask students to apply their knowledge in creative ways. For example, instructors could invite students to reimagine a topic, theme, or concept they are studying, putting it into an alternative form. Given enough latitude and time, students are quite adept at using the technology at their fingertips: they could make videos (e.g., through smartphones or iMovie) and then upload them to YouTube; use a comic-strip generator to teach a concept to their peers; or collaborate on research through blogs and wikis. These tools give students access to authentic, public audiences, and, when followed by reflection, increase their understanding of how course experiences connect to their lives and the world. Faculty should also maximize opportunities for students to confront multiple perspectives on relevant and complex situations, especially emerging and unanticipated events (Newell, 2010). The current Instagram and hashtag culture offers a range of possibilities for integrative learning: a discussion about the relationship between stereotypes and the media could be taken outside the classroom where students use their smartphones to photograph examples, add an agreed-upon hashtag in Twitter or Instagram, and then compile and analyze results.

One of the more flexible technologies encouraging integrative learning is the electronic learning portfolio (ePortfolio), which provides a valuable and relevant format for students to explore connections between their lives and educational experiences. Using an ePortfolio in a FYS/LC is especially valuable because it is designed to be a place where students connect all their goals, learning, and experiences, moving students "toward not only integrated learning, but also more integrated lives" (Arcario, Eynon, & Clark, 2005, p. 16). Preliminary findings from Connect to Learning (C2L), LaGuardia Community College's FIPSE-funded project that included 24 institutions, show that ePortfolio practice is "inherently connective and integrative" (Eynon, Gambino, & Torok, 2014, p. 98) and actually bolsters the already-strong effects of learning communities and first-year seminars. In short, because they allow students to organize their learning across time in one space, ePortfolios make learning more visible and, thus, are becoming known as a "signature pedagogy of integrative learning" (Gale, 2006, p. 7).

Maintaining Momentum

Once faculty take the risk to try new pedagogical strategies, they must stay the course and learn from setbacks and disappointments to avoid falling back into the cycle of disengaged teaching and learning. These setbacks should be expected in the first year of attempting integrative pedagogy, hence the necessity to take risks. At the same time, however, they allow the opportunity for faculty to learn what works for their community, which makes the following years more satisfying for all. As this chapter has emphasized, maintaining contact with other faculty in a combined program, encouraging one another, and brainstorming concerns is essential, as is setting aside time to personally reflect on the experience. Building a community of learners is the essence of learning communities, and the exceptional value of the social and intellectual bonding that takes place cannot be over-emphasized. However, instructors must take caution that this environment sometimes gives rise to what is known as *hyperbonding* (Lenning et al., 2013), a negative phenomenon that can manifest in several ways: the class can develop a Groupthink mentality where students are motivated more by collective and unanimous thinking than by critical analysis or evaluation; they can create cliques that isolate or exclude others; they can behave in disruptive ways or even harass others or challenge authority in defiant ways. One strategy to help prevent this occurrence is for faculty to establish a conflict resolution process at the beginning of the semester. But if hyperbonding arises, as it does in about 27% of classes, instructors need to remind learners of ground rules established at the beginning of the semester and, if possible, call on the community itself for regulation (Lenning et al., 2013). This practice in itself creates one more connection of class experiences to real-world meaning. Ideally student bonding can be directed into positive outlets, such as the community adopting a strong work ethic and taking advantage of opportunities made available to them.

Conclusion

Teaching in a FYS/LC is an ideal scenario that has transformative powers for students, faculty, and the institution. The shared goals and structure of this learning environment prime students to value interconnectedness with each other and their classes, and their shared experiences through the LC can be referenced in all their courses, thus deepening their abilities to make meaning of what they are learning.

Faculty are able to step outside the silos in which they usually teach and build a supportive and collaborative network with each other, breaking the all too common isolation that can accompany teaching. Just as FYS/LC faculty are challenged to think beyond their disciplinary boundaries, they must also be challenged to reconsider their pedagogical approaches. That is, they cannot simply rely on the fact that they share a cohort of students; they must move beyond parallel play and, through intentional strategies, help students "begin to operate with real facility in a borderless universe of contiguous ideas" (Burg, Klages, & Sokolski, 2008/2009, p. 66). By taking the risk to make even slight changes in their pedagogy and curriculum, FYS/LC faculty can capture the attention of today's college students. The rewards are substantial: new perspectives on their discipline, rejuvenated teaching, decreased feelings of isolation, shared purpose, and increased satisfaction with student learning (Fink, 2013; Mino, 2013). Taking these risks also contributes to breaking the cycle of disengagement in that doing so inevitably leads to enhanced student engagement and stronger student performance. Significantly, too, taking these risks moves faculty off the sidelines and makes them stakeholders in improving student retention.

The collective efforts of all the parts in a combined program can prompt a new direction for the institution: Bridges are built across academic and student affairs through the increased faculty investment in the shared goals of strengthening student success, engagement, and retention; through instructors for the FYS coming from both academic and student affairs; and through the cooperation, collaboration, and compromise necessary to fulfill the administrative processes. In sum, the rich learning and discoveries that occur across courses, disciplines, and departments pave the way to institutional transformation.

References

Arcario, P., Eynon, B., & Clark, J. E. (2005, Summer/Fall). Making connections: Integrated learning, integrated lives. *Peer Review,* 15-17.

Association of American College & Universities (AAC&U). (2004). *Statement on integrative learning.* Washington, DC: Author.

Association of American Colleges & Universities (AAC& U). (2007). Essential learning outcomes. In *College learning for the new global century.* Washington DC: Author. Retrieved from http://www.aacu.org/leap/documents/GlobalCentury_final.pdf

Barr, R. B., & Tagg, J. (1995). From teaching to learning—a new paradigm for undergraduate education. *Change, 27*(6), 13-25.

Bass, R. (2012). Disrupting ourselves: The problem of learning in higher education. *Educause Review, 47*(2), 23-33.

Baxter Magolda, M., & King, P. M. (Eds.). (2004). *Learning partnerships: Theory and models of practice to educate for self-authorship.* Sterling, VA: Stylus.

Beaulieu, E. A., & Williams, L. B. (2013). Micro-strategies: Small steps toward improved retention. *Learning Communities Research and Practice, 1*(1), Article 12.

Bloom, B. S. (Ed.). (1956). *Taxonomy of educational objectives. Handbook 1: The cognitive domain.* New York, NY: David McKay.

Brown, J. S., & Adler, R. P. (2008, January/February). Mind on fire: Open education, the long tail, and learning 2.0. *Educause Review.* Retrieved from https://net.educause.edu/ir/library/pdf/ERM0811.pdf

Burg, E., Klages, M., & Sokolski, P. (2008/2009). Beyond "parallel play": creating a realistic model of integrative learning with community college freshman. *Journal of Learning Communities Research, 3*(3), 63-73.

Christensen, C. M. (1997). *The innovator's dilemma.* New York, NY: HarperCollins.

Costa, A. L., & Kallick, B. (2004). Launching self-directed learners. *Educational Leadership, 62*(1), 51-57. Retrieved from http://www.ascd.org/publications/ educational_leadership/sept04/vol62/num01/Launching_Self-Directed_Learners.aspx

Davidson, C. N. (2011). *Now you see it: How technology and brain science will transform schools and business for the 21st century.* New York, NY: Penguin.

Dunlap, L., & Sult, L. (2009). Juggling and the art of the integrative assignment. *Journal of Learning Communities Research, 3*(3), 27-45.

Eisner, S. P. (2011). Teaching Generation Y college students: Three initiatives. *Journal of College Teaching and Learning, 1*(9), 69-84.

Eynon, B., Gambino, L. M., & Torok, J. (2014). What difference can ePortfolio make? A field report from the connect to learning project. *International Journal of ePortfolio, 4*(1), 95-114. Retrieved from http://www.theijep.com/ pdf/IJEP127.pdf

Fink, L. D. (2013). *Creating significant learning experiences: An integrated approach to designing college courses.* San Francisco, CA: Jossey-Bass.

Fink, L. D. (2014, January). *A self-directed guide to designing courses for significant learning.* Unpublished manuscript.

Friedman, D. B., & Alexander, J. S. (2007). Investigating a first-year seminar as an anchor course in learning communities. *Journal of The First-Year Experience & Students in Transition, 19*(1), 63-74.

Gale, R. A. (2006). Fostering integrative learning through pedagogy. *Integrative Learning Project.* Retrieved from http://gallery.carnegiefoundation.org/ilp/ uploads/pedagogy_copy.pdf

Graziano, J., & Kahn, G. (2013). Sustained faculty development in learning communities. *Learning Communities Research and Practice, 1*(2), Article 5.

Gross, C. M., Whitbred, R., Skalski, P., & Lui, Y. (2013, Spring). Influencing faculty willingness to participate in learning communities. *The Florida Communication Journal, 41*(1), 1-15.

Huber, M. T. (2006). Fostering integrative learning through the curriculum. *Integrative Learning Project.* Retrieved from http://gallery.carnegiefoundation. org/ilp/uploads/curriculum_copy.pdf

Huber, M. T., Hutchings, P., Gale, R., Miller, R., & Breen, M. (2007, Spring). Leading initiatives for integrative learning. *Liberal Education.* Retrieved from http://www.aacu.org/publications-research/periodicals/leading-initiatives-integrative-learning

Hutchings, P. (2006). Fostering integrative learning through faculty development. *Integrative Learning Project.* Retrieved from http://gallery. carnegiefoundation.org/ilp/uploads/facultydevelopment_copy.pdf

Klein, J. T. (2005). Integrative learning and interdisciplinary studies. *Peer Review, 7*(4), 8-10.

Kuh, G. D. (2008). *High-impact educational practices: What they are, who has access to them, and why they matter.* Washington, DC: Association of American Colleges and Universities.

Lardner, E. & Malnarich, G. (2008, July/August). A new era in learning-community work: Why the pedagogy of intentional integration matters. *Change.* Retrieved from http://www.changemag.org/Archives/BackIssues/July-August2008/full-new-ear.html

Lardner, E., & Malnarich, G. (2009, September/October). When faculty assess integrative learning. *Change,* 29-35.

Lenning, O. T., Hill, D. M., Saunders, K. P., Solan, A., & Stokes, A. (2013). *Powerful learning communities: A guide to developing student, faculty, and professional learning communities to improve student success and organizational effectiveness.* Sterling, VA: Stylus.

Mino, J. (2013). Link aloud: Making interdisciplinary learning visible and audible. *Learning Communities Research and Practice, 1*(1), Article 4. Retrieved from http://washingtoncenter.evergreen.edu/lcrpjournal/vol1/iss1/4

Montag, T., Camp, J., Weissman, J., Walmsley, A., & Snell , A. (2012). In their own words: Best practices for advising millennial students about majors. *NACADA Journal, 32*(2), 26-35.

Newell, W. H. (2010). Educating for a complex world: Integrative learning and interdisciplinary studies. *Liberal Education, 96*(4), 6-11.

Rodgers, C. (2002). Defining reflection: Another look at John Dewey and reflective thinking. *Teachers College Record, 104*(4), 842-866.

Rodgers, C. (2006). Attending to student voice: the importance of descriptive feedback on learning and teaching. *Curriculum Inquiry, 36*(2), 209-237.

Werth, E. P., & Werth, L. (2011). Effective training for millennial students. *Adult Learning, 22*(3), 12-19.

Chapter 5
What Should We Be Assessing and Why?

Michele J. Hansen and Maureen A. Pettitt

In Chapter 1, Finley and Kuh discuss the need for strategies to assess the synergistic effects of combined first-year seminar and learning community (FYS/LC) programs, which is especially urgent given that regional accrediting bodies have mandated learning outcomes assessment. Yet, the seemingly endless range of structures and approaches to first-year seminars, learning communities, and combined programs—while necessary to meet varied student and institutional needs—makes identifying common student outcomes, language, and assessment frameworks challenging.

The effort is further complicated by a lack of agreement about the purpose of assessment. The multiple—and sometimes conflicting—roles of assessment include (a) examining relevance (Are we doing the right things?) versus determining excellence (Are we doing things right?), (b) meeting accountability requirements (proving) versus improving, and, (c) learning versus participating in a conversation (Friedman, 2012; Moore, 2003; Smith, MacGregor, Matthews, & Gabelnick, 2004; Walvoord, 2010). Despite the variety of curricular structures and perspectives on assessment, this chapter approaches the assessment of FYS and LC programs with the conviction that it is valuable to collaboratively identify outcomes for institutions, programs, students, faculty, and staff and engage in conversations about how to effectively and efficiently measure those outcomes. Exploring these topics can encourage further discussions about student learning and success and, ultimately, enhance research, assessment, and practice. The chapter begins with a review of traditional approaches to assessing the outcomes of FYS/LC programs for students, faculty, staff, and institutions and proposes strategies for strengthening and deepening assessment efforts.

FYS and LC Outcomes

Established frameworks for assessing LC and FYS programs, individually or combined, may vary in terms of elements and sequence, but they have one thing in common: They start with specific, measurable outcomes related to cognitive, behavioral, or affective changes (Friedman, 2012; Smith et al., 2004;

Taylor, Moore, MacGregor, & Lindblad, 2003). While programs developed for special populations (e.g., conditionally admitted students, first-generation and/ or low-income students, engineering majors) may include population-specific outcomes, the majority of LC and FYS outcomes fall into one or more of the following four categories:

- **Student progress and performance** assessment generally involves quantitative measures of student retention, persistence, and academic performance. These are generally summative outcomes; that is, they are evaluated after the experience. As such, student progress and performance measures are more likely to be used for proving the value of the experience than improving courses or programs.

- **Student engagement** is generally defined as the effort students put into the educational process and is identified as key to student success. Kuh and his colleagues (2005) expanded the notion of engagement to include not only the time and effort students put into studies and other education-related activities but also the degree to which an institution allocates resources and organizes learning opportunities and services that encourage student participation in and benefit from such activities.

- **Integrative learning and interdisciplinary understanding**. Assessing integrative learning and interdisciplinary understanding is a critical practice for LC and FYS programs. Integrative learning is the broader term, which the Association of American Colleges and Universities (AAC&U) and the Carnegie Foundation for the Advancement of Teaching (2004) described in a joint statement as having several aspects, including connecting skills and knowledge from multiple sources and experiences, applying theory to practice in various settings, using diverse and even contradictory points of view, and understanding issues and positions contextually. These outcomes could apply to LC and FYS programs whether offered individually or in combination.

    A central outcome of curricular LCs is interdisciplinary understanding, demonstrated when students integrate knowledge and modes of thinking from two or more disciplines or well-established fields of study. Boix-Mansilla (2005) noted that the challenges associated with assessing student learning are particularly evident in interdisciplinary understanding where there is less clarity and definition about the indicators of quality.

- *Faculty and staff outcomes*. LCs and FYSs done well, whether offered individually or combined, will almost always involve a number of departments or units across campus, and promote robust, collaborative partnerships between academic affairs and student affairs. Consequently, assessment of LCs and FYSs should not be limited to the impact on students but might also include the assessment of the participation of and collaboration among faculty, student services staff, and other members of the academic community.

Assessment Approaches in FYSs and LCs

Each of the four outcomes categories described in the previous section can be associated with an assortment of assessment methods and tools. The list below is not meant to be exhaustive but rather illustrative of the strategies being used to address the outcomes of interest.

Student Progress and Performance

Whether the LCs or FYSs are offered alone or in combination, faculty and administrators are concerned with understanding how participation in these programs affects students' performance over time. Typically, these metrics include one or more of the following: (a) completion of term, (b) term-to-term retention, (c) year-to-year persistence and persistence to a degree, (d) course pass rates, (e) GPA, (f) academic standing, and/or (g) dean's list or honor roll status. In fact, several institutions featured in Henscheid's (2004) overview of the role of first-year seminars in learning communities—including the University of New Mexico and Texas A&M University-Corpus Christi—used student progress and performance data as part of their assessment plan. Iowa State was able to use their retention data for first-year students to show that learning community participation contributed to the university's tuition revenue (Henscheid, 2004).

The Washington Center for the Improvement of Undergraduate Learning's (Washington Center) National Survey of Learning Community Programs (NSLCP) asked participants to describe their assessment activities. More than 80% of the 66 respondents reported that they tracked grade point average, course completion rates, pass rates, or students' progress after completing the learning community (Lardner, 2014). Respondent comments indicated that these data were collected using student management systems, "often in collaboration with institutional research or institutional effectiveness offices" (Lardner, 2014, p. 4).

Student Engagement

Findings from the NSLCP also indicated that engagement was a commonly assessed outcome (Lardner, 2014). The National Survey of Student Engagement (NSSE) and the Community College Survey of Student Engagement (CCSSE) are the primary instruments for measuring student engagement in FYS and LC programs. Both surveys include questions that help faculty, staff, and administrators assess the impact of students' enrollment in learning communities. While there are no questions specific to FYSs on either survey, Hayek and Kuh (2004) suggested principles for using NSSE to assess the first-year seminar, including becoming familiar with the conceptual and empirical foundations of student engagement; ensuring the sampling scheme matches the intended use of the data; and linking NSSE results to other relevant information about seminars, such as the EBI First-Year Initiative Assessment. These principles could easily apply to the use of other survey surveys as well.

Practitioners recognized that a survey assessing students' experiences and perceptions in the learning community—as a companion to the assessment of student work—would be helpful. Subsequently, the Washington Center and Skagit Valley College collaborated to design and administer the Survey of Students' Experiences of Learning in Learning Communities (SSELLC, Washington Center, 2010), a web-based survey for students enrolled in learning communities. The SSELLC examines students' engagement in classroom activities, instructors' activities supporting learning, students' perceptions of gains made in their own understanding and abilities, and students' perceptions of cognitive activities in the learning community versus other courses they have taken. While there are similarities between the SSELLC and several other surveys, including NSSE, CCSSE, and the First-Year Initiative Assessment, the SSELLC is focused on curricular learning communities.

From the validation study of the SSELLC conducted in 2012-2013, a peer-to-peer reflection protocol emerged. The protocol provides students "an opportunity to explore the social and constructivist nature of learning and knowledge in one another's company" and provided LC programs and teaching teams "an opportunity to appreciate the deep and intricate connections between LCs done well and transformative learning" (Malnarich, Pettitt, & Mino, 2014, p. 24). While still in the field-testing stage, it has become clear that the protocol is a valuable tool for examining the collective learning of students in a variety of educational settings where learning together is encouraged.

Integrative Learning and Interdisciplinary Understanding

Two national projects during the past decade have supported institutions with a measurement of integrative learning and interdisciplinary understanding resulting from student participation in an LC. One national project, Assessing Learning in Learning Communities, was launched by the Washington Center in fall 2005. The purpose of this two-year effort was to develop collaborative assessment practices that focused on the quality of student learning made possible by LCs, whether or not they included FYSs. Twenty-two teams from two- and four-year institutions participated.

One of the major activities of Assessing Learning in Learning Communities was using a structured conversation protocol targeted specifically for interdisciplinary work. To that end, a version of the collaborative assessment protocol developed by Boix-Mansilla and Dawes Duraising (2007) was created for this project. Articles in a special issue of the *Journal of Learning Communities Research* (Lardner & Malnarich, 2008a) describe how participants adapted the protocol and other tools used in the project, and how they applied the knowledge and insights gained from their participation in the project to their assessment of integrative learning and interdisciplinary understanding. Long-term impacts described by one of the project participants include the development of integrative learning outcomes for general education and integrated assignment workshops for faculty (Dunlap & Pettitt, 2012).

AAC&U has also been actively involved in the promotion of assessment and integrative learning. Through their Valid Assessment of Learning in Undergraduate Education (VALUE) project, a rubric for integrative learning was developed. As part of AAC&U's LEAP (Liberal Education and America's Promise) initiative, the organization maintains a Campus Toolkit website with a variety of resources for high-impact practices (HIPs) and learning outcomes and assessment, including the VALUE rubrics (AAC&U, n.d.). The integrative and applied learning rubric is anchored by five outcomes: (a) connections to experience, (b) connections to discipline, (c) transfer of knowledge or skills to new situations, (d) integrated communications, and (e) reflection and self-assessment (AAC&U, 2009). These outcomes are similar to many espoused by LC and FYS programs and provide an excellent starting point for assessing student assignments focused on integrative learning or interdisciplinary understanding.

Despite these efforts, findings from the NSLCP suggested that fewer than half of the respondents reported that they assessed integrative or interdisciplinary learning (Lardner, 2014). Given that interdisciplinary and integrative learning "are strongly associated with learning communities," Lardner pointed out, "Our collective assessment practice with respect to this outcome is lagging" (p. 9). Further, the survey results suggest a strong need for "more clarification about the differences between integrative and interdisciplinary learning and the development of more readily accessible tools and practices for directly assessing student work" (p. 9).

Faculty and Staff Outcomes

As noted above, the very nature of LC and FYS programs promotes collaboration among faculty, student services staff, and other members of the academic community. While there are several instruments for assessing students' perceptions of their experience and educational gains and their satisfaction with those experiences, there are few for measuring outcomes for faculty and staff involved with LC work. Although a number of the tools mentioned earlier can be used to inform meaningful professional development programs (i.e., NSSE, CCSSE, and SSELC), few provide opportunities for faculty and staff to reflect on their own experiences, such as their interactions with other members of the college community. For example, in the NSLCP, expanded pedagogical strategies, increased knowledge of other disciplines, increased intellectual engagement in teaching, and increased collaboration among faculty and staff were identified as significant outcomes for LC programs (Lardner, 2014).

Challenges for the Assessment of LCs and FYSs

The preceding discussion suggests there are a variety of assessment activities being employed in both LC and FYS programs. While most of these methods have been used to examine individual programs, the same metrics can be employed in combined programs. Several observations can be made about the current state of LC and FYS assessment and the challenges for expanding these activities and enhancing their comprehensiveness and rigor. For example, it is clear that many institutions have been diligent about articulating a range of outcomes for their programs; some are addressing a number of assessment questions using multiple methods. While other institutions are examining multiple outcomes either within a single category (e.g., student engagement or faculty and staff outcomes), assessing outcomes across all categories appears to be less common.

Tracking students over time also appears to be a challenge for institutions. This is not surprising given the intricacies of developing a cohort and methods for following that group with regard to multiple performance outcomes from term-to-term and over an extended period of time. In addition, assessment plans and research designs using comparison groups to better measure the advantage of LC and FYS participation are not the norm. Endicott, Suhr, McMorrow, and Doherty's (2004) description of the University of Northern Colorado's FYS program offers a good institutional example of multilevel assessment, which includes student surveys, self-reports, and focus groups; faculty surveys; course evaluations; and measures of student academic performance and progress. The University also uses comparison data for academic measures and the student survey that examines students' perceptions of advising, campus services, academic planning, and engagement with the institution.

As noted earlier, engagement also includes an institutional component: the degree to which an institution allocates resources and organizes learning opportunities and services that encourage student participation in and benefit from such activities. The limited occurrence of goals or assessments related to such institutional engagement factors could be attributed in part to the barriers encountered when cross-departmental collaboration and information sharing is required.

This review of findings from the NSLCP also suggests that the degree of rigor associated with LC and FYS assessments varies considerably. Continued or increased collaboration with the institutional research (IR) office can help LC and FYS programs identify measures, assessment frameworks, and research strategies that better serve the needs of the program. The involvement of IR is particularly crucial to the development of assessment methods and techniques that help the institution understand how participation in multiple programs affects the array of outcomes associated with that engagement. The next section describes several approaches to strengthening LC and FYS assessments in the future with this challenge in mind.

New Directions: What Should We Be Assessing and Why

As more campuses focus on implementing HIPs, such as FYSs and LCs, to help students make a successful transition to college and progress toward degree completion, there should be an increased attention on developing assessment frameworks that tell campus leaders what programs are most effective, for which students, and how to best organize learning opportunities with limited resources. Given the current state of LC and FYS, the following approaches are proposed as new directions.

The Synergistic Effects of Participating in Multiple HIPs

Although positive outcomes are routinely associated with HIPs, the picture of which interventions are most effective in promoting student success is clouded by the difficulty of isolating the effects of individual initiatives. Because students participate in multiple educational experiences concurrently, assessment is needed to evaluate the potency of given interventions as well as the various combinations of interventions. For example, while many LCs include a FYS or college success skills course, participation in a seminar is not accounted for in many studies examining the impact of LCs on GPA (Andrade, 2007-2008). Assessment practitioners may consider the synergistic effects of these programs by conducting analyses that explore students' learning gains and academic success outcomes when they participate in a stand-alone FYS compared to one embedded in a LC.

Structure, Processes, and Strategies

Assessment practitioners should also focus beyond outcome studies to collect data on curricular structures, formats, pedagogy, and learning activities. This program process information will help clarify the reasons why (or why not) FYS/LC programs are successful and the features that should be improved or sustained. For example, it is vital that assessment activities include rich descriptions of local context and details of formats and curricular structures associated with FYS/LC programs. This will help ensure that institutions are effectively implementing FYS/LCs to produce desired outcomes and will help to enhance understanding of which strategies work. Brownell and Swaner (2009, 2010) found that a major limitation in assessments of HIPs, such as FYSs and LCs, was that they lacked descriptions of the interventions, thus limiting the utility of the findings. When assessment results did contain adequate descriptions of programs, Brownell and Swaner (2010) were able to identify conditions where positive outcomes were more likely to occur and which designs and implementation strategies to employ to maximize impacts. For example, they found that the following practices were associated with effective FYS implementation: (a) establishing goals before designing a program and choosing a seminar format to fit those goals; (b) building instructional teams comprising faculty, advisors, librarians, and technology professionals; (c) using engaging pedagogies that are active and collaborative in nature, such as group work, interactive lectures, experiential learning, and problem-based learning; and (d) helping students see that the skills they need to succeed in the seminar are ones they will use throughout college and after graduation. LCs were more effective if they included strategies, such as intentionality in linking courses, engaging pedagogies, investing in faculty development to ensure full integration of courses, and embedding seminar courses (Brownell & Swaner, 2010).

At the onset of assessment planning, practitioners should engage campus leaders and faculty members to think carefully about the student learning outcomes they want to develop or improve, and what types of FYS/LC structures, curricular and cocurricular activities, pedagogical strategies, and assignments will most likely lead to those ends. This step can be accomplished by engaging in a dialogue with program administrators and instructional teams in meetings, retreats, focus groups, or using questionnaires designed to illicit input. Simpson (2002) recommended that a variety of qualitative and quantitative instruments be employed to facilitate understanding regarding why programs and interventions produce specific outcomes. Effective assessment planning should also begin with clearly articulated program processes and intended outcomes as this will help guide the selection of instruments. With agreed upon goals clearly defined by key stakeholders, assessment planners will be able to select measures and instruments that are sensitive, valid, and reliable. Information on intended outcomes can be gathered directly from instructional team members or other key stakeholders and from documents, such as content analyses of syllabi, internal websites or resource sites that post information about intended program outcomes and activities, or even materials collected during faculty meetings and retreats. Systematic collection of program materials and descriptions of processes along with outcome assessment results will help increase understanding regarding what internal program operations need to be improved when selected outcome measures suggest that desired program outputs are not achieved (Huerta & Hansen, 2013).

Deeper and More Varied Outcomes

To understand the effects of LCs and FYSs individually and in combination and meet diverse information needs, practitioners must broaden the scope of outcomes when assessing FYSs and LCs. MacGregor (2003) suggested that LC assessment should consider multidimensional impacts, including effects on faculty, students, and institutions. Assessment results may reveal that faculty members teaching in FYS and LC programs have more opportunities to interact with colleagues and learn how to use multidisciplinary teaching strategies, link curricular and cocurricular activities, and implement effective integrative learning assignments. Analyses could be conducted to ascertain how LCs with embedded FYS programs provide these opportunities and how the FYS structure can offer students more comfortable spaces for deep learning, reflection, and integration. The institutional outcomes of improved student success and graduation rates may also be more fully understood from the combination of FYS/LCs rather than examining the impact of either program in isolation.

In addition to taking into account the multiple levels of impacts, assessment of LCs and FYSs should move beyond merely measuring program effects on student retention to investigating effects on student-to-student interaction, student-to-faculty interaction, learning objectives, attitudes, and behaviors (Barefoot 2000, 2001). Lardner and Malnarich (2008b) asserted that

> while improved retention is a welcome consequence of learning-community work, it has never been its aim. In the push to improve student retention, it is easy to overlook what research tells us: Students persist in their studies if the learning they experience is meaningful, deeply engaging, and relevant to their lives. (p. 32)

Lardner and Malnarich (2008b, 2009) have also emphasized the importance of assessing how LCs foster students' levels of critical thinking and integrative learning. Assessment practitioners should investigate both the indirect effects (e.g., facilitate student-student and faculty-student interactions) and direct effects (e.g., academic performance, retention) of LCs on students (Pike, 2008). As such, assessment activities should be aimed at examining the critical outcomes of programs, such as retention, academic achievement, and learning outcomes, and also capture the combined FYS/LC program processes that directly affect these outcomes, such as faculty-student interactions, peer interactions, a sense of belonging and community, and integrative learning experiences.

Using a combination of qualitative and quantitative assessment approaches may help us better understand the deep and varied outcomes of FYS and LC programs. To appreciate program impacts more holistically, students' cognitive, social, emotional, and attitudinal outcomes need to be considered. Mixed-method approaches could be employed to comprehensively assess the impacts of dynamic and complex FYS/LC programs synergistically and individually. These two methods will yield the most value if they are employed as complementary techniques, not as two independent strands of inquiry. The assessment process should bring an awareness of the different ways that programs are implemented and how students respond to those differences; qualitative research is critical here. Institutional improvement also requires developing common indicators of program effectiveness, measuring them over time, and using the results to make strategic and policy decisions at different higher education organizational levels (e.g., instruction, administration, governance). Quantitative results can be useful in making data-driven decisions. However, once decisions are planned and implemented, qualitative techniques can be employed to examine the cultural variations underlying different methods of implementation (Duckworth, Hansen, & Evenbeck, 2002).

Qualitative evaluations provide the kinds of in-depth process information that allow faculty, staff, and students to better understand when and how interventions are meeting intended goals (Huerta & Hansen, 2013). Conducting focus groups and one-on-one interviews, and observing classroom behaviors, can be helpful for understanding students' in-depth perceptions and exploring students' learning experiences. Protocols should be developed to investigate perceptions of how FYS and LC structures individually and collectively contribute to students' learning and instructional team members' teaching experiences. For example, semistructured interviews could be designed to examine experiences with FYSs and LCs individually as well as to explore synergistic effects. Content analysis of students' open-ended comments on questionnaires can provide insights about students' perceptions, attitudes, feelings about sense of community, and academic needs. Students' and instructional team members' voices, stories, or narratives need to be included in assessment strategies. The quantitative data along with the stories can help make a more compelling case for the value of FYS/LCs, and capturing these narratives also allows stakeholders to hear the diverse, deep, and meaningful experiences of students and faculty members.

Direct Assessment of Learning Outcomes

Direct measures of student learning are important to help institutions improve and show the effectiveness of FYS and LC programs. They require students to demonstrate their knowledge and skills and provide tangible, visible, and self-explanatory evidence of what students have and have not learned as a result of a course, program, or activity (Palomba & Banta, 1999; Suskie, 2004, 2009). Suskie (2009) argued, "no assessment of knowledge, conceptual understanding, or thinking or performance skills should consist of indirect evidence alone" (p. 19). Examples of direct measures of student learning that could be collected from students participating in FYS/LC programs include exams, tests, quizzes, written papers, oral presentations, group work, assignments, exit exams, or standardized tests. Integrative learning assignments may be ideal sources of direct assessment. The AAC&U VALUE rubrics or others designed locally to assess integrative learning and critical thinking could be useful tools for evaluating and understanding student learning outcomes.

Rather than practicing assessment as an add-on to the existing work of instructional teams and students, assessment activities should involve the collection of embedded, authentic measures of learning. The aim of many LCs and FYSs is for students to become lifelong learners by enhancing students' communication, critical thinking, and problem-solving abilities. With authentic, embedded assessment tasks students are asked to demonstrate what they know and are able to do in meaningful ways. These tasks are often multidimensional and require higher levels of cognition, such as problem solving and critical thinking. Embedded assessment means that "those opportunities to assess student progress and performance are integrated into the instructional materials and are virtually indistinguishable from the day-to-day classroom activities" (Wilson & Sloane, 2000, p. 82). An example of an embedded assessment would be asking students to integrate their experiences and concepts learned in different disciplinary courses using a written assignment, artistic performance, or service-learning project.

Indirect Assessment of Learning Outcomes

Assessments that measure opinions or beliefs about students' knowledge, skills, and abilities are indirect measures of learning. Students' perceptions of the extent to which courses and assignments have enhanced their achievement of the stated learning outcomes may be obtained by using the following methods: (a) self-assessment; (b) peer-feedback; (c) end-of-course evaluations; (d) national survey instruments, such as NSSE, CCSSE, or SSELLC; (e) focus groups; or (f) exit interviews. Other examples may include academic performance levels (e.g., GPAs), graduation rates, retention and transfer studies, graduate follow-up studies, success of students in subsequent institutional settings, and job placement data. While these types of measures are important and necessary, they do not measure students' learning outcomes directly. They supplement direct measures of learning by providing information about how and why learning is occurring.

Long-Term and Sustainable Impacts

Much assessment of FYS/LC programs does not examine long-term outcomes, such as graduation, degree completion, and application of learning to academic tasks at later points in time. Lardner and Malnarich (2008b) have emphasized the importance of collecting longitudinal assessment data and sharing it with key decision makers and actively using such data in making choices about the purposes and structures of programs, identifying curricular trouble-spots, and improving academic achievement. Follow-up assessment may be necessary to determine how students apply skills gained in different settings and contexts, especially since students may not be able to adequately report the benefits of FYS and/or LC participation until they have had the opportunity to experience the college environment without the academic and social supports associated with these programs. Finally, demonstrating that FYS/LC programs have sustainable effects on student learning, adjustment, and persistence is more likely to prove the value that these programs add than focusing only on short-term gains.

Rigorous Studies Investigating the Effects of FYS/LCs

Assessment practitioners are often charged with determining which educational programs and practices are the most effective in improving students' learning, engagement, academic performance, retention, and completion. Additionally, campus administrators and policy makers have to make decisions about which programs to implement in order to address the transitional educational needs of a wide range of students. Research designs that focus on deeper, more complex outcomes can help provide a more accurate picture of the effects of FYSs and LCs. Analyses should also be conducted to explore whether there are differential program impacts based on students' academic preparation levels, gender, first-generation status, income level, and race or ethnicity.

The research and assessment designs, as much as practical, should (a) employ appropriate comparison groups and use either matching or statistical techniques that take into account differences in academic preparation, demographic characteristics, and enrollment patterns; (b) be longitudinal and consider long-term outcomes, such as graduation, degree completion, and application of learning to academic tasks at later points in time; and (c) employ pre-post designs with comparison groups to assess changes in outcomes over time, particularly gains in learning or changes in behaviors or attitudes. A noteworthy limitation of many investigations on the effectiveness of initiatives, such as FYSs and LCs, is that students self-select into the programs. It is possible that the positive effects of the programs are due to the fact that students who decide to participate may have differed in substantial ways from students who decided to not to participate and these differences (not the intervention experienced) may have caused the positive outcomes.

Carefully designed studies employing random assignment and experimental designs that include both a treatment and a control group remain the gold standard in terms of being able to make causal inferences about educational programs and also rule out selection bias. However, the use of experimental design is extremely rare in the literature on FYS and LC assessment, with some noted exceptions (Goldberg & Finkelstein, 2002; Scrivener & Coghlan, 2011; Strumpf & Hunt, 1993) because of logistical or ethical considerations. Random assignment to an FYS or LC may not feasible when, for example, many students may be denied access to programs; placement of students in the experimental group into the correct sections presents logistical issues; or legislators exert pressure to ensure low-income, first-generation students have access to academic support interventions. Despite these challenges, assessment practitioners should explore possibilities for random assignment, especially when pilot programs are developed that do not involve denying academic support to large populations of students and alternatives to treatment can be offered to these students. There are also some statistical approaches that have been employed to address selection bias when random assignment is not possible, such as propensity score matching (Vaughan, Parra, & Lalonde, 2014), the Heckman adjustment (e.g., Heckman, 1979) and the use instrumental variables (Angrist, Lang, & Oreopoulos, 2009; Pike, Hansen, & Lin 2011).

As we have improved our capacity to measure a wide array of student outcomes, it has become increasingly important that we develop ways to assess how FYS and LC programs work to increase desirable educational outcomes. Mixed-method designs can be useful because the combination of quantitative and qualitative approaches provides a more comprehensive understanding of program impacts as information is captured about participants' unique experiences as well as indicators of program effects (Creswell, 2008). Quantitative program outcomes may include scores on rubrics designed to assess student learning directly, academic performance, and even retention rates. According to Creswell (2008) and Jick (1979), mixed-methods approaches can also provide strengths that offset the weaknesses of either quantitative or qualitative alone.

A mixed-method design with a triangulation intent seeks convergence of qualitative and quantitative measures (Greene, Caracelli, & Graham, 1989). The use of both a qualitative interview and a quantitative questionnaire to assess program participants' sense of belonging illustrates this triangulation intent. Quantitative data may include closed-ended information, such as that found on attitude, behavior, sense of belonging, or student learning measures. The collection of these quantitative data may also involve using closed-ended checklists, which assess students behaviors observed in the classroom; GPAs; retention rates; or degree completion numbers. Qualitative data may consist of open-ended information gathered through interviews with students, and questions asked should allow the participants to supply answers in their own words and tell their stories. Qualitative data may also be gathered by collecting audiovisual materials, such as videotapes or artifacts.

Assessment for Sustaining FYS/LC Programs and for Decision Making

FYS/LC programs may not be sustained if they are not viewed as critical to institutional goals about improving student learning and success. As such, assessment strategies should take into account institutional missions and the data needed to assess progress toward strategic planning priorities and goals. The intended goals of FYSs and LCs are likely to align with strategic planning goals related to improving student learning, academic performance, engagement levels, and persistence rates. While comprehensive program outcomes assessment is crucial, assessment practitioners should enact feedback mechanisms that provide accurate and timely information to support data-driven strategic planning decisions. As such, sharing assessment data with program implementers and faculty members involved directly with FYS/LC programs is critical for ensuring the information is used to make decisions about program improvements. It is also important to collaborate with those who manage FYS/LC programs and instructional teams when planning for assessment to ascertain their information needs, and this, in turn, is likely to facilitate more meaningful reports as well as use of results. The ongoing sharing of assessment results with those tasked with implementing the programs and delivering powerful pedagogies is also essential for making sure that program quality and fidelity is maintained.

Consequently, maintaining program fidelity—making sure that key program components are implemented as conceptualized—is paramount. These components are likely to include ensuring the involvement of both student affairs and academic affairs, developing and using quality integrative learning assignments, promoting ongoing professional development, and creating effective collaborative instructional teams. To meet this end, assessment activities should include measures to determine the extent to which FYS/LCs are being carried out with a high degree of quality.

According to Johnson (2013), "The Completion Agenda represents a complex set of intersecting priorities advocated by federal and state government, nonprofit organizations, colleges, and universities that shift the national focus from expanding access to degree completion" (p. 1). In fact, the Completion Agenda has prompted several states to enact performance-based systems designed to allocate funds to incentivize improvements in degree production (Reyna, 2010). As such, FYS/LC assessment should also be responsive to the expectations of diverse stakeholders around the issues of access, completion, quality, and efficiency.

Institutional leaders must be intentional about growing programs such as FYSs and LCs strategically. However, increased attention devoted to college completion must also consider a focus on student learning and a production of high-quality degrees (Evenbeck & Johnson, 2012), since a myopic focus on accumulation of credits, retention, and graduation rates risks turning a blind eye toward student learning outcomes. Ideally, assessment data and research will be used to inform decisions about allocating resources "to ensure that students' learning experiences are meaningful, relevant to their lives, and deeply engaging, and that a focus on quality teaching and deep learning is recognized as the basis of a curricular model that contributes to persistence and retention"(Johnson, 2013, p. 4). Assessments should demonstrate how quality FYSs and LCs help ensure that students not only earn degrees but that they have also gained the critical knowledge, skills, abilities, and habits of mind necessary for being productive and engaged citizens.

Conclusion

This chapter described some traditional approaches to assessing LCs with embedded FYS programs and examined some of the challenges and limitations associated with these approaches. New directions for assessment, such as exploring more varied outcomes at multiple levels, enhancing understanding of what FYS/LC features lead to desired outcomes, focusing on long-term outcomes using longitudinal studies, assessing student learning outcomes directly, and employing more rigorous research designs that account for selection bias, were proposed. Additionally, the need for new assessment techniques to investigate the synergistic effects of participating in multiple HIPs during college was explored. Finally, this chapter examined how assessment efforts can help sustain quality LC and FYS programs by helping policy makers understand that these programs are often mission critical in facilitating student learning and success.

Merely advocating for the implementation of HIPs is not enough. They must be done well and continuously assessed to ensure that participating students experience positive learning experiences. LCs and FYSs are done well if they are synergistic collaborative environments that allow students to thrive;

compel faculty and staff do their best work; and create opportunities for students to develop the dispositions, knowledge, and skills to tackle complex real-world issues and become engaged citizens.

References

Andrade, M. S. (2007-2008). Learning communities: Examining positive outcomes. *Journal of College Student Retention, 9*(1), 1-20.

Angrist, J. D., Lang, D., & Oreopoulos, P. (2009). Incentives and services for college achievement: Evidence from a randomized trial. *American Economic Journal: Applied Economics, 1*(1), 136–163.

Association of American Colleges and Universities (AAC&U). (n.d.). *LEAP campus toolkit.* Retrieved from http://leap.aacu.org/toolkit/

Association of American Colleges and Universities (AAC&U). (2009). *Integrative and applied learning VALUE rubric.* Retrieved from http://www.aacu.org/value/rubrics/integrative-learning.

Association of American Colleges and Universities and the Carnegie Foundation for the Advancement of Teaching. (2004, March). *A statement on integrative learning.* Washington, DC: Association of American Colleges and Universities.

Barefoot, B.O. (2000). The first-year experience: Are we making it any better? *About Campus, 4*(6), 12–18.

Barefoot, B. O. (2001). First-year experience jeopardy. In R. L. Swing (Ed.), *Proving and improving: Strategies for assessing the first-year of college* (Monograph No. 33, pp. 95-98). Columbia, SC: University of South Carolina, National Resource Center for The First-Year Experience & Students in Transition.

Boix-Mansilla, V. (2005). Assessing student work at disciplinary crossroads. *Change, 37*(1), 14-21.

Boix-Mansilla, V., & Dawes Duraising, E. (2007). Toward a framework for assessing students' interdisciplinary work: An empirically grounded framework proposed. *The Journal of Higher Education, 78*(2), 215-237.

Brownell, J. E., & Swaner, L. E. (2009). Outcomes of high impact educational practices: A review of the literature. *Diversity & Democracy, 12*(2), 4–6.

Brownell, J. E., & Swaner, L. E. (2010). *Five high-impact practices.* Washington DC: Association of American Colleges and Universities.

Creswell, J. W. (2008). *Research design: Qualitative, quantitative, and mixed method approaches* (3rd ed.). Thousand Oaks, CA: Sage.

Duckworth, K., Hansen, M. J., & Evenbeck, S. E. (2002, November). *Assessing programs to increase student retention: The dialogue of qualitative and quantitative approaches.* Paper presented at the 2002 Assessment Institute, Indianapolis, IN.

Dunlap, L., & Pettitt, M. (2012). Using program assessments and faculty development to deepen student learning. In M. Soven, D. Lehr, S. Naynaha, & W. Olson (Eds.), *Linked courses for general education and integrative learning* (pp. 189-218). Sterling, VA: Stylus.

Endicott, P., Suhr, D., McMorrow, S., & Doherty, P. (2004). The flexible first-year experience as the centerpiece of five learning communities programs. In J. M. Henscheid (Ed.), *Integrating the first-year experience: The role of first-year seminars in learning communities* (Monograph No. 39, pp. 151-169). Columbia, SC: University of South Carolina, National Resource Center for The First-Year Seminar & Students in Transition.

Evenbeck, S., & Johnson, K. E. (2012). Students must not become victims of The Completion Agenda. *Liberal Education, 98*(1), 26-33.

Friedman, D. B. (2012). *The first-year seminar: Designing, implementing and assessing courses to support student learning and success. Vol. V. Assessing the first-year seminar.* Columbia, SC: University of South Carolina, National Resource Center for The First-Year Experience & Students in Transition.

Goldberg, B., & Finkelstein, M. (2002). Effects of a first-semester learning community on nontraditional technical students. *Innovative Higher Education, 24*(4), 235-249. http://dx.doi.org/10.1023/A:1015876829313

Greene, J. C., Caracelli, V. J., & Graham, W. F. (1989). Toward a conceptual framework for mixed method evaluation designs. *Educational Evaluation and Policy Analysis 11,* 255–274.

Hayek, J., & Kuh, G. (2004, March-April). Principles for assessing student engagement in the first year of college. *Assessment Update, 16*(2), 11-13.

Heckman, J. (1979). Sample selection bias as a specification error. *Econometrica, 47,* 153-161.

Henscheid, J. M. (Ed.) 2004. *Integrating the first-year experience: The role of first-year seminars in learning communities.* (Monograph No. 39). Columbia, SC: University of South Carolina, National Resource Center for The First-Year Seminar & Students in Transition.

Huerta, J. C., & Hansen, M. J. (2013). Learning community assessment 101: Best practices. *Learning Communities Research and Practice, 1*(1), Article 15. Retrieved from http://washingtoncenter.evergreen.edu/lcrpjournal/vol1/iss1/15

Jick, T. D. (1979). Mixing qualitative and quantitative methods: Triangulation in action. *Administrative Science Quarterly, 24*, 602-611.

Johnson, K. E. (2013). Learning communities and The Completion Agenda. *Learning Communities Research and Practice, 1*(3), Article 3. Retrieved from http://washingtoncenter.evergreen.edu/lcrpjournal/vol1/iss3/3

Kuh, G., Kinzie, J., Schuh, J., Whitt, E., & Associates. (2005). *Student success in college: Creating conditions that matter.* San Francisco, CA: Jossey-Bass.

Lardner, E. (2014). What campuses assess when they assess their learning community programs: Selected findings from a National Survey of Learning Community Programs. *Learning Communities Research and Practice, 2*(2), Article 2. Retrieved from http://washingtoncenter.evergreen.edu/lcrpjournal/vol2/iss2/2

Lardner, E., & Malnarich, G. (Eds.). (2008a). National Project on Assessing Learning in Learning Communities [Special issue]. *Journal of Learning Communities Research, 3*(3). Retrieved from http://www.evergreen.edu/washingtoncenter/about/monographs/jlcr.html

Lardner, E., & Malnarich, G. (2008b, July-August). A new era in learning-community work: Why the pedagogy of intentional integration matters. *Change.* Retrieved from http://www.changemag.org/Archives/Back%20Issues/July-August%202008/full-new-era.html

Lardner, E., & Malnarich, G. (2009). When faculty assess integrative learning: Faculty inquiry to improve learning community practice. *Change: The Magazine of Higher Learning, 41*(5), 29-35.

MacGregor, J. (Ed.). (2003). *Doing learning community assessment: Five campus stories* (National Learning Communities Project Monograph Series). Olympia, WA: Washington Center for Undergraduate Education, The Evergreen State College.

Malnarich, G., Pettitt, M., & Mino, J. (2014). Washington Center's online student survey validation study: Surfacing students' individual and collective understanding of their learning community experiences. *Journal of Learning Communities Research and Practice, 2*(1), Article 1. Retrieved from http://washingtoncenter.evergreen.edu/lcrpjournal/

Moore, W. (2003). Assessment as an integral part of educational change: Assessment in and of learning communities. In J. MacGregor (Ed.), *Doing learning community assessment: Five campus stories* (National Learning Communities Project Monograph Series, pp. 1-4). Olympia, WA: Washington Center for Improving the Quality of Undergraduate Education.

Palomba, C. A., & Banta, T. W. (1999). *Assessment essentials: Planning, implementing, and improving assessment in higher education.* San Francisco, CA: Jossey-Bass.

Pike, G. R. (2008). Learning about learning communities: Consider the variables. *About Campus, 13*, 30–32. doi: 10.1002/abc.269

Pike, G. R., Hansen, M. J., & Lin, C-H. (2011). Using instrumental variables to account for selection effects in research on first-year programs. *Research in Higher Education, 52*(2), 194-214.

Reyna, R. (2010) *Complete to compete: Common college completion metrics.* Washington, DC: National Governors Association. Retrieved from http://www.completecollege.org/path_forward/common_metrics/

Scrivener, S., & Coghlan, E. (2011, March). *Opening doors to student success: A synthesis of findings from an evaluation of six community colleges* (Policy Brief). New York, NY: MDRC. Retrieved from http://www.mdrc.org/sites/default/files/policybrief_27.pdf

Simpson, M. L. (2002). Program evaluation studies: Strategic learning delivery systems. *Journal of Developmental Education, 26*(2), 2-10.

Smith, B., MacGregor, J., Matthews, R., & Gabelnick, F. (2004). *Learning communities: Reforming undergraduate education.* San Francisco, CA: Jossey-Bass.

Strumpf G., & Hunt, P. (1993). The effects of an orientation course on the retention and academic standing of entering freshmen, controlling for the volunteer effect. *Journal of The Freshman Year Experience, 5*(1), 7-14

Suskie, L. (2004). *Assessing student learning: A common sense guide.* Boston, MA: Anker.

Suskie, L. (2009). *Assessing student learning: A common sense guide.* (2nd ed.). San Francisco, CA: Jossey-Bass.

Taylor, K., Moore, W., MacGregor, J., & Lindblad, J. (2003). *Learning communities research and assessment: What we know now* (National Learning Communities Project Monograph Series). Olympia, WA: Washington Center for Improving the Quality of Undergraduate Education.

Vaughan, A. L., Parra, J., & Lalonde, T. (2014). First-generation college student achievement and the first year seminar: A quasi-experimental design. *Journal of The First-Year Experience & Students in Transition, 26*(2), 51-67.

Washington Center for the Improvement of Undergraduate Education. (2010). *Survey of Students' Experience in Learning Communities.* Olympia, WA: Author, Evergreen State College. Retrieved from http://www.evergreen.edu/washingtoncenter/survey/surveyfindings.html

Walvoord, B. E. (2010). *Assessment clear and simple.* San Francisco, CA: Jossey-Bass.

Wilson, M., & Sloane, K. (2000). From principles to practice: an embedded assessment system. *Applied Measurement In Education, 13*(2), 181–208.

Part II
Contexts for Implementation: Models From Two- and Four-Year Institutions

Case Study 1
Inviting the Mother Tongue and a First-Year Seminar to Promote Success Among Spanish-Speaking ESL Students

Andrea Parmegiani
Bronx Community College

The Institution and Its Students

Bronx Community College (BCC) is a two-year college located in the Bronx, New York. It is a public, open-admission institution that is part of the City University of New York (CUNY). In fall 2013, the full-time equivalent (FTE) for undergraduate students was 8,060. BCC does not provide on-campus housing. The racial or ethnic background of the student body is as follows: 61% of the students identify as Hispanic, 33% as Black, 3% as White, 3% as Asian/Pacific Islander, and 0% as American Indian/Native American. More than half (57%) of the student body is female, and 31% are over 25 years old. In 2012, about 40% of first-time students reported that English was not their first language, and the vast majority of these students were native Spanish speakers.

The Program

Success rates at BCC have been improving, but they still remain the lowest within the CUNY system. The one-year retention rate for the entering class of fall 2008 was 65%; the six-year graduation rate was 20%. Systemic barriers to students' success include the need for remediation in one or more basic skills areas for 85% of students; a household income of less than $20,000 for more than half of the students; and competing obligations—45% are employed and 23% support children (Office of Institutional Research, 2010).

As the result of a collegewide initiative to increase success rates among first-year students, 10 extended-orientation first-year seminars (FYS) were piloted at BCC in spring 2012. Extensive research has shown that well-designed FYSs can have a strong impact on success rates (Karp et al., 2012), especially in community colleges (Zeindenberg, Jenkins, & Calcagno, 2007). This has been the case at BCC: By the end of the term, students who had enrolled in the FYS pilot had an average GPA of 2.29 and accumulated an average of 6.57 credits. Students who were not in the FYS had an average GPA of 1.77 and accumulated an average of 4.73 credits (Office of Institutional Research, 2013).

Building on this successful FYS, an innovative learning community (LC) was created in fall 2013, including an advanced English-as-a-second-language course (ESL 03), a Spanish composition course for native Spanish speakers (SPN 121), and a FYS. The goal of this program is to increase success rates among Spanish-speaking ESL students. Prior to the creation of this cluster, there were no attempts to link ESL courses to the native-level Spanish courses offered by the department of modern languages.

The rationale for this link is the strong presence of Spanish-speaking ESL students (SS-ESL) at BCC and the plethora of evidence suggesting that academic literacy skills foundations in students' mother tongues are positively correlated with ability to learn how to read and write effectively for academic purposes in a second language (Baker, 2011; Cummins, 1979, 2000; Krashen, 1999). In the case of students who attended secondary schools in Latin America, there is also evidence suggesting that what is considered effective academic reading and writing in the United States differs from the way students were expected to read and write in their countries of origins. For example, Bartlett and Garcia (2011) found that "a much greater emphasis was put in U.S. schools on the development and expression of personal opinion" as opposed to a "focus on specific recounting of factual information" (p. 121). They also reported that in the United States, "teachers expect much more independent reading than students normally did in their previous schools" (p. 121). Given this academic literacy expectation gap and that SS-ESL students need to bridge this gap using a language in which they are still not fully proficient, it made sense to create a space within a LC where students could use their mother tongue to develop academic literacy skills in a second language.

The inclusion of a special FYS section built around the needs of ESL students in the LC was important for the success of the cluster. Seven of the students enrolled were from the Dominican Republic; the other three were from Honduras; all of them were recent immigrants. Research shows that "instruction that integrates language and content, courses and activities that orient students to U.S. school communities, qualified teachers [and] paraprofessional support" is particularly effective in helping ESL students succeed academically (Bartlett & Garcia, 2011, p. 9). The presence of two peer mentors in the FYS played a crucial role in helping students navigate the demands of college life in a new country. Peer mentors are successful BCC students who have made significant progress toward the completion of their degree. The fact that one of the peer mentors was a Dominican SS-ESL himself and that the other was a native English speaker who was fluent in Spanish helped students identify with these positive role models and establish a sense of community and belonging to their school. While all activities in the FYS were conducted in English, Spanish was used occasionally to express ideas students were not yet able to articulate in their second language. With the help of the tutors and the instructor, students reformulated these ideas into English while discussions were taking place.

The LC cluster was characterized by a wide of range of integrated language-based activities that revolved around the theme of students' empowerment through education. In keeping with BCC's slogan "transforming lives," the notion of empowerment was presented as a process of positive self-change rooted in students' agency, or their ability to take control of their lives. Thematic discussions, prompted by the reading of published texts, but also by the sharing of students' life experience in the form of personal essays, oral storytelling, and conversations, acknowledged the difficulties that students need to overcome to transform their lives. These discussions also emphasized human beings' ability to exercise agency by taking greater responsibility for their actions. The goal behind the choice of the theme was to help students create a better sense of themselves as learners and members of a community characterized by a "culture of achievement" (Bartlett & Garcia, 2011, p. 21).

In SPN 112 and ESL 03, students reflected on their life trajectories and investment in education. Integrated writing assignments, which students carried out in both Spanish and English, included a personal essay where students discussed their past achievements and potential as learners. These essays were shared during the writing process and brought into conversation with *Kaffir Boy* (Mathabane, 1998), a coming of age tale of a Black South African youth who, against all odds, managed to escape poverty, domestic violence, and apartheid through academic success. The ability to use both languages in the exploration of the theme allowed for a much greater complexity in terms of reasoning, analysis, and personal expression. In addition, it created opportunities for building vocabulary, addressing false cognates (words that are likely to be mistranslated), and exploring differences in usage and rhetorical styles. In particular, during the writing process, both the Spanish and the ESL instructors were able to help students develop those principles of academic writing that differed from the way students were taught to write in their countries of origin. For example, both ESL 03 and SPN 112 emphasized the importance of a thesis statement, of using textual evidence, and of citing sources.

In the FYS, the discussion of the theme was more practical and contextualized in students' present lives. The starting point was an honest look at BCC's low graduation and retention rates and an analysis of the factors that stand in the way of students' success. This analysis was based not only on reports compiled by BCC's Office of Institutional Research but also on personal essays previous ESL students had written about their processes of self-empowerment. With the help of the peer mentors who shared their personal experience, current students reflected on the challenges they were facing at that point in time. As the course progressed, they explored strategies for success through small-group discussions facilitated by the peer mentors. These discussions revolved around the following weekly microthemes, which were designed by the instructor specifically for this section: (a) taking responsibility for one's action, (b) juggling multiple responsibilities, (c) managing time effectively, (d) using the resources available at BCC, (e) developing good study habits, and (f) overcoming difficulties related to language. The microthemes helped the class address issues faced by immigrant students related to expanded family, financial, and academic responsibilities (Bartlett & Garcia, 2011), and their implications for college success.

Not only did these small-group discussions help create the sense of belonging and the culture of achievement that is so important for academic success but they also helped students develop the language and literacy skills that were emphasized in SPN 121 and ESL 03. Each microthematic unit was designed to generate and scaffold a discussion through activities that revolved around students' lives. While engaging in these discussions, students read, wrote, and spoke critically, using language to analyze, interpret, evaluate, and, if need be, challenge ideas.

Program Assessment

The goal of this LC is to increase the success rates of SS-ESL students at BCC. At the pilot phase, the only quantitative success indicators available were the average class GPAs of students in different ESL 03 cohorts. Qualitative data assessed how students' perception of their ability to achieve academic success evolved as a result of their enrollment in the LC. Students' self-perception is an important factor for academic success. The executive summary of the Freshmen Year Analysis and Recommendation, carried out by the Office of Institutional Research (2011) and investigating barriers to success, identified socio-affective variables in students' disposition, such as "motivation and sense of self-worth" as a major factor "contributing to the lack of students' success in the freshmen year and beyond" (p. 2).

The qualitative data emerged in class from the discussion of the theme. Throughout the learning process, there were metacognitive moments during which students reflected on the progress they had made. These reflections found expression through oral discussions and writing assignments. In addition, two writing assignments carried out in the FYS provided qualitative data. The first assignment, which was informal and not graded, asked students to discuss whether the work done in the FYS helped them become successful students. While the question was open, students were invited to consider fundamental aspects of the course, such as microthematic units that were covered, small-group discussions, information conveyed by the peer mentors, and the opportunity to share their personal experience and develop a personal relationship with the peer mentors. The second assignment was more formal and was administered as the final project for this course. It consisted of a multiparagraph letter addressed to a student who would be taking the FYS in the future. In this letter, current FYS students had to introduce themselves, share selected aspects of their first-year experience, and provide advice on how to be successful students. Both writing assignments were preceded by small-group discussions facilitated by the peer mentors.

A total of 20 writing assignments (two per student) were analyzed through a coding method that drew on grounded theory (Charmaz, 2006) in order to investigate how students' perception of their ability to achieve academic success evolved in the LC and to what factors students attribute this evolution. Three groups of factors that emerged from students' reflections as reoccurring themes are discussed in the next section.

Results

Table C1.1 shows that ESL 03 students who took the FYS had a significantly higher average GPA than ESL 03 students who did not. The average GPAs of ESL 03 students who took the FYS within the LC were also significantly higher those who took the seminar outside the cluster.

The qualitative data that emerged from students' metacognitive reflections shows that LC students developed positive perceptions of themselves as learners and that the inclusion of the FYS into the LC was crucial in this process. Three interconnected factors stood out in the way students constructed the role the FYS played in their academic success. That is, the course provided access to critical information; made students feel that they were "not alone;" and created a safe space where they could share their feelings, which is a factor that has been found to be crucial for student retention (Tinto, 1997).

Table C1.1

Comparative Outcomes for First-Time, First-Year ESL 03 Students

Cohort	GPA	*n*
ESL 03 students taking FYS	3.36	21
ESL 03 students not taking FYS	1.73	28
Difference	1.63**	
ESL 03 students in the LC	3.68	10
ESL 03 students taking FYS outside the LC	3.07	11
Difference	0.61*	

*p < .05. **p < .0001.

Students' reflections emphasized that the FYS provides critical information, which is hard for first-year students to access, especially if English is not their first language. One student referred to the FYS metaphorically as a "program that takes the student by the hand to move inside the complicated world of college with important information." Some of this information was practical and provided both by the peer mentors and the counselor students met with twice during the semester. Students expressed great appreciation for the advice they received on which courses to take, where to get extra help, how to relate to their professors, and which study skills to cultivate. The greatest emphasis, however, was placed on the "emotional information" that became available through the sharing of personal experience that was such a big part of the learning process. It was important for students to be able to see their struggle for academic success acknowledged and to be able to identify with the culture of achievement that was created through the interaction with the peer mentors and the other students in the class.

Another factor students highlighted was that the FYS helped them not feel alone since "there are other students who have troubles and who don't give up." One student wrote that because the FYS gave her "the opportunity to know that [she was] not alone," she found "the support, motivation, and courage not to leave college for any reason." Another student made a connection between feeling "not alone" and the need to improve BCC graduation and retention rates:

> When the peer mentors told us their personal experience, it helped me to continue with what I am doing. If they could do it, I can do it, too. They

went through the same things that we are going through now. I think if this class continues in the future, the percentage of students who drop out will change.

On a similar note, a different student mentioned feeling a greater sense of agency and responsibility after she was made aware of the contrast between BCC's low success rates and the stories embodied by the peer mentors and the personal essays written by previous ESL students:

> Taking the FYS made me see that things are not easy, but I can do every-thing I put my mind to. The stories we read help me see that everybody has problems, but reading how people succeed helped me to not let my troubles overcome my goals. When we looked at the dropout statistics I felt something that made me think 'I don't want to be part of the dropout statistics.'

A third factor that stood out was that the FYS created a safe space for students to share their feelings while developing their language skills. As these two students note, the creation of this safe space was often attributed to the small-group discussions facilitated by the peer mentors, during which the instructor faded into the background of the learning process:

> Working in small groups helped me express my ideas and share my per-sonal experience. We discussed topics that we can relate to in our lives, and these discussions helped me with my English skills. I felt comfortable talking to the peer mentors and the other classmates.

> The small groups helped us a lot to develop our speaking skills because we felt comfortable with the tutors. We could speak and not feel scared by our pronunciation because they understand that we are new ESL students.

Implications

The quantitative data presented suggests that ESL 03 students benefited considerably from the LC and from taking the FYS as a stand-alone class; students in the LC had the highest average GPA. Students' reflections show that the inclusion of the FYS in the cluster played a crucial role in their academic success by providing access to critical information, making students feel that they are not alone, and creating a safe space where students could share their feelings.

While the quantitative data is statistically significant, its implication cannot be generalized because students were not randomly assigned to the different groups examined in this study. It is possible the differences in average GPAs could also be attributed to different levels of student motivation and teacher effectiveness in different groups.

One-year retention rates are still not available for all the cohorts of ESL 03 students considered in this study, but for students in the LC, 9 of the 10 registered for fall 2014; one student took a leave of absence because of a pregnancy and came back in spring 2015. In the 2012-2013 academic year, the retention rate for first-time, first-year students was 55%. The fact that three semesters after starting college, none of the students in the LC dropped out and their average GPA was considerably higher suggests the cluster should be continued at BCC and that similar configurations can be recommended as pilots to other community colleges with large populations of ESL students.

The long-term impact of the LC at BCC will be evaluated through a longitudinal study that will monitor average GPAs, retention, credit accumulation, and graduation rates. Focus-group interviews will be used to investigate students' assessment of the role the LC played in developing more positive self-perceptions and how this affected their academic performance.

References

Baker, C. (2011). *Foundations of bilingual education and bilingualism*. Bristol, UK: Multilingual Matters.

Bartlett, L., & Garcia, O. (2011). *Additive schooling in subtractive times: Bilingual education and Dominican immigrant youth in the Heights*. Nashville, TN: Vanderbilt University Press.

Charmaz, K. (2006). *Constructing grounded theory*. London, UK: Sage.

Cummins, J. (1979) Cognitive/academic language proficiency, linguistic interdependence, the optimum age question. *Working Papers on Bilingualism, 19*, 121-129.

Cummins, J. (2000). *Language, power, and pedagogy: Bilingual children in the crossfire*. Clevedon, UK: Multilingual Matters.

Karp, M., Bickerstaff, S., Rucks-Ahidiana, Z., Bork, R., Barragan, M., & Edgecombe, N. (2012). *College 101 courses for applied learning and student success* (CCRC Working Paper No. 49). New York, NY: Community College Research Center, Teacher's College, Columbia University.

Krashen, S. (1999). *Condemned without trial: Bogus arguments against bilingual education*. Portsmouth, NH: Heinemann.

Mathabane, M. (1998). *Kaffir Boy: The true story of a youth's coming of age in South Africa*. New York, NY: Free Press.

Office of Institutional Research. (2010). *Making a case for improving the freshman year at BCC*. Bronx, NY: Bronx Community College.

Office of Institutional Research. (2011). *Freshman year analysis and recommendations: Executive summary*. Bronx, NY: Bronx Community College.

Office of Institutional Research. (2013). *Comparative first-year semester outcomes by first-semester course status*. Bronx, NY: Bronx Community College.

Tinto, V. (1997). Classrooms as communities: Exploring the educational character of student persistence. *The Journal of Higher Education, 68*(6), 599-623

Zeindenberg, M., Jenkins, D., & Calcagno, J. (2007). *Do student success courses actually help community college students succeed?* (CCRC Brief No. 36). New York, NY: Community College Research Center, Teacher's College, Columbia University.

Case Study 2
The Metro College Success Program: Redesigning the First Two Years of College

Vicki Legion
City College of San Francisco

Mary Beth Love
San Francisco State University

The Institution and Its Students

The Metro College Success Program is a redesign of the first two years of college, jointly developed by two diverse, urban institutions in San Francisco, California—City College of San Francisco (a community college) and San Francisco State University (SF State). As of 2014, City College has approximately 32,630 full-time equivalent students with a headcount of 77,000; SF State has about 26,360 full-time undergraduate students, with 3,807 students in its most recent entering class. Further, City College has no on-campus housing, while approximately 9.5% of SF State's students live in residence halls. At City College, 54% of students are over age 25 and their ethnic makeup is 26% White, 26% Asian, 20% Hispanic or Latino, 10% African American, 6.5% Filipino, 6.5% unknown, 3% Southeast Asian, 1.4% other non-White, 0.9% Pacific Islander, and 0.4% American Indian/Native (rounded percentages). At SF State, students' ethnic makeup is 33% White/non-Latino, 22% Asian, 15% Chicano or Mexican American, 9% other Latino, 6% African American, 8.5% Filipino, 6.0% two or more races, 0.3% Native American or Alaskan Native, and 0.6% Hawaiian/Pacific Islander.

The Program

The Metro College Success Program supports first-generation, low-income, and/or underrepresented recent high school graduates to achieve high rates of academic excellence; persistence; timely graduation; and, at the community college level, transfer. This study focuses on the first two years of college because data show that this is the critical period of highest attrition (Gandara, Alvarado, Driscoll, & Orfield, 2012; Moore & Shulock, 2007). Metro is unusual because of the very close alignment between the community college and university segments; the program itself is very similar at both institutions, and the leadership group is blended. Student recruitment and most faculty development are shared across the two institutions, along with student learning outcomes. Metro also aims to model a cost-efficient, sustainable approach that can be adapted at other public, postsecondary institutions, and the program has gained the interest of a number of California community colleges and universities.

As of 2014, the Metro College Success Program consists of nine Metro academies: Seven at SF State and two at City College. Each is a small school-within-a-school for up to 140 students—one cohort of 70 students in their first year and a continuing cohort of 70 in their second year. Since City College and SF State founded their first Metro academies in 2008, they have built a strong track record of improving persistence and graduation rates. As a result, both institutions are scaling up the number of their academies. SF State is in the process of expanding from seven to 16 academies, which will serve two thirds of the university's Pell-eligible, first-year students. In 2015, City College will open a third Metro Transfer Academy in a new campus location, envisioned as an anchor for multiple future academies.

Metro's outreach team has built permanent recruitment pipelines with high schools and community-based organizations in low-income communities. Incoming students must meet Metro's placement threshold, which is typically two to three semesters below college-ready at City College, and one to two semesters below college-ready at SF State. To be admitted to the University, SF State students must also be in the top third of their high school class. Incoming students need to carry 12 units or more per semester. Metro's outreach and orientation process stresses that students make a significant commitment of time and effort, and they sign a contract to this effect early in the first semester. With these criteria satisfied, Metro has open enrollment, and entrance is on a first-come, first-served basis. This recruitment strategy has resulted in virtually all Metro students being low-income (Pell-eligible), first-generation, and/or underrepresented. The majority—9 out of 10 City College Metro students and 8 out of 10 SF State Metro students—place at a developmental level in English, math, or both.

The program supports students' success through three main elements. The first is a learning community (LC) structured around a guided pathway of two linked general education (GE) courses per semester for four semesters, with students working together as a cohort. This design develops strong bonds among students, faculty, an academy coordinator, and a counselor who follows the students over time. Each Metro is led by a carefully selected and trained faculty member who is responsible for establishing a LC with high academic standards, accountability, and support between students and faculty. Students are encouraged to study together, and routinely help each other solve problems when personal complications arise (e.g., a car breaks down or someone needs to catch up after an illness).

Each academy has a broad career or topical theme, such as health, science, or ethnic studies. The linked pair of classes consists of one course focused on an academic foundation skill (i.e., writing, math, critical thinking, or oral communication) and one course tied to the academy's career or topical theme. In all the academies, the two courses share an overarching social justice theme, and most classes are writing intensive. In the Metro pathway, students move through a sequenced curriculum that allows them to repeatedly practice complex, foundation skills through increasingly challenging assignments. For example, over time, students move from writing a two-page paper to a 15-page research report with citations. Metro instructors infuse required GE content with real-world examples, readings, assignments, and issues connected with the academy's theme so that students engage with big questions in their broad field of interest early in their college careers. For instance, Metro Health students learn to create and interpret bar graphs using information about their own neighborhoods from real, public health databases and reflect on issues of health inequity. The courses target specific student learning outcomes and have associated grading rubrics.

In students' first semester, one of the two linked courses is a first-year seminar (FYS), which gives students an orientation to college and to the theme of the academy. They also learn college study skills, such as using a planner and managing time. In addition, students learn about issues of education equity and explore why so many of them begin higher education lacking confidence that they are college material. Each academy's faculty coordinator teaches this FYS, setting up a relationship that continues as students move through the program.

All of Metro's pathway courses satisfy GE graduation requirements for all 289 majors in the California State University (CSU) system, whether students take them at the community college or university. This ensures that, from the start, students earn high-value course credits that count toward graduation.

The second element that supports student success is having student services anchored in the linked Metro pathway classes. Services include proactive academic counseling, mandatory tutoring for students struggling in difficult gatekeeper courses, personalized access to financial aid advisors, and in-class reminders about financial aid deadlines. Community college students participate in a hands-on, in-class workshop led by a university admissions counselor. This is quite different from standard practice where it is common for students to seek services in remote locations for counseling, tutoring, and so on, and to experience long waits to talk to staff who they may never see again. In contrast, Metro mainly uses program-dedicated academic counselors, tutors, and financial aid advisors who stop by the Metro classroom to make appointments and announcements. Tasks that are critical to graduation, such as keeping an updated graduation plan, are required homework assignments.

The third support element is a 45-hour faculty development process where instructors across disciplines learn active-learning strategies, such as how to use structured small-group work. Instructors of linked classes plan how to integrate content from each other's courses, including shared readings or assignments. They are strongly encouraged to observe and discuss each other's classes. At monthly meetings of each academy's faculty, instructors review student attendance and grades, and plan how to intervene quickly if a student starts to falter.

Completing a postsecondary degree is a multiyear endeavor that places demands on students on many levels (i.e., academic, social, and financial). Metro is not a quick fix or add-on program but a comprehensive approach that combines the academic and social support of an LC with a structured course pathway, integrated student services, and faculty development.

Program Assessment

Metro assesses program results by measuring student outcomes and cost efficiency. At City College, the primary student outcome metrics are persistence (i.e., staying to the end of a semester and enrolling the following semester) and completion (i.e., graduation with an associate degree or transfer readiness). At SF State, two main metrics are used: persistence and graduation. Institutional Research (IR) directors at both schools have emphasized that persistence is an extremely important intermediate success indicator. Metro students stay in school, steadily clocking modest improvements that multiply into impressive gains, even as many similar nonparticipating students drop out.

Metro was designed for wide use in public, postsecondary institutions with tight resources, so its assessment methods needed to be cost efficient and sustainable. The Metro team, with IR departments, devised ways to compare Metro student outcomes to those of similar non-Metro students, using readily available institutional data. SF State's IR department compares Metro students to all SF State first-time, full-time, first-year students (FTFTF). City College's IR department compares Metro students to a group matched on eight variables:

(a) placement level, (b) race or ethnicity, (c) income, (d) ESL status, (e) course enrollment, (f) number of transfer units per semester, (g) total transfer units, and (h) whether they sought academic counseling in their first term (a proxy for motivation).

To assess Metro's cost efficiency, a study was completed with Robert Johnstone, a researcher from the National Center for Inquiry and Improvement (previously with the RP Group), in 2013. Adopting the Pro Forma Model, a method that has been used to analyze the cost efficiency at many colleges, Johnstone calculated annual spending on Metro and non-Metro students, attrition, and average time to degree for both groups (Metro College Success Program, n.d.). Nationally known cost-expert Jane Wellman vetted the study and presented the findings at a Congressional briefing.

Results

This section presents the overall student outcomes, including transfer preparation, persistence, and graduation rates. Findings from the cost-efficiency study are also addressed.

Student Outcomes

Overall, Metro students strongly outperform their peers. At City College's Metro Academy of Health, 7 out of 10 students are underrepresented, and 9 out of 10 require remediation. Although they started college at two or three semesters below college ready, after two years, students in the 2010 and 2011 Metro Health cohorts were almost three times more likely to be transfer prepared than a matched sample of non-Metro students (Figure C2.1). Transfer preparedness is defined as having completed 60 transferable units including college-level English and math, with a GPA of C or better. After three years, 54% of Metro Health students were transfer prepared, compared to just 21% of the matched sample.

Students in the 2010 and 2011 City College Metro Health cohorts were almost four times more likely to complete in three years versus a comparison group, with completion defined as graduation with an associate degree or transfer preparedness. Sixty-three percent of City College Metro Health students completed in three years versus 13% of the comparison group.

At SF State, 63% of Metro students are low-income and Pell eligible, 81% require remediation, and 49% are first-generation. IR assessed results for all three academies operating at that time—Metro Health, Metro Child Development, and Metro Science. Using the most recent institutional data, IR averaged the results for all Metro cohorts during the 2012-2013 academic year. As they entered their senior year, Metro students outperformed their more advantaged peers (i.e., non-Metro FTFTF) on persistence by 12 percentage points (76% for Metro students vs. 64% retention for all non-Metro FTFTF; Figure C2.2).

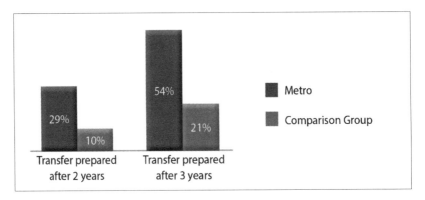

Figure C2.1. Transfer preparedness of Metro versus non-Metro students, City College Metro Academy of Health, 2010 and 2011 cohorts.

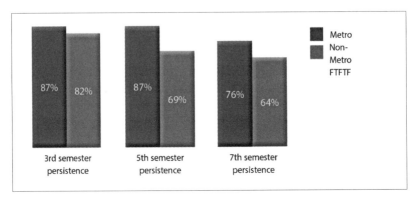

Figure C2.2. San Francisco State University Metro persistence rates as compared to all non-Metro first-time, full-time first-year students.

The two most mature academies, SF State's Metros of Health and Child Development, are now producing students who have gone on to complete bachelor's degrees after their two-year Metro experience. More than one third of these students graduated in four years as compared to less than one fifth (18%) of their non-Metro peers and just 14% of historically underrepresented first-year students (Figure C2.3).

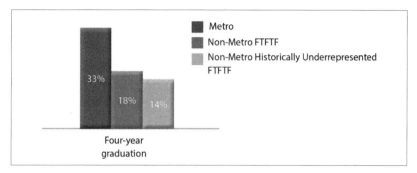

Figure C2.3. San Francisco State University Metro Academies of Health and Child Development four-year graduation rates as compared to all non-Metro first-time, full-time first-year students and non-Metro historically underrepresented first-year students, 2010 cohorts.

Cost Efficiency

In 2013, a cost efficiency study of the most mature academies at both institutions was carried out. Metro requires a modest, up-front institutional investment to cover program coordination time, outreach and recruitment, academic counseling, tutoring, and faculty development. The main program expense (i.e., required GE courses) represents no additional cost for institutions, which simply designate existing required courses as Metro sections. The purpose of this study was to test the hypothesis that extra program costs are more than offset by cost reductions. These reductions flow from (a) sharply lowered attrition, which saves the resources lost when students drop out; (b) reduction of excess units, or students taking courses that do not lead toward graduation or a credential; and (c) reduced time to degree. These early findings bore out this hypothesis, as shown in Figure C2.4.

At City College, Metro requires an additional investment by the institution of $740 per student per year—an 8% increase over current practice—yet reduces overall costs by $22,714 per completer (graduation and/or transfer preparedness), leveraging each dollar of investment 15 times. Even though Metro students starting at City College place at one to three semesters below college ready, they have an average completion time of three years versus five years for comparable students—shaving off two full years. In 2013, only 6% of the comparison group completed in two years versus 34% of Metro students. This has significant implications for students' living expenses, foregone wages, and other economic factors.

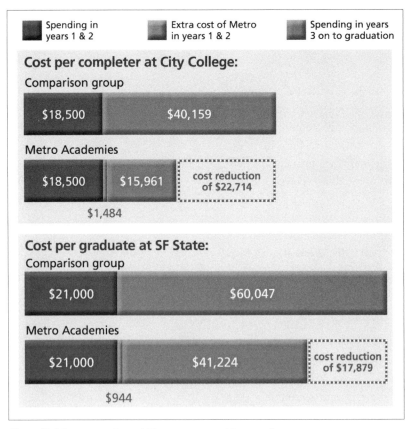

Figure C2.4. Cost comparison of Metro versus non-Metro students.

At SF State, Metro requires an additional institutional investment of $470 per year per student for two years—a 4.5% increase over current practice—yet reduces overall costs per graduate by $17,879, leveraging each dollar of investment 19 times. Throughout the CSU, the most common time to graduation is now six years. In contrast, despite starting at below college ready, disadvantaged Metro students are projected to shave off one year to graduation. Nearly two thirds of Metro students are projected to graduate in five years and to save one year of tuition as well as earn an extra year of wages.

A limitation of these data is that only the two most mature Metro Academies of Health were studied in a one-year period. Future research will include a more comprehensive cost study.

Implications

The research literature shows there are very substantial hidden costs in current practice: (a) attrition, (b) students taking courses off-path, (c) course repetition, and (d) delayed time to degree (Schneider, 2010; Skinner, 2011; Wellman, 2008, 2010a, 2010b, 2011). Excess units are one important reason for delayed completion, especially for community college students. Students may enroll in off-path courses when they have inadequate access to academic advising or when the courses they need are not available and they enroll in random courses to maintain their financial aid eligibility. Students also accrue excess units when their community college courses are later not accepted at the CSU, or if they need to retake a course for a passing grade. For the California community college system, the Legislative Analyst's Office estimates that excess units cost the state of California $160 million per year (Skinner, 2011). Metro represents an efficient alternative. By investing a small amount on the front end (i.e., the first two years of college), the state can realize a much larger cost reduction per graduate on the back end.

As Pascarella and Terenzini (2005) concluded in their review of two decades of educational research, "Discrete, un-integrated, and uncoordinated efforts are likely to be only marginally successful" (p. 643). As previously stated, Metro is not a small add-on program—it is a comprehensive transformation of the way an institution serves disadvantaged students. This redesign requires changes to outreach and recruitment, class scheduling and enrollment, modification of GE courses, integration of tutoring into selected classes, and attention to faculty development over time. Starting the program requires a strong hands-on leadership team with time to focus, along with a funded set-up period of one year and technical assistance from the Metro office. A strong commitment from institutional leaders is also very important—deans at both institutions in this case study became long-term champions of the work.

During our years with Metro, we have learned three main lessons. First, initially Metro was a *department-based* program. However, many 18- and 19-year-old students are not clear on their specific major, and, in Metro's early days, some students had to leave the program when their intended majors shifted. In early 2011, it was determined that Metro should instead be a general education pathway for the lower division in very broad areas that are *college-based* (e.g., College of Science and Engineering or School of Health and Human Services). Now that Metro is a GE pathway, students can change their intended majors without leaving the program.

Second, careful faculty selection is imperative. The program seeks instructors who enjoy teaching low-income students, are enthusiastic about learning new pedagogies, and like collaboration, even though the general consensus is that it is more work. It is important that faculty *volunteer* to work with Metro rather than being assigned by their chairs. Metro's faculty development coordinator observes and vets potential faculty members. Each instructor signs a memorandum of understanding to make sure he or she understands the commitment involved. With a very ethnically diverse group of Metro students, it is particularly important to have diverse faculty and program leaders.

Last, a hard-learned lesson was not to impose exact details of one model in all situations. Initially, the focus was to have the Metros be identical at the University and community college, and an experienced academic counselor was not included in the pathway planning. As a result of the pilot experiences and discussion, the course pathways were adjusted to be quite similar, but not identical, better reflecting reality on the ground.

A major challenge has been that Metro's early development coincided with five years of deep, state budget cutbacks with loss of enrollment and (in the CSU) a doubling in tuition. Because of improvements in the California state budget starting in 2014-2015, the governor announced a four-year program to rebuild enrollment in the state's university systems, and in 2015-2016, a 2% increase for rebuilding enrollment in the community colleges. Because of Metro's strong results, and with expanded funding in hand, the CSU Chancellor's Office recently awarded $675,000 a year of general funds, to permanently scale up Metro Academies at SF State.

Another challenge was an accreditation sanction at City College. This led to major college leadership turnover, and necessarily became a focus of many people at the college, slowing Metro's development. As this situation clears and state funding improves, it is hoped the community colleges will see an expansion similar to that at SF State.

In closing, Metro is bringing about change at a serious scale through steady, long-haul work. The project is leading from the middle tier of postsecondary education—with faculty leaders, department chairs, and deans who work closely with senior academic leaders at the level of vice chancellor and provost. The Metro project is big enough to be visionary, yet is also down to earth, with every step being tested in the trenches, where the real work of education happens.

References

Gandara, P., Alvarado, E., Driscoll, A., & Orfield, G. (2012). *Building pathways to transfer: Community colleges that break the chain of failure for students of color.* Retrieved from http://www.eric.ed.gov/ERICWebPortal/detail?accno=ED529493

Metro College Success Program. (n.d.). *Cost efficiency.* Retrieved from http://metroacademies.org/cost-efficiency/

Moore, C., & Shulock, N. (2007). *Beyond the open door: Increasing student success in the California community colleges.* Sacramento, CA: Institute for Higher Education Leadership and Policy.

Pascarella, E.T., & Terenzini, P.T. (2005) *How college affects students: A third decade of research.* San Francisco, CA: Jossey-Bass.

Schneider, M. (2010). *Finishing the first lap: The cost of first-year student attrition in America's four-year colleges and universities.* Washington, DC: American Institutes for Research. Retrieved from http://www.eric.ed.gov/ERICWebPortal/contentdelivery/servlet/ERICServlet?accno=ED512253

Skinner, E. (2011). Challenges of college transfer: Senate bill 1440: the student transfer reform act. *iJournal: Insight into Student Services, (27).* Retrieved from http://www.ijournalccc.com/articles/issue_27/content/senate-bill-1440-student-transfer-achievement-reform-act

Wellman, J. V. (2008, November/December). The higher education funding disconnect: Spending more, getting less. *Change.* Retrieved from http://www.changemag.org/Archives/Back%20Issues/November-December%202008/full-funding-disconnect.html

Wellman, J. V. (2010a). *Connecting the dots between learning and resources* (Occasional Paper No. 3). Champaign, IL: University of Illinois at Urbana-Champaign, National Institute for Learning Outcomes Assessment. Retrieved from http://www.learningoutcomesassessment.org/documents/wellman.pdf

Wellman, J. (2010b). Making it real: Incorporating cost management and productivity improvements into financing decisions. *New England Journal of Higher Education, 24*(3), 30–32.

Wellman, J. (2011). *Financial characteristics of broad access public institutions* (Paper prepared for The Changing Ecology of Higher Education Project). Stanford, CA: Center for Education Policy Analysis, Stanford University. Retrieved from https://cepa.stanford.edu/conference-papers/financial-characteristics-broad-access-public-institutions

Case Study 3
The Targeted Learning Community: A Comprehensive Approach to Promoting the Success of First-Year Students in General Chemistry

Hillary H. Steiner, Michelle L. Dean,
Stephanie M. Foote, and Ruth A. Goldfine
Kennesaw State University

The Institution and its Students

Kennesaw State University (KSU) is a growing, comprehensive, four-year public institution located in the suburban community of Kennesaw, Georgia, 30 miles north of Atlanta. The university currently enrolls more than 32,000 students, a large majority of whom are undergraduates. A commuter campus until 2007, the University now offers on-campus housing that accommodates 15% of undergraduate students. The most recent entering class of first-year students totaled 3,088. Almost half (53%) of the current student population is made up of traditionally aged students, and 58% of the total cohort are women. Of the total undergraduate population, 31% are minority, broken out as follows: 0.2% American Indian or Alaskan Native, 4% Asian, 16.4% Black non-Hispanic origin, 7% Hispanic, 3.2% multiracial, and 0.2% Native Hawaiian or other Pacific Islander.

The Program

First-year students interested in the sciences often begin college with high aspirations, only to become frustrated and overwhelmed by large, lecture-based, entry-level science courses. The resulting low achievement and retention problems lead many students to adopt a negative view of college-level science, and many leave the sciences altogether. At KSU, General Chemistry is the prerequisite for all courses in the chemistry, biochemistry, and biology degree programs. In an average semester, 43% of students withdraw from General Chemistry or earn a D or F; this percentage is even higher when first-year students are considered separately. These numbers reflect a nationwide problem: high-risk, gateway courses, such as General Chemistry, may prevent students from pursuing degrees in the sciences. Universities often approach these achievement and retention issues by attempting to correct a deficit in students' preparation through remediation and supplemental instruction, but these initiatives only address part of the problem. To engage and retain students in the sciences, it is important to address other aspects of the learning environment that contribute to students' learning outcomes (Light & Micari, 2013).

All students at KSU must meet a first-year requirement by choosing either a first-year seminar (FYS) or a learning community (LC), many of which include an FYS. Learning communities include two or more courses linked by a common theme. FYSs in LCs may be tailored to meet the needs of the cluster while retaining the learning outcomes common to all seminars. In the case of the Targeted Learning Community (TLC) described herein, the FYS learning outcomes served as the scaffolding for the LC's theme: helping entering science students achieve success in General Chemistry.

The TLC seeks to meet this goal by drawing on what is known from the educational psychology and chemical education literature. It has been shown, for example, that enhancing students' metacognition significantly impacts their problem solving ability (Pintrich, 2002), a major hurdle for many students in General Chemistry (Cooper & Sandi-Urena, 2009; Schoenfeld, 1992). The transfer of universal critical-thinking skills to General Chemistry is typically rare and ineffective (Rickey & Stacy, 2000). As such, the critical-thinking skills associated with metacognition must be developed within the context of the subject area. The TLC addresses this reality by tailoring the curriculum in the FYS to develop learning strategies specific to General Chemistry. Additionally, the TLC promotes a strong working relationship among faculty teaching in the LC, thereby fostering a collaborative effort to ensure that the strategies presented in the seminar are implemented within the General Chemistry lecture and laboratory.

Following the definition of Smith, MacGregor, Matthews, and Gabelnick (2004), the TLC for General Chemistry was intentionally designed "to build community, enhance learning and foster connections between students, faculty, and disciplines" (p. 20). It includes the entry-level General Chemistry course and an FYS tailored to the needs of first-year science majors, allowing for a comprehensive approach to supporting these students. The first-semester General Chemistry course is taught through the Chemistry and Biochemistry Department and typically enrolls 775 and 500 students each fall and spring, respectively. The course uses a common textbook, syllabus, and grading scheme. The FYS is housed in the Department of First-Year and Transition Studies that includes full- and part-time faculty dedicated to research on and the teaching of first-year students and students in transition.

Two TLCs, each including 24 students, were first offered in fall 2013 and consisted of three classes: (a) the FYS, (b) a large General Chemistry lecture class (including students from both TLCs and 75 students not enrolled in a TLC), and (c) a General Chemistry lab taught by a part-time instructor. Pairing General Chemistry with an FYS proved ideal because the seminar is, by design, a small class and its content, which focuses on student success, provided the foundation for addressing the goals of the TLCs. The instructors of the FYS and General Chemistry course worked closely to build curricula that met these specific objectives. Additional suggestions for curricular interventions were collected from a focus group of students who had previously completed General Chemistry as first-year students.

In addition to ensuring the learning outcomes common to all seminars and LCs were met, the TLC creators sought to improve students' grades and retention in chemistry, metacognitive abilities, and attitudes toward science, while building a supportive community of budding scientists. Several curricular and cocurricular activities contributed to meeting these learning outcomes. For example, as noted above, one critical need of first-year science students is metacognitive ability appropriate to college-level work. Drawing on a background in educational psychology, the FYS instructor covered the general processes of metacognition, learning, and memory and taught students how to use specific strategies for deep learning. These strategies were then applied to the General Chemistry course via a semester-long strategy project assignment that required students to apply the learning strategies introduced in their FYS to their chemistry course and to reflect on and report the results of their efforts. This activity proved crucial for convincing students that self-regulation and good metacognition were necessary for college-level work. The revised version of this assignment as tailored for the General Chemistry TLC is included as Appendix C3.1.

Recognizing the need for students to be motivated by potential careers in science, a finding clearly expressed in the student focus group, the FYS incorporated career exploration activities, such as career assessments and assignments as well as guest speakers on the topics of entrance into medical or graduate school, internships and shadowing opportunities in science, and the typical life of a practicing scientist. The instructors organized and accompanied students on field trips to the Centers for Disease Control; Arylessence, Incorporated (manufacturer of fragrances); and Cryolife, Incorporated (devoted to the preservation of human tissues). These field trips catalyzed student interest in the various ways their science degrees might be applied.

Two peer leaders were included in the TLCs at the recommendation of the student focus group. These peer leaders, who supported both sections of the FYS, served as social architects and academic cheerleaders, organizing out-of-class events and facilitating a student-only LC Facebook page. One peer leader had been successful in her General Chemistry course as a first-year student, while the other successfully passed the course on his second attempt after learning from his mistakes. The addition of these two very different peer leaders, who were chosen intentionally by the instructors, was important for making students feel comfortable about the challenges they encountered and their progress in the course.

Although this LC was open to all first-year students during registration, the target group were those interested in pursuing a degree in science. Since science majors usually take General Chemistry, the inclusion of that course in the TLC helped restrict it to only those considering a science major. To ensure all potential first-year majors were aware of the TLC, the instructors sent a video clip describing the LC to all students who indicated an interest in science upon admission to KSU. Many students remarked that they first were attracted to the LC because of the potential for achieving success in General Chemistry but later realized it impacted them in ways beyond simple academic assistance.

Program Assessment

Although there is ample evidence that LC participation positively affects students' cognitive and affective development (Laufgraben, 2005; Zhao & Kuh, 2004), there is little existing research that specifically investigates the efficacy of pairing a targeted FYS with a high-risk course in an LC. The primary focus of the study described here was to investigate the impact of this pairing on students. To that end, several outcomes of the LC were assessed, including retention and achievement in General Chemistry as compared with non-TLC participants and changes in metacognition and attitude toward science among TLC participants.

Each of these outcomes was assessed through quantitative and qualitative measures. To measure retention and achievement in General Chemistry, semester grades, including withdrawal rates, and scores on the normalized American Chemical Society (ACS) First-Term General Chemistry Exam, used as the final exam for this course, were collected from all first-year students taking General Chemistry. To measure metacognition and self-regulation, an abbreviated version of the Motivated Strategies for Learning Questionnaire (MSLQ ; Pintrich & DeGroot, 1990) was distributed to TLC participants at the beginning and end of the semester in which students were enrolled in the TLC.

Along with the MSLQ, the Attitude Toward the Subject of Chemistry, Version 2 (ASCI-V2; Lewis, Shaw, Heitz, & Webster, 2009) was also administered as a pre- and post-assessment.

Qualitative data sources provided a more nuanced understanding of quantitative results. These included metacognitive reflection papers from the strategy project assignment, which were analyzed for emerging themes, students' self-assessments of General Chemistry learning objective mastery, and group interviews with LC participants at the close of the semester. To encourage honest reflection, a member of the research team who did not teach in the LC conducted these interviews. The responses gathered were coded for emerging themes. Additional data sources included end-of-semester course evaluations, other course artifacts, and thank-you notes written by students to field trip hosts.

Results

The results of the TLC pilot implementation demonstrate how this model for an LC may positively impact achievement and retention among students enrolled in a high-risk course. All of the results reported herein compare members of the TLC to other first-year students who were enrolled in General Chemistry during the same semester. To ensure accurate group comparison, it was established there were no significant differences between the SAT Math scores of the two groups and the distribution of declared majors upon entering KSU.

One of the most significant results was the final letter grade distribution. A comparison of the distribution for students enrolled in the TLC to all other first-year students taking General Chemistry is shown in Figure C3.1. This comparison reveals that the TLC had a substantial impact on achievement and retention rates. Regarding retention, the *DFW* rate for students in the LC was nearly half that of the comparison group (20% and 37.8%, respectively). Although the students in the TLC earned fewer *A*s, they earned significantly more *B*s and *C*s than their peers not in the LC. The ACS First Term General Chemistry Exam was also used to compare these two groups. This exam accounts for 20% of the final grade, equivalent to a unit exam. When the final exam scores were compared, using an independent samples *t*-test, no significant difference was observed among the scores. Taken together, these two findings may demonstrate that, even though the students in the TLC did not outperform their peers on a normalized test of content knowledge, they may have engaged in consistent study habits throughout the semester that better enabled them to meet the learning goals of the course, resulting in the difference among the grade distributions.

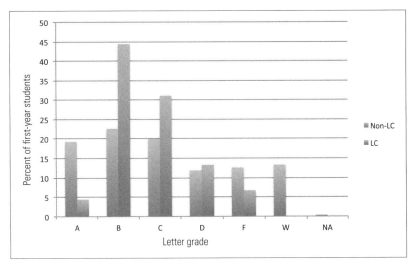

Figure C3.1. Letter grade distribution among first-year students enrolled in TLC as compared to all other first-year students enrolled in General Chemistry I.

The difference between the grade distributions may also be accounted for in the development of metacognitive skills that were addressed and fostered by the TLC. The students enrolled in the TLC ($n = 44$) completed an abbreviated version of the MSLQ that measured the following factors: (a) controlling of learning beliefs, (b) test anxiety, (c) self-efficacy for learning and performance, (d) metacognition and self-regulation, (e) peer learning, (f) effort regulation, and (g) help seeking. The results of the pre- and post-MSLQ scores for each factor were compared using the Wilcoxon Signed Rank Test and are displayed in Table C3.1. These results demonstrate that TLC students made gains in those factors (i.e., controlling of learning beliefs, self-efficacy for learning and performance, metacognition and self-regulation, and effort regulation) that best aligned with the instruction delivered in the TLC. For example, students completed the strategy project assignment in the FYS, which allowed them to critically engage in each of the factors where growth was observed. Additionally, in the chemistry course students ranked their level of mastery on a scale of 0 to 5 for each learning objective that was assessed weekly. The results of this suggest that students were able to self-regulate their learning on topics with which they were familiar but struggled to assess their own understanding on new topics, such as thermochemistry and quantum numbers.

Table C3.1
Comparison of Pre- and Post-MSLQ Scores

Factor	Z	p
Controlling of learning beliefs	-2.912	0.004*
Test anxiety	-0.039	0.969
Self-efficacy for learning and performance	-2.828	0.005*
Metacognition and self-regulation	-3.028	0.002*
Peer learning	-1.197	0.231
Effort regulation	-2.451	0.014*
Help seeking	-0.560	0.576

* $p < 0.05$.

Developing the ability to assess one's level of understanding is an important component of metacognition that can lead to greater mastery and retention of course content (Schraw, 1998). Although the ACS exam scores did not necessarily reflect this, the ranking of learning objective mastery described above reveals that there may be a delayed impact of the metacognitive skills presented in the FYS. This is further illustrated by qualitative data from the strategy project, which was completed between the first and second General Chemistry exams. Many students, despondent after the first exam, recognized that their test-preparation strategies had proven unsuccessful. However, they lacked the confidence to try new study strategies, stating that despite their low grades on the first exam, they would not have tried new strategies had they not been required to do so to complete the strategy project. Although the content of the second exam moved beyond what is typically introduced in the high school curriculum, and, therefore, is perceived by students as being more difficult, 48% of the TLC students were able to increase their grade on the second exam, with the greatest gain by one student being an increase of 40% from the first to the second exam. A large number of students commented on the benefits of completing the strategy project. One student stated:

> The strategy project was of a great help to me; it aided in compiling all the study techniques learned in class and utilizing them on the test. KSU 1101 taught me how to truly study through avenues such as metacognition and active note taking, and this project allowed me to show it off. Hopefully, I can continue to employ these strategies throughout the rest of my college career.

Although not all students were able to improve their grades, many mentioned that their new skills gave them the confidence to continue to strive for improvement in future science courses. Another student commented,

Just because I got the same grade, does not mean I feel that the strategies that I tried did not work. I still recognize that the way I felt during and after the test was more comfortable and more confident.

Overall the TLC model for a LC appears to be a promising holistic approach to supporting student success in a high-risk course. The feedback received from students during a focus group interview (Table C3.2) demonstrates the perceived benefits of their involvement in the TLC.

Table C3.2
Student Feedback to Focus-Group Questions

Focus group question	Major theme in responses
How do you feel your KSU 1101 course or the LC helped you succeed in CHEM 1211?	• Able to create study group with peers • The FYS instructor/peer leaders taught us how to study, gave options for study strategies, forced us to study via strategy project. • Bonding with other students who had common interests • Integrated KSU 1101 and CHEM with strategy project and other assignments
How do you feel your KSU 1101 course or the LC helped you build your identity as a science major?	• Helped with setting priorities/time management • Getting to know faculty, science administration, upperclassmen, and future employers in science • Guest speakers were important. • Field trips showed us what was available and how we could apply our learning to the real world. • Showed us the importance of research • Helped us bond with students in the same major
Are you continuing to pursue a major in science?	• Nine of 47 students commented they would possibly or definitely change their majors.

Implications

The TLC described in this case study drew from existing first-year programs to develop a model aimed at fostering the success of first-year students enrolled in General Chemistry at KSU. Although not conclusive, the findings from the pilot implementation of the TLC suggest that participation in the LC contributed to students' success and retention in chemistry, as well as their metacognitive abilities. Based on these findings, the TLC is a viable approach and, because of this, consideration will be given to expanding the scope of the TLC to infuse the framework into other disciplines, such as biology and math. Moving forward, few changes will be made to the content or structure of the TLC, although modifications will be made to allow for additional in-depth analysis and comparison of outcomes during future data collection. Furthermore, longitudinal data will be collected and analyzed to determine what, if any, long-term outcomes are associated with participation in the TLC.

Much of the initial success of the TLC can be attributed to the instructors' intentional cross-disciplinary approach as they planned and taught the courses in the community. Working together on a common goal enabled the instructors to model this integration for their students. As other institutions consider implementing similar TLCs, it is important to consider the time and expertise needed to successfully integrate the curricular and cocurricular content across multiple disciplines. In the absence of a dedicated TLC, instructors teaching any type of FYS may wish to consider incorporating instruction on discipline-specific metacognitive strategies to help students succeed in high-risk courses.

References

Cooper, M. M., & Sandi-Urena, S. (2009). Design and validation of an instrument to assess metacognitive skillfulness in chemistry problem solving. *Journal of Chemical Education, 86*, 240-245.

Laufgraben, J. L. (2005). Learning communities. In M. L. Upcraft, J. N. Gardner, & B. O. Barefoot (Eds.), *Challenging and supporting the first-year student: A handbook for improving the first year of college* (pp. 371-387). San Francisco, CA: Jossey-Bass.

Lewis, S., Shaw, J. L., Heitz, J. O., & Webster, G. H. (2009). Attitude counts: Self-concept and success in general chemistry. *Journal of Chemical Education, 86*(6), 744-749.

Light, G., & Micari, M. (2013). *Making scientists: Six principles for effective college teaching.* Cambridge, MA: Harvard University Press.

Pintrich, P. (2002). The role of metacognitive knowledge in learning, teaching, and assessing. *Theory Into Practice, 41*(4), 219-225.

Pintrich, R. R., & DeGroot, E. V. (1990). Motivational and self-regulated learning components of classroom academic performance. *Journal of Educational Psychology, 82,* 33-40.

Rickey, D., & Stacy, A. M. (2000). The role of metacognition in learning chemistry. *Journal of Chemical Education, 77*(7), 915-920.

Schoenfeld, A. H. (1992). Learning to think mathematically: Problem solving, metacognition, and sense-making in mathematics. In D. A. Grouws (Ed.), *Handbook of research on mathematics teaching and learning: A project of the National Council of Teachers of Mathematics* (pp. 334-370). New York, NY: Macmillan.

Schraw, G. (1998). Promoting general metacognitive awareness. *Instructional Science, 26,* 113-125.

Smith, B. L., MacGregor, J., Matthews, R. S., & Gabelnick, F. (2004). *Learning communities: Reforming undergraduate education.* San Francisco, CA: Jossey Bass.

Zhao, C. M., & Kuh, G. D. (2004). Adding value: Learning communities and student engagement. *Research in Higher Education, 45*(2), 115-138. Retrieved from http://tlc.uc.iupui.edu/Portals/161/Articles(PDFs)/AddingValueLearningCommunitiesAndStudentEngagement.pdf

Appendix C3.1
Strategy Project

This assignment will help you put the information you have learned in this course into action. In this project, you will apply the strategies and hints that we've learned in this course to preparing for your next test in CHEM 1211. This assignment will require you to submit all your test preparation and other strategies along with a written metacognitive reflection about your experience. You may scan or take a picture of your notes, annotations, and other test preparation strategies for submission to the drop box. All reflection papers should also be submitted to the drop box.

Strategy Project Timeline:

Professor Interaction (15 points). Attend an office-hours session with Dr. Dean. Write a one- or two-paragraph description of the questions you asked, what you learned, and why attending office hours might be helpful.

Plan of Study (15 points). Using the suggestions from your professor as well as what you have learned in KSU 1101, please outline your plan of study for this test. You should create a **detailed** study schedule that describes *what* you will do and *when* you will do it.

Active Note Taking (15 points). Use the Cornell or a modified Cornell method to take notes on Dr. Dean's PowerPoint lectures during the entire pretest period, making sure to set aside space for self-quizzing.

Active Reading (15 points). Preview and annotate all textbook chapters associated with this test, combining information from the lectures with your text. Summarize these annotations by distilling all important information into a one-page study sheet.

Additional Test Preparation Strategies (60 points). Select and complete at least *four* test preparation strategies. You may choose from the following list, or create one of your own, with my prior approval:

- ACS Study Guide
- Concept map
- Pencast
- Tutoring
- Flashcards
- Self-quizzing
- Textbook website activity

Written Reflection (30 points). After you take your test but before you receive it back, please estimate the grade you think you received. When you receive your feedback, please write a reflection paper 3-5 pages in length about your experiences with the strategy project. In particular, please reflect on which elements of the project you think helped and which did not. Please also reflect on the grade you received, whether it was an improvement over your last grade, and whether it matched what you thought you would receive.

Case Study 4
Common Courses: A Developing Linked Coursework Perspective

Hilary L. Lichterman, Daniel B. Friedman, Amber Fallucca, and Jason E. Steinas
University of South Carolina

The Institution and Its Students

The University of South Carolina (UofSC) is a large, public, four-year research institution located in the capital city of Columbia. As the flagship institution of South Carolina, UofSC enrolls more than 23,000 undergraduates. The first-year class in 2012 consisted of 4,625 students, of whom approximately 56% were women, 46% were from out-of-state, and 18% were non-White. UofSC enrolls a largely traditional first-year class, with 96% living on campus and 99% being 19 years old or younger. Admission has becoming increasingly more selective, and the number of applications has doubled (to more than 21,000) over the past 10 years. In addition, the academic profile has improved significantly, with a current average SAT score of 1206.

The Program

The Common Courses program at the UofSC seeks to enhance first-year students' academic experience and persistence through purposeful collaboration between academic departments and student affairs. University Housing, University 101 Programs (U101), and the College of Arts and Sciences (A&S) are invested in this program as a strategy to enhance the academic mission of the institution and create residential learning environments that provide opportunities to students both within and beyond the classroom. This program is undergirded by research suggesting that students who participate in linked courses tend to earn higher grades (Friedman & Alexander, 2007) and are more likely to benefit from greater academic achievement and retention (Pascarella & Terenzini, 2005; Taylor, Moore, MacGregor, & Lindblad, 2003).

The three stated goals of the Common Courses program include (a) cultivating peer relationships that foster strong residential communities, (b) increasing student-faculty engagement in general and beyond the classroom more specifically, and (c) creating residential environments that support peer-to-peer learning.

Residential Component

Living-learning communities are an integral part of the first-year experience at UofSC as they provide students with the opportunity to live in an environment that promotes diversity, encourages insightful faculty-student interaction, and works to develop a strong sense of community. The Common Courses program allows first-year students to take both a U101 course and a core introductory course (i.e., CHEM 111) in A&S with peers who live in their residence hall. The structure of the Common Courses program is such that students who participate are required to enroll in one of the designated links, including a U101 seminar and an introductory course. Students live in a specific residence hall with others who will be enrolled in the same two courses for the fall semester. Residence life staff, including professional, graduate, and student staff, facilitate community development experiences to integrate the 19 students in each Common Courses link into the broader living-learning community. These staff partner with faculty and academic staff to design events and experiences with the intent to offer seamless learning opportunities for students both within and beyond the classroom. To that end, the residence life staff collect syllabi for both courses in the link to effectively coordinate peer study groups. When needed, the housing staff will bring Supplemental Instruction sessions to residence halls, act as a liaison to promote positive student behavior, and encourage faculty and/or instructors to visit residence halls (Friedman & Lichterman, 2013).

Curricular Component

The Common Courses program contains two academically based components that accompany the residential living-learning environment: (a) a first-year core course based out of A&S and (b) the U101 first-year seminar. All of the A&S courses selected for the Common Courses program are either part of the Carolina Core (UofSC's general education curriculum; UofSC, n.d.) or are required courses for a high percentage of incoming first-year students. In the 2012-2013 academic year, only 10 sections of the U101 seminar were part of the Common Courses program.

The purpose of the U101 seminar, now in its 42nd year at the University, is to help new students successfully transition to UofSC, both academically and personally. This extended orientation course aims to foster a sense of belonging; promote engagement in the curricular and cocurricular life of the University; articulate the expectations of the University and its faculty; facilitate the development and application of critical-thinking skills; and help students continue to clarify their purpose, meaning, and direction. The role of the U101

Common Courses seminar is to provide a classroom setting where students engage closely with one another while enhancing content learned from their respective linked course. The U101 Common Courses instructors act as the primary catalyst for instructional collaboration. For the Common Courses program, this is defined as the responsibility for ensuring curricular integration; fostering intentional beyond-the-classroom activities; regularly communicating with students and the faculty partner in A&S; and assuming responsibility for dissemination of assessment, such as student surveys. A&S courses can be taught by a graduate student, instructor, or professor, while U101 instructors are either a full-time employee or retiree from UofSC possessing a master's degree or higher.

Communication and integration of assignments and activities between A&S and U101 instructors are crucial to successfully meet goals of the program. U101 instructors and their respective A&S partners encourage their students to attend events relevant to course material. For example, students enrolled in the PHIL 110: Introduction to Logic I and U101 link attended a political campaign watch party to debrief the logic underlying the candidates' arguments. U101 instructors also have students bring articles to class that complement material from the A&S course or use A&S course material when discussing study skills and time management. It is recommended that instructors for the linked courses attend each other's class at least once, promote residential study groups, and share textbooks and readings (Friedman & Lichterman, 2013).

To further enhance partnerships between A&S and U101, a planning session organized prior to the beginning of the academic semester allows A&S partners and U101 instructors to explore opportunities for within- and-beyond-the-classroom learning. Instructors of the A&S course and respective U101 section are urged to share syllabi to help ensure the seminar integrates material from the A&S core class. Instructors for linked courses are also encouraged to communicate frequently about student classroom participation, continued integration, and overall collaboration within the program.

Student Recruitment

Incoming, first-year residential students may opt in to the Common Courses program via the University Housing Application. Students are able to select and rank their preferred courses on a drop-down menu within the application. Preferences for courses are based primarily on academic major and general interests. Students are recruited for the Common Courses program through printed marketing materials distributed to students during Admitted Students Day, Scholars Day, Minority Students Day, and other recruitment events. The

University Housing staff also have an opportunity to explain the benefits and goals of the program at these events. The Office of Admissions provides assistance in recruitment efforts by sending targeted e-mails to students with academic majors that complement the Common Courses program. Once officially enrolled in the program, students receive e-mails with further information and are encouraged to ask additional questions or voice comments they have about the process, events, or overall components of the program.

Program Assessment

The 2012-2013 academic year acts as the baseline for data collection and informs the program assessment shared throughout this case study. As noted earlier, Goals for Common Courses are to (a) cultivate peer relationships to foster residential community development, (b) promote engagement with faculty in beyond-the-classroom settings, and (c) create residential environments to support peer-to-peer learning. Achievement of these goals will inform larger institutional outcomes, including first-to-second-year retention and academic performance in affiliated A&S courses.

Participants

The fall 2012 Common Courses cohort consisted of 179 first-year students. Total number of males (76) and females (103) in the program mirrored the total first-year population living on-campus (43% male and 57% female). Predictive grade performance analysis by quintile categories found an approximate normalized distribution of Common Courses participants as compared to the overall first-year population.

Measures

Figure C4.1 describes the alignment of each program goal to the measures as described in this section.

Student participant survey. A paper survey was distributed to Common Courses participants during the last week of the fall 2012 semester. This mixed-method survey design included Likert-scale and open-ended questions. Overall response rate for the survey was 89%, ranging from 72% to 100% across each of the 10 sections.

Faculty and instructor participant survey. Participating U101 and A&S course instructors were sent an online survey during the last week of the fall 2012 semester. A total of 15 surveys were usable (10 U101 instructors and 5 A&S instructors), for an overall response rate of 75%. This mixed-method survey included Likert-scale and open-ended questions.

Focus group. A focus group of five student participants was facilitated at the end of the fall 2012 semester to explore participant perceptions of the program, including performance across the three program goals and overall satisfaction. Current Common Course participants were invited to attend the focus group via e-mail at a predetermined time and location. The attendees originated from two residence halls and three different linked course sections.

The First-Year Initiative Survey. This survey was administered near the conclusion of the fall 2012 semester to all U101 sections. Participants in Common Course sections ($n = 97$-105 across survey factors) were compared to a random sample of all University 101 sections ($n = 144$-157 across survey factors).

Persistence and retention rates. Enrollment data for entering first-year students (fall 2012 cohort) were categorized by Common Courses participation (yes/no). Retention rates for fall 2012 were analyzed across the entire first-year cohort.

Academic course performance. Academic course performance (4.0 scale) in the designated A&S course was gathered for Common Courses participants and a control group. The control group included students taking the same A&S course from the same instructor, albeit a different section, during the same semester. Grades were aggregated by course section and categorized as Common Courses ($n = 159$) and control group ($n = 1,181$).

	Goal 1: Residential community development	Goal 2: Engagement with faculty	Goal 3: Peer-to-peer learning	Academic performance	First-to-second year retention
Student participant survey	X	X	X		
Student focus group	X	X	X		
Survey for A&S faculty		X			
Survey for University 101 instructors		X			
First-Year Initiative Survey		X	X		
Institutional datasets				X	X

Figure C4.1. Alignment across Common Courses, goals, and assessment methods.

Results

The multipronged assessment approach provided insight into the current status and future direction for the developing Common Courses program. Summative assessment methods were employed to measure the three stated program goals.

Goal 1: Residential Community Development

With regards to fostering residential community development, student respondents scored positively across survey questions specific to peer relationships developed as part of their linked course (90.6%), residential community environment (75.8%), and Common Courses supporting social (75.5%) and academic (75.5%) transitions to college (Table C4.1). Specific to the survey open-ended responses, one student participant acknowledged the frequency of visits with peer Common Course students as she "would see the group almost every day that in turn led to strong relationships with my classmates." Furthermore, the physical environment helped promote engagement for another student since "the people in my class lived right down the hall. So if I needed help, they were there." One focus group participant noted the quality of the residential environment and described her residence hall as "the nicest. I don't know if I'd want to live anywhere else." A further benefit of living together in a shared space was acknowledged by another student who stated, "I was able to make friends immediately."

Goal 2: Faculty Engagement

Student survey responses revealed medium to low agreement across questions regarding faculty engagement, including questions related to comfort with talking with professors (66.7%), satisfaction with course integration (69.8%), connections beyond the classroom with A&S faculty member (44.03%), and connections beyond the classroom with U101 instructor (64.8%). Participants desired increased integration across the selected A&S and U101 classes and noted "material in each class was vastly different." A focus group participant also shared a similar sentiment: "I think the one thing that integrated the two (linked courses) was the fact that we were in the same classes."

From the teaching perspective, A&S faculty participants demonstrated a satisfactory teaching experience through participating in the Common Courses program (range of 3.0 to 4.8 across six questions on a 5-point Likert-scale). One faculty remarked on his enjoyment "working with a small group of students who

Table C4.1
Common Courses Student Survey Responses, Fall 2012 Cohort (N = 159)

	Percent reporting agree or strongly agree
Social	
I made friends with one or more of the students in my Common Courses link (link defined as attending UNIV 101 AND A&S course).	90.6
Being part of my Common Courses link helped support my social transition to college.	75.5
Living with students in my Common Courses link was beneficial to creating a sense of community on my residence hall floor.	75.8
Academic	
I participated in study groups with other students in my Common Courses link.	57.9
Being involved with Common Courses assisted me with my academic transition to the University of South Carolina.	75.5
Being in the Common Courses program helped make me more comfortable talking with my professors.	66.7
Integration	
Overall I was satisfied with the level of integration of course material between my A&S course and my UNIV 101 course.	69.8
Being enrolled in UNIV 101 contributed to my academic success in the [A&S] course.	64.8
I discussed course material related to Common Courses link with my classmates outside of the classroom.	79.9
I made connections beyond the classroom with the [A&S] faculty member.	44.0
I made connections beyond the classroom with my UNIV101 instructor.	64.8

have a connection outside of class." Another faculty member noted the program was "kin to my previous experiences" from a smaller institution. Suggestions for program improvement included increased communication between instructors of the linked courses and greater selectivity across A&S courses to ensure balance among instructor expertise, fulfillment of core curriculum, and the interests of students. U101 instructor survey results also revealed a positive teaching experience (range of 3.7 to 4.5 across four questions on a 5-point Likert-scale). A U101 instructor shared,

> The students found a lot of value being in the same classes with the same people and living together. It made the sense of community stronger, and I could tell they were a bit more motivated and engaged academically due to the connection.

Goal 3: Peer-to-Peer Learning

Beyond the social benefits perceived by the participants, students acknowledged the opportunity to combine the living and study environment through the residential setting. One participant reported "living in the same building with people I had classes with made it easier to ask for help during exams." Student participants scored positively with regards to course material discussion outside of the classroom (79.9%), but not as well with study-group development (57.9%). Qualitative responses elicited a similar theme regarding structured study time. One participant stated, "We didn't always utilize each other as study resources." Participants described positive outcomes associated with the close proximity, including "being able to walk into a class and know people made the adjustment significantly easier."

The First-Year Initiative Survey

Two survey factors aligned with Common Courses program goals (Table C4.2). Independent sample t-tests were conducted comparing the survey factor scores of Common Courses participants and a randomized sample of all U101 sections. Common Courses participants ($M = 5.4$, $SD = 1.4$) scored slightly higher than the randomized sample of all U101 participants ($M = 5.1$, $SD = 1.6$) specific to the Connections with Faculty factor, but not to the level of statistical significance, $t(238) = 1.319$, $p = 0.19$. Common Courses participants ($M = 5.76$, $SD = 1.4$) scored slightly less than the randomized sample of all U101 participants ($M = 5.80$, $SD = 1.5$) specific to the Connections with Peers factor, but not to the level of statistical significance, $t(236.8) = -0.204$, $p = 0.84$.

Table C4.2

EBI First-Year Initiative Survey Responses (Common Courses Versus Randomized Sample of All U101 Sections)

	U101 Status	n	M	SD	t	df	p (2-tailed)
Connection with faculty	Common Courses	105	5.40	1.442	1.319	238	0.19
	Random-All	154	5.15	1.601			
Connection with peers	Common Courses	105	5.76	1.366	-0.204	236.8	0.84
	Random-All	154	5.80	1.503			

*$p < .05$

Retention Performance

Return rate of Common Courses students to the institution from fall 2012 to fall 2013 was 83.1% compared to the overall institutional return rate of 88.1% (a difference of -5.0%). Students enrolled in U101 only (i.e., not in Common Courses) returned at a rate of 88.5% (-5.4%). Given the one cohort year of data, in conjunction with the smaller cohort for retention comparisons, staff are hesitant to initiate immediate change. This difference will be continually reviewed with consideration for Common Course participant motivation and opt-in behaviors.

A&S Course Performance

As depicted in Table C4.3, independent-samples t-tests were conducted to evaluate the fall 2012 differences between the aggregated grade performance across the 10 A&S Common Courses sections and the aggregated grade performance across the 10 corresponding A&S courses control group. Students enrolled in the A&S Common Courses sections ($M = 3.36$, $SD = 0.23$) scored slightly better than the A&S control group ($M = 3.19$, $SD = 0.37$), but not to the level of statistical significance, $t(18) = 1.20$, $p = 0.25$.

Table C4.3

Independent Samples t-Test for Academic Performance Differences for A&S Course Sections

	A&S status	n	M	SD	t	df	p (2-tailed)
Fall 2012 grade	Common Courses	10	3.36	.2265	1.20	18	0.25
	Control	10	3.19	.3726			

Implications

Based on qualitative and quantitative data analysis, UofSC is optimistic about the growth of the Common Courses program with four implications. First, the selection criteria for the program can be refined to better consider student motivation while still balancing the priority of access and inclusion. Future assessment topics should include students' intent to return to the institution.

Second, increasing coursework integration between the U101 instructor and A&S partner will foster synergy associated with linked or paired courses. When the participating students see the intentional connection between their linked classes, they may be more engaged within and beyond the classroom with peers, faculty, and staff.

Third, as one of the goals for the program is engaging faculty beyond the classroom, the need for integration between the academic component (U101 and A&S) and residential component is crucial for continued success. Increased participation from residential life professional and student staff to promote peer study groups, Supplemental Instruction, and sequentially based residence hall programs themed around overall concepts taught in Common Courses links is needed.

Finally, with a priority being placed on integration of coursework and activities, a natural outcome of this process would be an increase in overall communication between the three main entities of the program: University Housing, U101, and A&S. The communication would not only serve to facilitate conversation of corrective action, but also provide a platform to explore future iterations of the program. Moreover, these opportunities have the potential to increase synergy across people and programs within the university.

References

Friedman, D., & Alexander, J. (2007). Investigating a first-year seminar as an anchor course in learning communities. *Journal of The First-Year Experience & Students in Transition, 18*(1), 63-74.

Friedman, D., & Lichterman, H. (2013, May). *Ideas for integrating your courses.* Instructional document presented at Common Courses program planning session, Columbia, SC.

Pascarella, E. T., & Terenzini, P. T. (2005). *How college affects students: A third decade of research.* San Francisco, CA: Jossey-Bass.

Taylor, K., Moore, W. S., MacGregor J., & Lindblad, J. (2003). *Learning community research and assessment: What we know now* (National Learning Communities Monograph Series). Olympia, WA: The Evergreen State College, Washington Center for Improving the Quality of Undergraduate Education.

University of South Carolina (UofSC). (n.d.). *Carolina Core*. Retrieved from http://www.sc.edu/carolinacore

Case Study 5
Need a Little TLC? Incorporating First-Year Seminars in Themed Learning Communities

Stephanie Zobac, Kelly Smith, Julia Spears, and Denise Rode[5]
Northern Illinois University

The Institution and Its Students

Northern Illinois University (NIU) is a four-year, public, research university in DeKalb, Illinois, offering 63 undergraduate majors in its six degree-granting colleges. In the fall 2012 semester, NIU had an enrollment of 21,869 students of whom 16,552 were undergraduates. Among undergraduate students, 70% are White, 15% African American, 8% Hispanic, 6% Asian, and less than 1% Native American. Approximately 16% of NIU's undergraduate students are over the age of 25, 47% are male, 28% live in campus housing, and many are first in their family to attend college.

The Program

NIU supports high-impact practices (HIPs) with the goal of having nearly 100% of students participate in one or more academic enrichment programs. The University's recent curricular revisions, collectively called PLUS (Progressive Learning in Undergraduate Studies), reflect the intent to infuse Kuh's (2008) educationally effective initiatives into the baccalaureate program. This case study examines the synergistic influence of pairing two HIPs to create a more comprehensive and influential first-year experience. This pairing required a collaboration between the Office of Student Engagement and Experiential Learning (OSEEL) and First- and Second-Year Experience (FSYE). Housed in Academic Affairs with oversight by the vice provost, both offices strive to engage students in curricular and cocurricular experiences. Currently FSYE administers the first-year seminar, UNIV 101 (The University Experience), and OSEEL coordinates Themed Learning Communities (TLC). Both TLCs and UNIV 101 are offered to the entire first-year student population. They are marketed primarily via admitted student days, admissions open houses, direct mailings, orientation programming, advising sessions, and social media.

---

[5] We want to thank Greg Barker, Director of Testing Services at NIU, for his assistance in gathering the data used in this case.

NIU TLCs consist of two to four courses, at least one of which is a general education class in which students are co-enrolled. Each TLC requires a minimum of two integrated assignments. Class sections are limited to 25 first-year students, allowing incoming students a unique opportunity to engage deeply with a course theme, connect learning across courses in collaborative and active ways, and develop relationships with peers and faculty to ease the transition to college. UNIV 101 at NIU is an elective, 12-week seminar emphasizing the experiences and skills expected to help each student in his or her transition to NIU, such as getting involved, setting goals, managing time, making healthy decisions, and living in a multicultural community. TLCs and UNIV 101 also serve subpopulations, including honors students, student athletes, a special scholars program, and students admitted to the university by academic review (nontraditional admits). This study focuses on traditionally admitted students in TLCs linked with UNIV 101 sections.

Although UNIV 101 has been a consistent practice at NIU since being piloted in 1985, it has recently become increasingly significant due to declining persistence and graduation rates. TLCs were purposefully implemented in 2009 to affect change in student retention. In an effort to augment the impact of both programs, the majority of TLC bundles include UNIV 101 (7 of 13 and 9 of 17 TLCs were linked with UNIV 101 in 2012 and 2013, respectively), blending two high-impact practices. This combination was an effort to increase student engagement, which is predictive of satisfaction with the entire college experience and correlates highly with persistence and graduation (Kuh, Kinzie, Schuh, & Whitt, 2005).

Many TLCs and UNIV 101 goals and objectives intersect, as both seek to increase peer connections, integration, academic success, and retention among participants. General education courses taught by faculty, instructors, and some graduate students focus primarily on disciplinary content, whereas UNIV 101 is taught predominately by academic and student affairs staff and emphasizes academic success skills, community building, and other retention-related content. TLCs connected with UNIV 101 enhance the linked-course experience by highlighting reflection, relevant developmental goals, and practical skills. To ensure courses are integrated and students in these programs received increased support, TLC and UNIV 101 instructors attend a daylong faculty institute. Sessions at the institute focus on key strategies for student success and include information on college readiness, integrative learning, the campus early-alert system, faculty collaboration, and other campus resources. Professional development is provided to faculty throughout the semester via working lunches, newsletters, and conference attendance.

TLC bundles address integrated assignments in a variety of ways. In this case, the fall 2012 Explorations of Perception TLC, linking Psychology 102, English 103, and UNIV 101, engaged students in reflective writing and discussions that challenged them to make meaning of and integrate their experiences into their identity. One of the integrated assignments asked students to write a literature review using five-to-seven scholarly sources on a psychological concept of personal significance. They included an analytical reflection that incorporated their individual views and life experiences pertaining to their chosen topic. The instructors looked for various elements that met the objectives for each of their course sections and assigned separate grades for each course. Student could earn 10 points toward the final grade in each linked course based on the integration and quality of

- key psychological concept and pertinent research (Psychology 102);

- critical thinking and the ability to analyze and apply concepts to personal experience (UNIV 101); and

- the ability to read, summarize, and explain scholarly research in a college-level format (English 103).

This assignment is typical of how TLC courses create and review integrated projects.

Program Assessment

Data presented in this case study were collected by administrators of UNIV 101 and TLCs via Registration and Records, Institutional Research, and the MAP-Works Fall Transition Survey. These data reflect students who participated in UNIV 101 and TLCs linked with UNIV 101 as well as students that did not participate in either program during fall 2012. MAP-Works, a key component of retention initiatives at NIU, is an early-alert system that gathers data on student academic, social, and personal transition issues. TLC and UNIV 101 students are strongly encouraged, and often required, to take the online survey as a course assignment. Instructors in TLCs and UNIV 101 have access to MAP-Works data and are able to intervene in a timely and collaborative way with each other and University personnel, including residence life staff and academic advisors, who can help with addressing identified student issues. Students who are at risk for leaving the institution or performing poorly academically benefit from having multiple points of contact that build layers of support.

MAP-Works measures items by questions associated with various factors to reveal a composite score for that factor (e.g., peer connections). Participants measure their level of association with each question on a 1 to 7 scale (1 = low association; 7 = high association). First-year NIU students complete MAP-Works during the fall semester, providing faculty and staff real-time data. Administrators are able to separate UNIV 101 and TLC student data from the entire student population completing the MAP-Works survey to determine which students need referral or intervention to help them succeed at the University.

The following overlapping objectives and outcomes were considered: (a) peer connections, (b) integration, (c) academic success, and (d) retention. Peer connections and integration were assessed using factor ratings from MAP-Works. The questions associated with each factor are listed in Table C5.1. Academic success was assessed using semester GPAs. Retention was measured by the number of students enrolled in the subsequent semester for at least 10 days, and overall risk of leaving the institution was revealed via student responses on the MAP-Works survey.

Table C5.1

EBI MAP-Works Factors and Associated Questions

Factors	Associated questions
Peer connections	On this campus, to what degree are you connecting with people • who share common interests with you? • who include you in their activities? • you like?
Academic integration	Overall, to what degree are you • keeping current with your academic work? • motivated to complete your academic work? • learning? • satisfied with your academic life on campus?
Social integration	Overall, to what degree • do you belong here? • are you fitting in? • are you satisfied with your social life on campus?

Results

The following data are presented in four categories that illustrate the overlapping objectives of UNIV 101 and TLCs. This information was gathered from the first-year population, including students enrolled in TLCs with a UNIV 101 course. These data are used during and after the semester to continue to increase synergies between these two HIPs.

Peer Connections

As shown in Table C5.2, compared to first-year students not enrolled in a UNIV 101 section or TLC and students enrolled in UNIV 101 without a TLC connection, students who enrolled in a TLC section with UNIV 101 embedded tended to rate peer connections at a higher level (5.31, 5.60, and 5.74, respectively). This suggests that as students became more engaged with NIU via the synergy of these HIPs, their sense of peer connection (e.g., people they shared a common interest with, feelings of inclusion, interactions with individuals they liked) increased.

Table C5.2
Students' MAP-Works Factors by Program Type

Program type	Peer connections	Academic integration	Social integration
TLC with UNIV 101 embedded	5.74	5.79	5.59
UNIV with no TLC component	5.60	5.73	5.46
Not enrolled in TLC or UNIV 101	5.31	5.65	5.28

Integration

Academic and social integration factors were used to measure integration among students enrolled in TLCs with UNIV 101 embedded. Students who participated in either a TLC or a stand-alone UNIV course reported higher levels of academic and social integration than student enrolled in neither intervention (Table C5.2). Similar to the pattern observed in the peer connections factor, students involved in a TLC with a UNIV 101 embedded reported the highest levels of both academic and social integration.

Academic Success

Fall 2012 and spring 2013 GPA data indicated that the highest level of academic success was demonstrated by students enrolled in a TLC that included a UNIV 101 course (Table C5.3). Average fall 2012 GPAs for students enrolled only in UNIV 101 and in UNIV 101 embedded in TLCs were higher than the average for first-year students not enrolled in either program. Furthermore, across both fall and spring terms, students in TLCs that included UNIV 101 had the highest average GPA compared to students enrolled in neither program and those enrolled only in UNIV 101.

Table C5.3
Students' GPA and Retention by Program Type

Program type	*n*	Fall 2012 term GPA	Spring 2013 cumulative GPA	Enrolled in fall 2013
TLC with UNIV 101 embedded	141	2.91	2.91	74%
UNIV with no TLC component	857	2.64	2.75	72%
Not enrolled in TLC or UNIV 101	1,001	2.55	2.72	70%

Retention

Students enrolled in the combined HIPs showed an approximately 2% higher retention rate than students only enrolled in UNIV 101 and 4% higher than students who participated in neither program (Table C5.3). MAP-Works also revealed that students enrolled in a TLC with an embedded UNIV 101 course were 13% more likely to report that they planned to return the following semester compared to students in stand-alone UNIV 101 courses. Additionally, students enrolled in the combination of UNIV 101 and TLC reported a 17% higher likelihood of returning the following semester than students not enrolled in either program. Similarly, program participation appears to have some impact on whether students are rated as being at a very high risk for leaving the institution. Students who participated in neither intervention had the highest risk (16%) followed by those who participated in a stand-alone UNIV (10%) and those who participated in the TLC (6%, Figure C5.1).

Implications

The outcomes of pairing TLCs with UNIV 101 courses indicate that connecting these two best practices adds synergy in terms of peer connections, integration, academic success, and retention. Increasing the number of TLCs bundled with UNIV 101 sections would allow more students to experience the positive outcomes discussed above and support the larger university goals of

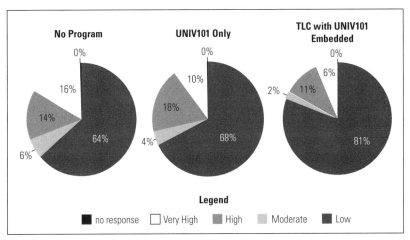

Figure C5.1. MAP-Works risk factors for withdrawal by program participation.

higher persistence and graduation rates. In part, these positive outcomes may be due to increased support for students from two or four instructors. To achieve this level of increased support, it is necessary to offer professional development, training sessions, and ongoing workshops.

In addition to increasing the frequency of these partnerships and enrollment in TLC courses linked with UNIV 101, greater efforts will be made to promote the use of MAP-Works among these programs. Use of early-alert information systems will add an additional layer of support for student participating in HIPs.

The findings suggest synergy exists between these two initiatives in that they reinforce the institutional commitment to engaged learning opportunities. Moreover, through student participation in HIPS, increased retention allowed for a culture of engaged learning to be fostered among all stakeholders. More intentional research is necessary to explore the potential influence of TLCs and UNIV 101 at NIU. Examples of further research include involvement in multiple HIPs, increased use of MAP-Works among instructional teams, and outcomes of subpopulations' involved in TLCs with UNIV 101. It is important to continue documenting the efficacy of blended HIPs.

References

Kuh, G. D. (2008). *High-impact educational practices: What are they, who has access to them, and why they matter.* Washington, DC: Association of American Colleges and Universities.

Kuh, G. D., Kinzie, J., Schuh, J. H., & Whitt, E. J. (2005). *Student success in college: Creating conditions that matter.* San Francisco, CA: Jossey-Bass.

Case Study 6
Writing Across the Curriculum Through Community Engagement: Exploring the Foster Care System in a Thematic Living and Learning Community

Richie Gebauer and Michelle Filling-Brown
Cabrini College

The Institution and Its Students

Cabrini College is a small, Catholic, liberal arts college located in Radnor, Pennsylvania. This private, four-year institution is dedicated to academic excellence, leadership development, and social justice. The student body is composed of approximately 1,300 undergraduates, with a gender distribution of 35% male students and 65% female students. Of these, 65% live in on-campus housing. The racial or ethnic makeup of undergraduates is such that 77.9% of students identify as White, 5.7% as Black or African American, 1.4% as Hispanic or Latino, 1.2% as Asian, 0.1% as American Indian or Alaskan Native, 0.6% as biracial or multiracial, and 0.4% as nonresident alien; 12.6% declined to identify their race or ethnicity. A typical entering class of first-year students ranges from 325 to 380 students, with 329 students entering in fall 2013.

The Program

Cabrini College received a Title III grant in 2006 that allowed the college to develop its Living and Learning Community (LLC) program. Each LLC includes a faculty director (who typically serves as the first-year academic advisor), two faculty fellows, and a master learner (an upper-class student who lives with the students as a peer tutor and mentor). Incoming students have the opportunity to apply to an LLC, and on average 40-45% of the incoming class enroll in one. Typically, an LLC comprises a one-credit college success seminar (a nonacademic course that assists students in the transition from high school to college and acclimates students to campus resources) and four general education courses, including ECG100, an academic first-year seminar (FYS) discussed below.

The centerpiece of this case is the Realizing Dreams (RD) LLC, which was inspired by Mother Cabrini. The RD LLC focuses on the aspirations of our ancestors and explores why their dreams were or were not realized due to considerations of race, class, gender, or other cultural factors. In addition, the RD

LLC examines the goals of the students and what they would like to accomplish in their four undergraduate years and beyond. RD launched in fall 2009, led by an interdisciplinary team of three faculty members from English, psychology, and history and includes five courses: ECG 100, College Success Seminar, American Studies, Modern American Literature, and Psychology. These courses are integrated and have assignments that bridge content across academic coursework throughout the first year. Enrollment is limited to the students in the RD LLC. At the conclusion of each semester, the faculty team participates in a professional development retreat in which they continue to strengthen the curricular and cocurricular opportunities of this common intellectual experience offered to first-year students.

Engagement with the Common Good (ECG) 100, part of the Justice Matters general education curriculum, is the first course of a sequence of three interdisciplinary, theme-based writing courses that move students from an awareness of social justice issues to action and advocacy. In this course, individual instructors select a unique lens that allows students to explore concepts of social justice, power, privilege, and difference while developing foundational proficiencies in writing and information literacy. Because the ECG series is the hallmark of the core curriculum, ECG 100 organically became a part of every LLC at the College, providing a lens for the thematic culture of the LLC to which it is linked. This course not only develops important skill sets, such as written communication, but it grounds the mission of the College—"education of the heart"—in an academic course context.

In the RD LLC, ECG 100 exposes students to foster youth, ages 18-21, who struggle to realize their dreams within the child welfare system. Students learn about the policies related to emancipation from the foster care system, which vary from state to state, and that impact an individual's capacity to transition to independent living. The negative outcomes related to foster care placement are staggering: high rates of homelessness and incarceration and low rates of high school and college graduation. These statistics and policies come alive for the RD LLC students as members of the Pennsylvania Youth Advisory Board (YAB) —current and former foster youth ages 16-21—visit the class several times to share their personal stories. LLC students, as part of their research on the changes and policies needed to improve the quality of life for foster youth, also interact with leaders of the Pennsylvania Child Welfare Resource Center and the Casey Family Programs. This community engagement prepares students for deeper service-learning and community-based research as they progress through the ECG series.

There are intentional links between this ECG 100 course and the other RD classes. For example, at the end of the fall semester, students complete an integrated portfolio in which they include their papers from both ECG 100 and American Studies. In addition, students write reflective essays on their writing process and contemplate their awareness of others' (deferred) dreams across both courses. Additionally, throughout the semester, students complete online hot-topic discussion prompts that help them integrate concepts across courses. The year culminates with an RD symposium in which students create interdisciplinary presentations that combine the concepts taught across the four major LLC courses. During this symposium, it is clear that the values from the ECG 100 course impact how they approach their other course subjects.

Part of why the ECG 100 has become so central in the LLC program is that the course learning outcomes are closely aligned with the LLC goals. For example, one program goal is that students will develop a disposition for engagement as they build a commitment to leadership, service, diversity, and academics. Similarly, the ECG 100 course asks students to reflect upon and critique their disposition toward social justice, especially in light of the College mission, and explore the foundations of civic literacy by analyzing concepts like human dignity, solidarity, human rights, environmental sustainability, the common good, and concern for the needs of the poorest and most vulnerable. The goals of the LLC and ECG 100 intersect in ways that ask students to engage with their community and build their capacity to appreciate diversity.

Another direct intersection between ECG 100 and the LLC program is in terms of students' interfacing with diverse people and communities. RD comprises a diverse group of students, so part of the work involves unpacking their unique strengths, biases, and challenges. In ECG 100 students are asked to inspect their connectedness to social groups beyond their immediate communities, as well as to analyze the complexities of their interactions within their community groups. These two learning outcomes intersect with the goal of the LLC to help students develop the skills and habits for effective community building. Throughout the year, there are opportunities outside the classroom to work on these skills. At the start of the semester, the RD students attend a leadership retreat, facilitated by a consultant who helps them strengthen communication skills and create an inclusive community bond. These skills are honed throughout the year at group dinners where the LLC works through any issues that might arise in the community. Additionally, these skills are applied in the ECG 100 classroom, as students interact with foster youth in ways that are empathetic and respectful.

Learning outcomes of community building are also enhanced in the LLC through cocurricular programming. One of the activities in the ECG 100 class is to create a budget based on a minimum wage salary that might reflect the financial reality for a foster youth aging out of care. The students quickly realize that it is nearly impossible to live without assistance on a minimum wage salary. Students are then taken to the local mall to reflect on the psychological impact of advertising and consumerism, especially in light of the foster care budgeting activity. This experience is complemented by other cocurricular programs that build student appreciation for communities that are different from their own. For example, RD faculty and students travel to Lancaster, Pennsylvania, to participate in interfaith conversations with the Amish, sample Pennsylvania Dutch cuisine, and spend time with each other outside the classroom. Students' leadership capacity continues to develop in the spring semester by allowing them to plan their own cocurricular experience, such as a trip to New York or Baltimore. These experiences help students to build relationships with their faculty and peers in ways that enhance their confidence and motivation in the classroom.

Program Assessment

As evidence by the RD LLC, Cabrini's LLCs are devoted to preparing students to be more active on the campus and in the community beyond college. Through campus and community involvement, LLCs provide opportunities for students to engage with people from diverse backgrounds. The LLC experience offers a curricular structure that allows students to see connections across academic courses and teaches the skills necessary for students to successfully write college-level essays. It is through this academic journey that the LLC program creates an environment for students to become more active learners as they are challenged to question their own primary beliefs and assumptions.

Assessment of the program was related to two central questions:

- What are the value-added benefits of LLCs to the first-year experience?
- Do LLCs at Cabrini College teach students the skills to successfully write college-level essays?

A range of methods was used to answer these questions, including evaluation of writing assignments and a locally designed assessment instrument.

As noted above, the curricular structure of each of the LLCs is made up of a first-year writing seminar titled Engagements With the Common Good (ECG) 100. Every ECG course consists of at least one writing assignment (designated as the signature assignment) that meets the following criteria:

- is 4-6 pages in length,
- incorporates at least three outside sources (e.g., scholarly articles, theoretical texts),
- is argumentative in nature, and
- draws on themes of social justice and pluralism as appropriate for the course.

Every ECG course must also meet the following learning outcomes to ensure students will

- use reading and writing to become more critical thinkers,
- enlarge the scope of their rhetorical knowledge (i.e., to understand how writing genres shape communication),
- develop a mastery of writing conventions,
- demonstrate the importance of process (i.e., drafting, editing, and revising) to the development of successful texts,
- develop the ability to effectively assess the quality of their own and others' work, and
- improve their communicative capacities in light of the social justice curriculum.

A team of six evaluators read and score artifacts from the ECG courses using the ECG Social Justice/Writing rubric (Appendix C6.1). These artifacts are read twice by two separate readers. Third readers are used when initial reader scores differ by more than 2 points in any given domain. The work of LLC students is compared to non-LLC students (all of whom will have completed an ECG 100 by the conclusion of the first year) to gauge the impact of the LLCs on writing.

For comparative purposes a First-Year Student Assessment tool (Appendix C6.2), created internally, is administered to both LLC and non-LLC first-year students at the end of each semester. This tool qualitatively assesses the first-year experience and allows for review and, potentially, revision of the LLC program's learning outcomes to ensure that the College is appropriately assessing the first-year experience.

Though this assessment only provides qualitative data pertaining to each student's perception of their first-year experience, it nonetheless allows the College to understand the impact (either positive or negative) of a students' LLC experience on their first-year at Cabrini. Questions are designed to provide insight with regard to the learning outcomes of the college's LLC Program.

Results

Over the past five years, the message communicated by students via the data extracted from the First-Year Student Assessment Tool has been consistent. Students in the RD LLC reported, as have students across the college's other LLCs, (a) strong relationships with faculty, (b) improved writing skills (in addition to improved public speaking, debate, and communication skills), (c) an increased sense of belonging and feeling of community on campus, (d) better academic preparation, and (e) an appreciation of peer-to-peer support through an established student leader network. Though student success does occur for those who are not participants in an LLC, these students have been less likely to attribute their success to specific college initiatives.

RD students communicate, through this assessment tool, that faculty have helped improve their outlook on college, have been extremely accessible and helpful, and have been available for relationships that extend beyond the classroom. The relationships developed with LLC faculty help explain why RD students in their first year feel closer to their LLC faculty than to those outside the LLC. These relationships lead students to a sense of belonging and increase their confidence in their ability to succeed academically.

Numerous students applying to the RD LLC, similar to all LLC applicants, do so because of high levels of anxiety with respect to making friends and connecting with the campus community. At the conclusion of both the fall and spring semester, students spoke about their LLC as a family. Having a secure community of friends and sharing both academic and cocurricular experiences helped students connect with one another in ways they were not expecting. By considering the struggle that foster youth experience, students are able to think critically about the ways in which we need to support each other in community.

Many of the College's RD LLC students enter the institution doubting their academic abilities, yet they attribute the close support of faculty and student leaders to an increase in their academic preparation. These students report that it was not that they did not have the skills to be successful; rather, that they had not recognized their potential until LLC faculty instilled in them the confidence to succeed. This increased level of support was eye opening for RD students in light of the lack of support evident in their exploration of the foster care system.

Arriving at this Aha! moment did not happen overnight for the RD students. The fall semester ECG course played a significant role in providing students with opportunities to flourish. RD students reported that this curriculum encouraged high levels of involvement and offered a different lens to explore social justice issues. Most felt that they now knew more about the foster care system and understood how it exists as a social justice issue in society. This became apparent through the relationships developed between RD students and foster youth who served on the Pennsylvania Youth Advisory Board. The curricular focus on the current foster care system, especially when RD students in the classroom had themselves experienced being a foster care youth, offered new perspectives and contributed to students viewing life through a new lens.

While exploring new ideas and gaining new perspectives on social justice issues, RD students were simultaneously developing their writing skills. Through the ECG course, students engage regularly in the writing process, revising through multiple drafts, working with classmates in peer review writing workshops, and communicating with the instructor through one-on-one conferences. These were experiences that most students did not have prior to college. Being challenged with assigned research writing, as well as other forms of writing, helped students feel more confident about their abilities.

The signature assignment completed in the ECG was assessed across five domains: (a) argument, (b) analysis, (c) development and support, (d) structure, and (e) grammar and mechanics. These data were drawn from all ECG 100 courses, which included writing from both LLC and non-LLC students, and yielded results that showed students were weak in their ability to integrate sources. Based on these data, the RD LLC faculty converted their three-credit ECG course to a four-credit course that included a comprehensive, one-credit, information literacy instruction module designed to build student understanding of a fully developed argument through well-chosen evidence.

Implications

For any institution considering introducing a social justice curriculum or a writing-across-the-curriculum initiative into their LLC or first-year experience, it is important to create opportunities to make writing real for the students. Whether it is finding a community partner, as the RD LLC has forged with the Pennsylvania Youth Advisory Board, or creating a digital project for students' writing, it is crucial for students to understand that their voices matter. Working in collaboration with the community provides students with greater motivation to produce their best work and deepen their connections within their LLC community. Ultimately, assessing the needs of the community partner as well as those of the college or university is the key to a successful program. At Cabrini, the cycle of assessment—whether it be assessing students' writing, community partners, or the LLC program as a whole—has been essential to the evolution and growth of the first-year experience.

At the conclusion of every academic semester, all faculty and staff involved in the College's LLC program organize for a faculty development day retreat that allows participants to reflect on and improve upon the program. Changes to the LLC program have been accomplished through a collective process involving the entire LLC community of faculty, student leaders, and staff. In preparation for the next academic year, the director of the First-Year Experience will begin working closely with the College's Assessment Committee to revisit the LLC program's assessment process. In the midst of this process, individual LLCs will set annual goals, identify strategies to achieve them, and complete end-of-year reports to show progress.

It is important to note that the development of a learning community or even the creation of individual communities, such as the RD LLC, is not an overnight project. The growth of Cabrini's learning community program has been a seven-year journey with faculty and staff better understanding, through both trial and error and assessment, how to best meet the needs of first-year students. Institutional needs and student interests may also play a large role in decision making as a learning community program expands. To ensure success, a learning community program must become ingrained in the culture of the institution. To achieve this, administration must support, both in their communicated message and in the way of financial resources, such programming. It is also essential that campuswide buy-in at the faculty and staff level occur through energy and enthusiasm. Even after seven years, faculty and staff at Cabrini College recognize that the success of a learning community program is an ongoing process that is constantly evolving with the ever-changing needs of students.

Appendix C6.1
Engagements with the Common Good (ECG) Social Justice/Writing Rubric

Grading Criteria	Achievement levels				Points
	Excellent – 4 points	Good – 3 points	Fair – 2 points	Poor – 1 point	
Argument (sense of "motive" through interrogation of own core values and/or privilege, audience and intent)	Essay is based on a precise and well-defined original argument (grounded in a sense of writer's core values and/or power/privilege expressed through vivid images appropriate for audience and intent).	Essay is based on a clear yet general argument (posing a clear "motive"). The argument may lack a consistent awareness of core values and/or power/privilege, audience, and intent.	Essay is based on a vague or tangential (irrelevant) argument that shows some focus, but lacks continuity, and does not show why the writer cares or why the readers should read.	Essay has an unfocused argument or rationale for exploring this issue or analytic approach. Writer seems unsure of direction.	
Analysis ("nuanced" articulation of the value of and dignity shown through the understanding multiple cultural perspectives)	Essay offers a strong analysis of significant, fresh and varying perspectives (acknowledging the value of diverse cultural perspectives influence how people see and interact in the world).	Essay offers an analysis that shows an understanding of the ideas and information involved in the assignment. Analysis offers some sense of nuance and/or the dignity of diverse cultural perspectives.	Essay offers a basic, yet incomplete, analysis, factual/ interpretative errors, and little understanding of main ideas. Analysis offers little to no acknowledgment of nuance and/or dignity in diverse perspectives.	Essay lacks analysis and does not respond to the assignment. Essay contains little to no consideration of original thought and/or offers no acknowledgment of nuance and/or dignity in diverse difference.	
Development & support (Showing a sense of equality via just analysis of how social, historical, cultural or political "paradigms" shape(d) individual and group "dispositions"")	Essay consistently advances a fully developed argument through well-chosen evidence (showing a sense of equality by judiciously examining how, and in what ways paradigms shape(d) individual and collective dispositions).	Essay advances a clear argument equally weighing well-chosen evidence, but needs shaping to deepen and develop support that teases out ties between paradigms and dispositions.	Essay lacks a clear argument failing to include sufficient evidence. Essay shows a lack of a clear reading or a misreading of sources and/or limited consideration of equality in the links between paradigms and dispositions.	Essay makes statements without supporting evidence, relying too heavily upon personal opinion or summary and/or lacks consideration of equality in the links between paradigms and dispositions.	
Structure (Showing "interconnectedness" and "interdependency" through shared language and solidarity)	Essay moves smoothly from one paragraph to another (with clear introduction, supporting paragraphs, and conclusion). Approach points up interconnections (in structure and content) and solidarity.	Clear structure, but essay has some awkward transitions between paragraphs. Interconnectivity in approach is lacking because claims are not fully elaborated and/or themes of solidarity are not elucidated.	Essay has some poorly connected (awkward) transitions between paragraphs; essay lacks a clear introduction, supporting paragraphs, and/or conclusion. Interconnectivity and solidarity are weak if offered at all.	Essay has many poorly connected (awkward) transitions between paragraphs, lacks structure and/or fails to establish interconnections and solidarity.	
Spelling, grammar, syntax, & mechanics	Essay uses rich style, proper syntax and mechanics, and appropriate documentation format. Essay lacks major errors in grammar and/or spelling.	Essay offers evidence of strong, apt verbs; concrete nouns; and proper syntax, mechanics and documentation. Essay has some errors in grammar and/or spelling.	Essay offers little evidence of proper syntax, mechanics and documentation, containing awkward sentences, grammatical and spelling errors, and incorrect word choices.	Essay contains major grammatical errors and spelling mistakes; essay contains many awkward sentences and phrases.	
				Points Total	

Appendix C6.2
Cabrini College First-Year Student Assessment Tool

1) Gender:
   a. Male
   b. Female

2) Which best describes the relationships you have developed with other students here at Cabrini College?
   a. I have made friends that I will continue to keep in touch with, no matter where I live.
   b. I have made some friends.
   c. I have not made any friends here at Cabrini College.
   d. I have had primarily negative interactions with my peers.

3) How often do you participate in academic-related events (e.g., on- and off-campus speakers, off-campus trips tied to the curriculum)?
   a. Always
   b. Most of the time
   c. Occasionally
   d. Never

4) How often do you participate in social activities or events on campus (e.g., game nights, movie nights, Bingo, on-campus performers)?
   a. Always
   b. Most of the time
   c. Occasionally
   d. Never

5) In which of the following have you been involved? (Circle all that apply.)
   a. Major- or academic-related clubs or organizations
   b. Cabrini Day
   c. Service-learning, community service, or community partnerships
   d. Campus Activities Programming Board
   e. Other club or organization involvement (Please specify.)
   f. Athletics (varsity)
   g. I am a Classroom Coach.
   h. I am a Peer Tutor.
   i. I have used the services of the Writing Center.

    j.   I have used the services of the Math Resource Center.
    k.   I have used the services of the Peer Tutor Center.
    l.   I have used the services of Academic Counseling.
    m.   I have used the services of Co-Op and Career Services
    n.   None of the above

6) How many hours do you commit to each of those involvement opportunities that you have circled in question #5 (e.g., 2 hours per week on the Campus Activities Board, 5 hours per week as a member of the varsity soccer team)?

7) Do you have a job off campus? On campus? Work Study? How many hours a week do you devote to this job?

8) Please explain what your faculty have done to enhance your college experience.

9) Which best describes your interactions with your faculty? (Circle all that apply)
    a.   I have met with my academic advisor during scheduling.
    b.   I am comfortable meeting my faculty members to discuss class concerns.
    c.   I have met a faculty member I consider to be a mentor.
    d.   None of the above

10) Due to your college experience, do you feel:
    a.   More academically prepared
    b.   Less academically prepared
    c.   My academic preparedness has not been affected.

11) How many hours do you devote to your academic work per week?
    a.   1-5 hours
    b.   6-10 hours
    c.   11-15 hours
    d.   16-20 hours
    e.   21-25 hours
    f.   26-35 hours

12) What specific suggestions would you provide to improve your college experience?

13) How did your *expectations* of Cabrini College compare to your actual *experience* at Cabrini College?
   a. Exceeded my expectations
   b. Met my expectations
   c. Fell below my expectations
   d. My expectations were not met at all.
   e. Did not have any expectations

14) How comfortable do you feel approaching your faculty members outside of class?
   a. Very comfortable
   b. Somewhat comfortable
   c. Not comfortable at all

15) My experiences at Cabrini College have made me more likely to:

		Strongly agree	Agree	Neutral	Disagree	Strongly disagree
a.	Be more active in the campus community at Cabrini College					
b.	Be more active in the community beyond Cabrini College					
c.	Engage with people from diverse backgrounds					
d.	Take a leadership role					
e.	See the connections among different courses					
f.	Become a more active learner					
g.	Successfully prepare for and write college essays					
h.	Approach college-level writing assignments with confidence					
i.	Question my own beliefs and assumptions					

Case Study 7
Advancement via Individual Determination (AVID)
Lauren Smith, Aslinn Arcuri, and
Matthew Farina
Mt. Hood Community College

The Institution and Its Students

Chartered in 1965, Mt. Hood Community College (MHCC) is one of 17 community colleges in Oregon. Located in Gresham, MHCC is the only public, postsecondary institution serving the area, with an average annual student body of 30,790 students, representing a diverse population, including teens; adults; senior citizens; urban and rural dwellers; high school graduates; General Education Development (GED), Adult Basic Skills (ABS), and/or English-as-a-second-language (ESL) learners; adults changing their career directions; and a full range of socioeconomic backgrounds. In addition, many of the neighborhoods within the district have large populations relying on governmental assistance for basic needs, which makes for a very diverse, yet underrepresented and underserved student population.

According to the student profile from fall 2013, enrollment by gender at MHCC is 43% male and 55% female students with an average age of 31. The student body is diverse, with 12% of students reporting an ethnicity of Hispanic/Latino, 1% American Indian, 7% Asian, 5% African American, 57% Caucasian, and 6% multiracial; 11% failed to respond. Because MHCC does not have on-campus residence halls, all students are known as commuter students, and many also hold jobs in addition to attending school, with 18% of students reporting that they are working full time and 30% stating they are employed part time. Due to family, work, and personal obligations outside the school day, many students opt to take classes part time (below 9 credits). As such, more than half (53%) of MHCC students are part-time attendees. MHCC also has a fairly large percentage (23%) of students taking noncredit courses, such as ESL, ABS, or GED. Fifty-one percent of students that attend MHCC do so with the objective of earning a certificate or degree.

The Program

As part of their mission to promote college access and success, the nonprofit organization known as AVID (Advancement Via Individual Determination) offers support for college readiness through a program called AVID *for* Higher

Education (AHE). In spring 2012, MHCC was designated an AHE site. AHE directly impacts students through its Student Success Initiative (SSI)—a comprehensive approach to college success that combines faculty development in instructional best practices with a holistic student support program. This program includes the AVID Center—a resource and tutoring center where program-dedicated learning specialists, knowledgeable about course content and materials, stay in contact with instructors and build relationships with students—as well as thematic learning communities (LCs) in which a first-year seminar (FYS) is embedded.

Given the mission of AVID, first-year seminar and learning community (FYS/LC) programs at MHCC are primarily developmental education LCs that serve students who may be at risk, first-generation, nontraditional, or unfamiliar with the hidden curriculum of college and who therefore need extra support in their transition to college. The students who test into developmental reading and writing courses often begin levels below the gateway or transfer-level courses and need extra support to navigate the lengthy pipeline of coursework necessary to earn an associate degree, certification, or transfer degree to a four-year institution. Thematic LCs support and empower students who have multiple life and learning challenges by creating an environment where fundamental reading and writing skills are complemented by an FYS where students can build confidence, organization and time management skills, self-awareness, and other academic and study skills to help ensure their success in college and in life.

MHCC offers two levels of LCs, depending on students' developmental education coursework needs. The sequence of courses appears in Figure C7.1 and serves as a first-year experience for students. All of the courses are offered each fall, spring, and summer, so a student may enter and exit the program any semester.

If a student fails to persist beyond the first term of courses, advising takes place within the AVID Center to identify and address the barriers to success the student faced. A plan of action is developed, and students are encouraged to register for the next term—perhaps with a smaller course load and with additional assistance from the AVID Center. Combining student services and resources with content support greatly strengthens the FYS/LC program and helps each student in developing a foundation for success.

Level 1	Level 2	Level 3
90 LC **(12 Credits)**	**115 LC** **(10 Credits)**	**Stand-alone AVID supported class options**
Writing 90 – Writing Skills: Paragraph to Essay (4 credits)	Writing 115 – Introduction to College Writing (4 credits)	WR121 – English Composition (4 credits)
Reading 90 – Effective Reading and Learning Strategies (5 credits)	Reading 115 – Reading for College Success (3 credits)	RD117- Critical Reading (3 credits)
Human Development 100C – College Success. (3 credits)	Educational Literacy 115C – Academic Success Strategies (3 credits)	WR132 – Practical Grammar for Writers (3 credits)

Figure C7.1. First-year course sequence featuring LC and stand-alone course tracks.

All FYS/LC instructors are offered professional development, either on campus or at AVID National's Summer Institute, which focuses on teaching strategies that are based on best practices in five core areas—also known as WICOR (i.e., writing, inquiry, collaboration, organization, and reading). WICOR is a learning model that faculty use to guide students through advanced concepts, helping them build skills in comprehension, communication, critical thinking, collaborative learning, and writing as a tool for reflection and communication. In addition, the program offers informal lunch-and-learn workshops throughout the year, where faculty and staff have a chance to discuss best practices for bringing content to life in their classrooms. Faculty and staff members explore implementing WICOR strategies at increasingly complex levels (scaffolding) within developmental education, general education, and discipline-based curricula in specific programs and majors. Professional development is also provided through the faculty-led Teaching and Learning Center at MHCC. The engagement of faculty and staff in AVID strategies is having an impact on instructional practices throughout campus. This has resulted in a transformation of pedagogy and student support at the College.

FYS/LC instructors collaborate with the other faculty members within their LC, and the team selects a theme and then aligns their reading, writing, and academic skills or college success assignments to address this common inquiry topic, such as Sustainable Food and Agriculture, Sports, Lyin' and Cheatin', Money, and Diversity and Equality. Furthermore, the instructors within the FYS/LC also agree upon a set of classroom expectations for behavior, and grading and attendance policies, in order to offer a consistent experience for students who are learning the rules of formal, higher education.

The embedded FYSs serve to complement and enhance what students are doing in their reading and writing courses. These seminars—HD100C in the first term and EL115C in the second term—are primarily taught by faculty counselors and are the cornerstone of the FYS/LCs, incorporating lessons on taking notes, annotating course texts, using academic language in dialogue and debate, asking high-level questions, developing skills in organization and time management, using technology effectively, developing emotional intelligence, and regulating behavior. Students learn how to be creators of their educational path, rather than victims, and they emerge with a wealth of knowledge about their college and the programs offered to them, as well as strong relationships with classmates, their instructors, and staff in the AVID Center. In addition, all students are required to complete an academic plan and explore the myriad resources and services available to them on campus. The FYSs are truly holistic and student-centered and give FYS/LC students the skills necessary to be successful at MHCC.

Program Assessment

The AVID FYS/LC program has a place within campuswide assessments and plans at MHCC, such as the Strategic Program Assessment (SPA), Master Academic Plan, and Student Success Plan. In addition, as part the AVID for Higher Education National Center, the AVID program is required to collect data on course completion rates, course grades, and one-year retention rates (i.e., fall-to-fall enrollment). Beyond the quantitative data, the program also administers a pre- and post-survey to FYS/LC students each term to assess academic preparedness and skills gained, overall satisfaction with the AVID program, and student confidence. These surveys are developed using outcomes from the LC courses, such as student confidence in identifying the organizational patterns in a textbook and being able to type and format essays. Students are also asked to rate how frequently they use academic skills, such as Cornell notes and a planner or schedule.

Results

The initial findings related to the program are very promising. The one-year (fall 2012 to fall 2013) retention rate for all of the FYS/LCs combined was 49% compared to an average yearly retention rate of 32% for non-AVID developmental education students. Persistence rates from term to term show even greater gains, with a persistence rate of 82% from fall to winter term for AVID LC students versus 65% for non-AVID LC students. Furthermore, MHCC students who participated in an AVID FYS/LC program for their first term of developmental education coursework (RD/WR90) consistently outperform students that do not (Figure C7.2). The students who continue to the next term often do so within an AVID LC because they have found a system that works for them and classroom peers who share their goals. Unfortunately, there are also students who are unsuccessful and do not persist beyond the first term. Students may not persist to the next term for many reasons, such as moving to a new school, taking a term off, or experiencing a traumatic life event.

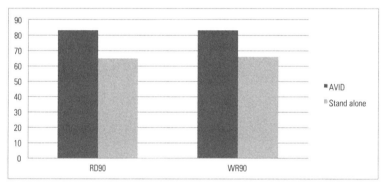

Figure C7.2. Retention of developmental reading and writing students in AVID LC versus stand-alone courses, winter 2013 – winter 2015.

To assess whether students starting in a LC fall term performed at a higher level in non-LC courses (WR121) spring term due to the skills that they gained from the FYS or college success or academic skills course and AVID Center support, the average passing rates of the six stand-alone courses (i.e., WR090, WR115, WR121, RD090, RD115, and RD117) were compared with the average passing rates of the same courses that were populated by AVID students in spring

2013 (Figure C7.3). With the exemption of WR115, AVID courses had higher average passing rates than comparable stand-alone courses, and the student's success in WR121, once they exited an LC, should also be noted.

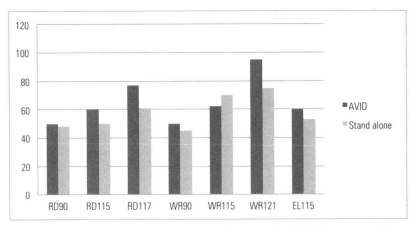

Figure C7.3. Average pass rates for developmental coursework, AVID LC versus stand-alone courses, spring 2013.

A pre- and post-survey was administered to all of AVID LCs each term. This case highlights changes for the winter 2013. Students reported an increase in academic organization (+22.7%), a decline in late or missing assignments (+28.1%), and greater understanding of how and where to get academic support on homework and assignments (+15.7%, Table C7.1).

Table C7.1
Pre- and Post-Survey Comparison for AVID LC Students, Fall 2012 – Winter 2013

Question	Pretest strongly agree or agree %	Posttest strongly agree or agree %	Increase %
My binder and planner help me to be organized and successful.	72.0	94.7	22.7
I only have 2-3 missing/late assignments per term at most.	45.6	73.7	28.1
I know where to go to get help with my homework	84.3	100	15.7

Instructors were also surveyed to assess the effectiveness of AVID and non-AVID high engagement pedagogical techniques and identify possible areas of improvement within the LCs. Feedback from faculty who teach within the FYS/LCs has been overwhelmingly positive, with many saying that they have never felt more supported during their work in a classroom and that they have enjoyed creating deeper, more meaningful relationships with the students in their LC. Furthermore, by working with two other instructors within a LC, learning outcomes and skills can be reinforced in all three courses. For example, when "writing in the margins" is addressed in a reading course, the students will receive homework on that skill in their academic success course, which frees up time in the reading courses to cover other topics. Instructors are also encouraged to communicate with AVID and Learning Success Center staff so that if a student's attendance begins to decline or he or she faces a major life challenge, interventions and appropriate referrals can be made.

Implications

MHCC'S program is framed around the success of a highly at-risk population with a national reputation of being unsuccessful academically. Yet, this does not imply watering down the curriculum or providing excuses for these students; rather, it means giving access and services to all students. Once they are AVID students, they can expect rigor with support and transformative pedagogy during their first year of college and development of skills that will assist them in completing a degree or certificate program.

One challenge has been asking faculty to critically examine their teaching methodologies. Fortunately, many faculty and staff at MHCC have recognized the need for more engaging pedagogies in their classrooms, and many have attended the AVID professional development sessions and have given positive reviews on the facilitation of those sessions and of the teaching tools that they have received. They leave the professional development session with a connection to the program's resources and strategies that can easily be implemented in their courses. When conducting professional development sessions, it is important to showcase the MHCC staff and faculty who are already using high-engagement strategies. Including AVID strategies with other instructional and institutional best practices, such as flipped classrooms and the acceleration of developmental education reading and writing courses, has produced promising initial outcomes.

Before implementing a first-year experience and LCs at MHCC, it became evident that collaboration with Student Services, TRiO, Learning Success Center (LSC), Student Outreach and Advising would be critical to the success of the program. Therefore, it was critical to include key campus partners and stakeholders on the Student Success and Retention Campus Team and invite many of these entities to attend the AVID Summer Institute to immerse themselves in professional development on best instructional practices, resources, and new trends in education. This has positively impacted the MHCC campus and increased the use of innovative teaching techniques and given the College a solid program for the entering developmental education student.

Looking to the future, there are many plans being created that involve the FYS/LC program, including a mandatory first-year experience for all students, LCs or concurrent course enrollment in multiple disciplines, accelerated developmental education coursework, and the creation of summer bridge programming for students that will assist them in transitioning into their first term of college. The FYS/LC program at MHCC has truly grown into a campuswide retention and completion effort, and the work of the program will only increase in scope as the state and federal governments look to community colleges to prepare and produce a highly functioning workforce for the future.

Conclusion
Lauren Chism Schmidt and Janine Graziano

In an effort to foster student success, many colleges implement high-impact practices (HIPs), with learning communities (LCs) and first-year seminars (FYSs) being two of the more popular choices. This volume explores what it means to bring these two HIPs together in FYS/LC programs. In Part I, authors from both two- and four-year institutions considered the rationale for creating combined FYS/LCs programs and discussed what it meant to do these programs well with respect to models, administration, teaching, and assessment.

In Part II, contributors offered examples of what it looks like to put FYS/LCs into action on real campuses, showing the versatility of these structures, implemented in varying contexts for different student populations and responding to a wide range of institutional concerns and goals. For example, at Cabrini College, FYS/LCs are designed to reflect institutional culture, embodying Mother Cabrini's vision of "education of the heart" through an integrative social justice curricula. At other institutions, FYS/LCs are implemented to address the needs of a particular group of students. As a Hispanic-Serving Institution, Bronx Community College uses FYS/LCs to help introduce cultural components of writing for academic purposes concurrent with English and Spanish language coursework. The programs at Mt. Hood Community College, designed to serve students most at risk, include a number of support features. Finally, at the University of South Carolina, where the vast majority of first-year students live on campus, the residence life staff are actively involved in creating learning experiences and opportunities in the FYS/LC initiatives. Still other FYS/LC structures are designed to address a particular curricular trouble spot, such as the intervention at Kennesaw State University, which includes a required course for science majors that nearly half of the students are unable to successfully complete as a stand-alone course. And still other FYS/LC programs are implemented to help students fulfill degree requirements, as can be seen in the Metro Academies of City College of San Francisco and San Francisco State University, where FYS/LC courses are deliberately chosen to fulfill general education requirements that will transfer to the nearly 300 degree programs throughout the Cal State

University system. In addition to program variation among institutions, programs also vary within institutions, as can be seen at Northern Illinois University, where FYS/LCs are specifically designed for nontraditional students, honors students, athletes, and others.

Although the descriptions of these unique interventions suggest advantages of the diverse landscape of FYS/LC structures, it is not all roses. The tremendous amount of variation in FYS and LC initiatives themselves, further illustrated in Chapter 2, which are then magnified in combined programs, pose notable challenges to maintaining program identity. Variations in administrative challenges are highlighted in Chapter 3, which notes that the flexibility of FYS/LC programs invites pressure to incorporate a variety of campus initiatives. Also, in FYS/LCs, teaching approaches can be expected to vary greatly as a number of disciplines are represented and instruction may be provided by student affairs professionals as well as faculty—both full and part time. FYS/LCs call for a particular understanding of teaching, learning, and collaboration, discussed in Chapter 4, and instructors also vary in the degree to which their approaches and practices answer this call. Finally, and not surprisingly, the array of structures and outcomes across FYS/LCs can pose challenges for assessment. In Chapter 1, it was noted that while the positive effects of FYSs and LCs are clear, variation in program features makes it difficult to determine which features, individually or in concert, contribute to these positive effects. Further, Chapter 5 points out that variation limits not only the assessment process but also the ability to use results to inform programmatic improvements.

While some degree of customization is needed to adjust to institutional context and to serve different student populations, the challenges that accompany this adaptation risk compromising quality. This is also true within any single institution, as variation in both content and quality is common within programs. Finley and Kuh argued in Chapter 1 for a relentless focus on quality, which is paramount as FYS/LC programs commonly adapt and expand to increase access. This growth must be balanced with a commitment to ensuring that FYS/LCs are truly integrated and do not simply reflect two programs operating in parallel. To find this balance, we must work in places where FYS and LC programs intersect—both ideologically, in terms of shared core values, and logistically, in terms of shared program components. In this way, FYS/LC collaborative work is integrative and not additive, and program integrity can be maintained.

Working in the Intersections: Core Values of FYS/LC Programs

As has been noted throughout this volume, institutions combine FYSs and LCs not simply because both are HIPs, but because, in their own ways, each supports the aim of integrative learning and thinking—goals for a liberal education in the 21st century—through developing an intentional community of learners. As a result, integration and community are central values of FYS/LC programs, and must be reflected both in the classroom and in their administration. Below, we consider ways to ensure that these values are evident.

Integration

In combined programs, integrative learning involves contextualizing academic and student success concepts from the FYS into the larger LC curricula. It means connecting the disciplines and incorporating real-world applications involving complex questions in a way that grounds the content of the FYS and enhances the LC. In other words, it requires reframing the curriculum and intentionally connecting the courses of the FYS/LC to deepen learning and metacognitive practices. It means providing integrative learning experiences that reflect the plethora of knowledge, skills, and experiences students possess and inviting students to use these to engage with new ideas, capitalizing on the self-awareness focus pervasive in many FYSs. It means replacing decontextualized discussions of academic skills with tasks that demand the use of those skills in ways that are meaningful and engaging to new college students. It means asking students to go beyond simply identifying the location of various campus resources, to actually experiencing the use of these resources in their work, and seeing the campus holistically as an extended support network. It means allowing additional time and space for cocurricular experiences and powerful learning opportunities that extend beyond the classroom. It means introducing students, concurrently, to their roles as new college students and as cocreators of knowledge in a setting that asks them to assume these roles intentionally and with an eye toward integration.

Community

Creating opportunities for integrative learning to take place and for students to demonstrate integrative thinking is not the responsibility of the FYS instructor, the writing instructor, or any other instructor in isolation—it is a collective responsibility shared by all members of the FYS/LC team. Likewise, FYS/LC programs offer students opportunities, not only to integrate course skills and content but also to do so by becoming part of a community of knowledge builders. As a cohort enrolled in multiple classes, occasionally even living in close proximity, students have an automatic network of study partners. The social and academic connections and multiple perspectives integral to FYS/LC programs are readily available, but must be cultivated. In other words, as noted in Chapter 4, it is not enough for instructors to share a cohort of students; they must also use intentional strategies to encourage students to connect in real and powerful ways. To do this, faculty must be willing to take risks and abandon traditional methods of teaching that do not foster community and the co-construction of knowledge, in favor of strategies, such as collaborative and active learning, that do.

Another strategy for instructors, as they work to create and deliver FYS/LCs, is to model the kind of collaboration they want students to exhibit. Faculty can demonstrate collaboration by working together before the FYS/LC is offered to develop shared student learning outcomes, align course content, create a shared syllabus, and design shared assignments and rubrics. Once the semester begins, instructors can meet regularly to stay current with each others' courses and reference each others' content in their classes, grade shared assignments collaboratively, visit each others' classes, and invite students to participate in establishing classroom policies and bringing outside materials into course discussions. Such activities send a coherent message of community to students. And at the end of the semester, instructors can together assess the success of the shared assignment in evoking integrative thinking from students and the success of the FYS/LC itself. While students may not see this end-of-semester collaboration directly, they will feel its effects in subsequent semesters.

Community extends beyond the course curricula, as success in FYS/LC programs requires administrators, faculty, and staff to work together, crossing college divisions and abandoning silos. True collaboration goes beyond merely cooperating, as it is not simply making room for others. Instead, it involves discovering shared goals and interests and proceeding in accordance with them. This involves a strategic approach to logistics that capitalizes on the cost effectiveness of combined efforts in terms of scheduling, recruitment, advisement, registration, and professional development. As a result, administrators, faculty, and staff are working together, defying the separation between departments and units to operate more collaboratively and holistically. This collaboration often has a transformative effect—changing the way an institution does business. Ultimately, then, these core values of integration and community, not only enrich the teaching and learning experience in FYS/LC programs, but can also become the impetus for institutional transformation.

Going Forward: Expanding Work in the Intersections

Examples of successful approaches to and implementation of FYS/LC programs may be found throughout this volume. Drawing from the experiences and insights of our contributors, we believe that moving forward—individually at our campuses and together as a community of practitioners—it is important to stay true to the shared core values as we expand our ideas about assessment to better reflect program goals and explore synergistic effects, and consider ways to integrate—not simply add on—other HIPs.

Staying True to Core Values

It is important that FYS/LC initiatives, regardless of institutional flavor, are driven by the core values of community and integrative thinking and learning. From the classroom or out-of-class learning experience, to the policies and procedures that maintain it, the FYS/LC must be committed to bringing together different perspectives to form a shared vision. It is this kind of collaborative approach that drives the cultural transformation experienced at institutions that have successfully implemented FYS/LC programs.

Expanding Assessment

To be most effective, there needs to be continuous assessment and documentation of the synergistic effects of FYS/LC programs. This process also reflects the core values above, as it must integrate different perspectives and involve the community. Assessment is not an addition or afterthought, but an integral, connected process involving stakeholders in both formative and summative processes that guide their work. Done well, it requires institutional researchers to collaborate with their constituents in designing the research, collecting the data, and interpreting the results. Further, both qualitative and quantitative data must be examined, and assessment should move beyond simply considering indirect effects, such as grade point averages and persistence, retention, and graduation rates, which often fail to reveal less quantifiable, but equally important, impacts. Instead, assessment must focus on data more directly indicative of the kinds of differences in learning we expect to see given the FYS/LC focus on integration and community. Finally, while single institution studies are important, particularly in light of the variation in program implementation, there is a need to examine the larger landscape of FYS/LC programs to more fully explore their impact and implications in a way that is generalizable and connected to the larger FYS/LC community.

Integrating HIPs

As this work progresses, programs may benefit from incorporating a third HIP where appropriate. As with truly integrated FYS/LC programs, this is not to suggest an additive process of one more thing to include in an already full curriculum. Rather, it is to discover which practices enhance FYS/LCs through providing another vehicle for learning that shares core values. Certainly other HIPs, such as service-learning, can be seamlessly infused in FYS/LCs in a way that deepens and extends the learning experience. Well-designed service-learning opportunities can deepen the sense of community through shared experiences, while providing a new context in which to experience the ways various disciplines connect to each other and the world around us.

Final Thoughts

This publication has united chapter authors from uniquely different institutional and academic backgrounds, forming new partnerships that embody the core values of FYS/LC programs. We thank the many contributors from the community of FYS/LC practitioners who collaborated to make this book possible and whose leadership will be essential in addressing the issues outlined above. We hope the ideas presented here support others in successfully developing FYS/LCs on their campuses, adapting these to their particular contexts while staying true to the core values of FYS/LCs.

Index

NOTE: Page numbers with italicized *f* or *t* indicate figures or tables respectively.

A

AAC&U. *See* Association of American Colleges and Universities

academic affairs administration
  bridge-building with FYS/LCs and, 79
  core values of integration and community and, 182
  FYS/LCs located within, 47
  scheduling FYS/LCs and, 51–52

academic exploration
  student metacognition and, 31
  at University of Nevada, Reno, 29

academic performance and progress measures. *See also* GPAs; letter-grade distribution
  as Common Courses measure, 143, 143*f*, 147, 147*t*
  MAP-Works survey on, 154, 155–156
  multilevel assessment and, 89
  Realizing Dreams LLC at Cabrini and, 164

academic planning, student survey on perceptions of, 89

academic seminars with uniform content across sections, xvii, 20, 24*t*. *See also* theme-based block-scheduled courses

academic seminars with variable content across sections, xvii, 20, 24*t*, 25, 25*t*

academic standing, assessment of, 85

academic support partners
  FYS/LCs and, 51–52
  professional development and, 54

academies. *See* Metro College Success Program

active-learning environments
  faculty as model, 182
  integrative learning and, 75
  service-learning and FYS/LCs and, 32

administration of FYS/LCs. *See also* academic affairs administration; environmental scanning; student affairs professionals
  conclusion to, 57
  environmental scanning and, 42–52
  introduction to, 41
  professional development for, 53–56

Adult Basic Skills (ABS) students, at Mt. Hood, 171

advising, 89, 117–118, 172, 177–178

Alexander, J. S., 67, 68

American Chemical Society (ACS) First-Term General Chemistry Exam, 130, 131

Annual Conference on The First-Year Experience, 55–56

anonymity, meaningful learning and, 7

Appalachian State University, 35

Assessing Learning in Learning Communities, 87

assessment
  challenges, 88–89
  conclusion on, 98–99
  continuous, of FYS/LCs, 183
  deeper and of more varied outcomes, 91–93
  direct, of learning outcomes, 93–94
  flexible approach to, integrative learning and, 75
  of FYS and LC outcomes, 83–85

of high-impact practices, 15–16
indirect, of learning outcomes, 94
inquiry-based professional development and, 54
introduction to, 83
of long-term and sustainable impacts,
  94–95
multiple HIP participation synergy
  and, 90
new directions for, 89–98
rigorous, on FYS/LCs' effects, 95–97
of shared assignments, 182
of structure, processes, and strategies,
  90–91
for sustaining FYS/LCs and for decision making, 97–98
variations in, 180
assignments
  common, integrative learning and
    sharing of, 22
  designing, for integrative learning,
    75–76
  faculty sharing of, 76
  integrative, technology and, 76–77
  integrative learning, direct assessment
    of, 93
  reflective practice and, 68, 70
  relevance of learning and, 68–69
  shared, collaborative assessment of, 182
Association of American Colleges and
  Universities (AAC&U)
  on challenges to higher education in
    global century, 61
  on integrative learning, xix–xx, 84
  LEAP initiative, 28, 87
  on learning communities, 21
  Statement on Integrative Learning
    (2004), 62
  VALUE project, 87, 93
Attitude Toward the Subject of Chemistry,
  Version 2 (ASCI-V2), 131

AVID (Advancement Via Individual
  Determination)
  college readiness support by, 171–172
  data collection for, 174
  LCs at Mt. Hood and, 175–176, 175f,
    176f, 176t
AVID Center, Mt. Hood's, 172
AVID for Higher Education (AHE),
  171–172

B
Barr, R. B., 57
Bartlett, L., 106
basic study-skills seminars, xvii, 20, 24t
Bass, R., 14, 73
Baxter Magolda, M., 70
Beaulieu, E. A., 68
Berger, J. B., 46
best practices, on FYS/LCs, 56
Blake, J. H., 50
Blake, Jerry L., 30
block-scheduled courses, with common
  theme, 9–10, 23, 24
blogs, integrative assignments using, 76
Bloom, B. S., 73
Boix-Mansilla, V., 84, 87
Bronx Community College
  assessing program at, 108–109
  FYS/LCs at, xxiii
  implications, 111–112
  institution and student profile, 105
  program at, 105–108
  results, 109–111, 110t
Brownell, J. E., 4, 11, 12, 90
Brusi, R., 4
building community. See community and
  community-building
Bunker Hill Community College, Success
  Coach Advisors at, 51

C

Cabrini, Mother, 159, 179
Cabrini College
    assessing program at, 162–163
    ECG Social Justice/Writing Rubric,
      167
    First-Year Student Assessment Tool,
      168–170
    FYS/LCs at, xxiii
    implications, 165–166
    institution and student profile, 159
    program at, 159–162
    results, 164–165
California State University (CSU), 117,
  124
California State University, Northridge,
  6, 11
campus culture, FYS/LCs and, 43, 46–47,
  57
campus services. *See also* student affairs
  professionals
    student survey on perceptions of, 89
career exploration
    FYS at Kennesaw State and, 129
    FYS/LCs and, 28
    learning community themes and topics
      and, 23
    student metacognition and, 31
Carnegie Foundation for the Advancement of Teaching, xix–xx, 84
case studies
    Bronx Community College, 105–113
    Cabrini College, 159–170
    integrative learning and, 75
    Kennesaw State University, 127–138
    Metro College Success Program,
      115–126
    Mt. Hood Community College,
      171–178
    Northern Illinois University, 151–157
    University of South Carolina, 139–149
Casey Family Programs, 160

Cerritos College (California), Konstructing Kafka: Radio Theater Project at, 29
Chandler-Gilbert Community College,
  Perception and Communication in Meet
  the Parents at, 29
changing world, acknowledging realities
  of, 75
chemistry, general, at Kennesaw State
  University, 127–138
Christensen, C. M., 73
City College of San Francisco, 115. *See also*
  Metro College Success Program
City University of New York (CUNY),
  105
clusters, learning communities as, xvi
co-enrollment
    FYS/LCs and, 24–25, 25*f*
    relevance of learning and, 68
cohort models, learning communities as,
  xvi
collaborative leadership, organizational
  theory and, FYS/LC administration
  and, 46
collaborative learning, 67, 72, 182
collaborative teaching, 53, 182
College Learning for the New Global Century
  (AAC&U), xix
College of Arts and Sciences, University of
  South Carolina
    grade performance in Common
      Courses program and, 147, 147*t*
    UofSC's Common Courses program,
      139, 140–141, 148
college survival, as extended orientation
  seminar, xvii
college transition, as extended orientation
  seminar, xvii
Colorado Northwestern Community
  College, 32
comic-strip generators, integrative assignments using, 76

Common Courses program. *See also* University of South Carolina
  about, 139
  curricular component, 140–141
  residential component, 140
  student participant survey, 142, 143*f*
  student recruitment for, 141–142
common experiences, learning communities and, 72
communication skills, lifelong learners and, 94
communications
  Common Courses program at UofSC and, 148
  integrated, assessment of, 87
community and community-building
  Common Courses program and, 144
  FYS in LC structures and, 26–27, 26*f*
  FYS/LCs and, 182
  FYS/LCs as site for, 22
  integrative learning and, 75, 77
  of knowledge, FYS/LCs and, 181–182
  learning communities and, xx
  Living and Learning Community at Cabrini and, 162
  Realizing Dreams LLC at Cabrini and, 164
  relevance of learning and, 67–68
  service-learning and FYS/LCs and, 32, 184
Community College Survey of Student Engagement (CCSSE), 86, 94
comparison groups, assessing FYS/LCs' effects using, 95–97
compensation, for FYS/LC faculty, 49–50
Completion Agenda, 97–98
concepts from other courses, pulling together
  FYS in LC structures and, 27
  as FYS/LC element, 22
conflict resolution process, early establishment of, 78

Connect to Learning (C2L) LaGuardia Community College, 77
connecting personal and/or social concepts with linked course concepts, 22
Connecting the Dots study, 4
cooperative learning, FYS/LCs and, 66–67
core values
  of FYS/LCs, 181–182
  staying true to, 183
Cornerstones Program, New Century College at George Mason University, 32–33
cost efficiency
  California FYS/LCs and, 123–124
  of Metro College Success Program, 121–122, 122*f*
Costa, A. L., 72
course evaluations, 89
course loads, for FYS/LCs, 50
course pass rates, assessment of, 85
Creswell, J. W., 96
critical thinking
  direct assessment of, 93
  ECG 100 at Cabrini and, 163
  FYS/LCs and, 43–44
  Kennesaw State LC and, 128
  lifelong learners and, 94
  Northern Illinois University and, 153
cross-disciplinary pedagogy. *See also* interdisciplinary education; interdisciplinary understanding
  learning communities and, xvi
  Targeted Learning Community at Kennesaw State and, 135
curriculum
  for FYS/LCs, clarity of, 44
  inquiry-based professional development and, 54
  intentional learning using, 62
  social justice, at Cabrini College, 159–170
  UofSC's Common Courses program, 140–141

D

Dawes Duraising, E., 87
dean's list, assessment of, 85
debate, integrative learning and, 75
decision making, assessment for, 97–98
deep learning, 5–6, 6*t*, 34, 129
degree, persistence to. *See* student persistence
Delaware Technical Community College, 28
Dewey, John, 67–69
Dillard University, Early Alert Program at, 51
discipline-linked seminars, xvii, 20
    learning communities and, 24*t*
    residential component and, 25, 25*t*
    at University of La Verne (California), 34
disciplines
    connections to, assessment of, 87
    permeability of, 66–67
discussions, relevance of learning and, 68–69
disruptive behavior, hyperbonding and, 78
disruptive innovations, 73, 75. *See also* high-impact practices
diversity
    ECG 100 and LLC program at Cabrini College and, 161
    experiences with, high-impact practices and, 13
    Metro College Success Program and, 115, 124
    at Mt. Hood Community College, 171
Doherty, P., 89
Dresdner, Lisa, xxii
Dunlap, L., 62–63

E

Early Alert Program, at Dillard University, 51
Eastern New Mexico University, 28
EBI First-Year Initiative Assessment, 86

ECG Social Justice/Writing rubric, 163
educational objectives taxonomy, in cognitive domain, Bloom's, 73
effort investment, for high-impact practices, 13
effort regulation, TLC student gains at Kennesaw State in, 132, 133*t*
electronic learning portfolios (ePortfolio), 77
embedded assessments, 94
empowerment, at Bronx Community College, 107
Endicott, P., 89
end-of-course evaluations, 94
Engagement with the Common Good (ECG) 100
    at Cabrini College, 160–163, 164–165
    Social Justice/Writing Rubric, 167
English-as-a-second-language students
    at Bronx Community College, 105, 106–107
    at Mt. Hood Community College, 171
Enriching Educational Experiences, 3–4
enrollment management division, 47, 48. *See also* registrar
environmental scanning
    of academic support partners, 51–52
    of campus culture, 46–47
    definition of, 42
    of faculty, 48–50
    identifying target population and, 44–45
    locating the program and, 47
    of mission and program alignment, 43–44
    of resource allocation, 45–46
    of stakeholder engagement, 47–48
    of student affairs professionals, 50–51
    of student partners, 52
Ernest, Roger, 29
Escalera, Liya, xxi–xxii

Evergreen State College
National Summer Institute on Learning Communities at, 56
Washington Center for the Improvement of Undergraduate Education, 10
exit interviews, as indirect assessment, 94
expectations
classroom, at Mt. Hood CC, 173
for high-impact practices, 13
experience, assessment of connections to, 87
experiential learning, FYS/LCs and, 90
experimental designs, for FYS/LC studies, 95–96
expert faculty. *See also* faculty
professional development for, 53–54
Explore, Discover, Decide Living-Learning Community, at Slippery Rock University, 29
extended orientation seminars, xvii, 20, 24*t*, 25, 25*t*

F
Facebook page, student-only, for Kennesaw State LC, 130
faculty. *See also* teaching
from other courses, FYS as link to, 22
allocating, for FYS/LCs, 45
assessment of participation and collaboration by, 85
as collaborative and active learning models, 182
from different departments, professional development expectations of, 54
of disengaged teaching and learning and, 63–64, 64*f*
FYS/LCs and, 48–50
incentives, learning communities and, 9
inquiry-based professional development and, 54–55
institute, at Northern Illinois University, 152

integrative assignments by, 75–76
integrative learning and, 62–63
interactions, Common Courses program and, 142, 143*f*, 144, 145*t*, 146
interactions, high-impact practices and, 13, 77
interactions, LCs and, 30
LC, contact information for, 68
Living and Learning Community at Cabrini and, 164
metrics for assessing involvement by, 88
Metro College Success Program and, 124
multidimensional impacts on, 91–92
risk-taking and, 65
Student Success Initiative at Mt. Hood and, 172
surveys, for multilevel assessment of, 89
Teaching and Learning Center at Mt. Hood and, 173
variations in teaching methods by, 180
feedback. *See also* focus groups
consistent, high-impact practices and, 13
from peers, 94
Ferrari, J. R., 43
field trips
by RD faculty and students at Cabrini College, 162
science-based, Kennesaw State's use of, 129
financial stress, environmental scanning as FYS/LC protection during, 42
Fink, L. D., 62, 72, 73
Finley, Ashley, xxi, 4, 6, 10–11, 35, 83, 180
First- and Second-Year Experience (FSYE), at Northern Illinois University, 151
First-Year and Transition Studies, Department of, at Kennesaw State University, 128
first-year experience, components of, 7
The First-Year Experience (FYE) movement, 8

First-Year Initiative Assessment, 86
    at Cabrini College, 163, 164, 168–170
    at University of South Carolina, 143,
        143f, 146, 147t
first-year learners, risk-taking and, 65–67
first-year seminar/learning community
    (FYS/LC) programs. *See also* adminis-
    tration of FYS/LCs; assessment; case
    studies; high-impact practices; teaching
    campus-based studies of, 35
    characteristics of, 21
    conclusion on linking, 13–16
    contexts for implementing, xxii–xxiii
    core values, 181–182
    definition of, 36
    electronic learning portfolios and, 77
    as high-impact practices, xv, 3, 7–10,
        33–35
    as institutionally transformational, 41
    integrating, the case for, 11–12
    introduction to implementing, xx–xxi
    rationale and implementation of,
        xxi–xxii
    reasons for, xviii–xx, 3
    structure on American college
        campuses, 23–35
    synergistic payoff of linking, 10–11
    unlearning traditional instructional
        methods and, 66–67
    variations in, 179–180
first-year seminars (FYSs). *See also* first-year
    seminar/learning community programs
    assessment approaches in, 85–88
    characteristics of, xv, xvi
    characteristics shared by HIPs and, 35f
    definition and types of, xvii
    General Chemistry at Kennesaw State
        and, 128–129
    as high-impact practices, 7–8
    NSFYS 2012–2013 definition of, 20
    role in learning communities, 21–23
FLEX (First-Year La Verne Experience)
    learning community, 34

focus groups
    with Common Courses participants,
        143, 143f
    as indirect assessment, 94
    on learning outcomes, 93
    on structures, processes, and strategies,
        91
    for student assessment, 89
    with TLC students at Kennesaw State,
        134, 134t
formats, assessment of, 90–91
foster care, Cabrini student's studies of,
    160–161, 164–165
foundational knowledge, content renamed
    as, 62
four-year institutions
    Cabrini College case study, 159–170
    FYS/LCs at two-year institutions vs.,
        23
    implementing FYS/LCs at, xxii–xxiii
    Kennesaw State University case study,
        127–138
    Metro College Success Program,
        115–126
freshman orientation, as extended
    orientation seminar, xvii
Freshmen Year Analysis and
    Recommendation, at Bronx Community
    College, 108
Friedman, D. B., 67, 68
full-time faculty. *See also* faculty
    professional development and, 54
FYSs. *See* first-year seminars

G
Gabelnick, F., 19, 30, 128
Garcia, O., 106
Gardner, John N., xvi, 8, 36
Geijsel, F. P., 53
General Education Development (GED)
    students, at Mt. Hood Community
    College, 171

general education (GE) courses, Metro College Success Program and, 116, 117, 121, 123

George Mason University, New Century College, service-learning and FYS/LCs at, 32–33

goals and objectives
  assessment planning and, 91
  of FYS/LCs, 43
  for pilot FYS/LCs, 45
  prior to program design, 90

Google searches, for learning communities, xv

GPAs (grade point averages)
  assessment of, 85
  at Bronx CC, 105, 109, 110t, 112
  as indirect assessment, 94
  MAP-Works survey on, 154, 155–156, 156t
  measuring FYS's impact of LCs on, 90

graduation rates
  at Bronx Community College, 105, 107–108, 110–111, 112
  FYS/LCs and, xvii, 92
  high-impact practices and, 6
  as indirect assessment, 94
  Metro College Success Program and, 118, 119, 121f
  multiple HIPs and, 11
  at Northern Illinois University, 152
  student learning outcomes and, 98

grant funding, for pilot FYS/LCs, 45–46

Graziano, J., 55, 64

Greece, ancient, first-year seminars and, 7

Greenfield, G. M., xvi, 36

grounded theory, coding writing assignments using, 109

group work, for FYS/LCs, 90

Groupthink, hyperbonding and, 78

H

Hansen, Michele, xxii

hashtag culture, integrative learning and, 77

Haydel, Nia, xxi–xxii

Hayek, J., 86

Heckman adjustment, for FYS/LC studies, 96

help seeking, TLC students at Kennesaw State and, 132, 133t

Henscheid, Jean M., xxi, 85

higher education, integrative learning as challenge for, xx

Higher Education National Center, 174. *See also* AVID

Higher Education Research Institute, 33

high-impact practices (HIPs)
  AAC&U on FYSs and LCs as, 3
  assessment using LEAP Campus Toolkit website, 87
  brief history of, 3–6
  characteristics shared by LCs and FYSs and, 35f
  first-year seminars as, 7–8
  FYS/LCs as, xxi
  integrating, to enhance FYS/LCs, 184
  intentionally communicating purpose for, 15
  learning communities as, 8–10
  multiple, cumulative benefits of, xviii, 10–11
  multiple, measuring synergistic effects of, 90
  at Northern Illinois University, 151–157
  quality issues with, 12–14
  staying true to core values vs. adding on, 183
  student engagement and performance and, xv

Hill, D. M., 71

honor roll status, assessment of, 85

Horn, Heather, 29

Hutchins, Robert Maynard, 7

hybrid seminars, xvii, 20, 24t, 25, 25t

hyperbonding, cautions against, 77–78

I

Illinois College, 31

immigrant students. *See* Bronx Community College

Indiana University Center for Postsecondary Research, 4

Indiana University-Purdue University Indianapolis (IUPUI)
 first-year seminars at, xvi
 FYS/LCs at, 35
 testing FYS/LC impact at, xix
 Themed Learning Communities (TLCs), 9–10, 27

initiative fatigue, planning FYS/LCs and, 10

inquiry-based professional development, 54–55

Instagram, integrative learning and, 77

institutional engagement, assessment of, 89

Institutional Research, assessing Metro College Success Program and, 118–120

institutions
 assessment for decision making by, 97–98
 Metro as department-based vs. college-based program and, 123
 multidimensional impacts on, 91–92

instructors and instructional teams
 Common Courses participants' survey of, 142, 143*f*
 for FYS/LCs, 90
 at University of South Carolina, 148

instrumental variables, for FYS/LC studies, 96

Integrated Studies Program, New Century College at George Mason University, 33

integration
 academic, MAP-Works survey on, 154, 154*t*, 155, 155*t*
 in FYS/LCs, institutional challenges for, 41
 high-impact practices and, 13

integrative learning
 assessment of, 84
 at Cabrini College, 160–161
 designing assignments for, 75–76
 direct assessment of, 93
 disruptive innovations and, 75
 as FYS/LC core value, 181
 FYS/LCs and, xviii, 62–63
 LC instructors and, 68
 learning communities and, 21
 metrics for assessing, 87–88
 types of, xix–xx

integrative thinking
 FYS/LCs and, xx
 high-impact practices and, 5–6, 6*t*
 post-college success and, xix

intellectual connections, common experiences and, 72

intellectual dexterity, embracing, 75

intentionality
 faculty, to abandon traditional methods, 182
 learning communities and, 71, 78, 91
 linked courses at UofSC and, 148
 Targeted Learning Community at Kennesaw State and, 135

interactive lectures, for FYS/LCs, 90

interdisciplinary education
 at Cabrini College, 160
 FYS/LC administration and, 46
 LC instructors and, 68

interdisciplinary understanding
 assessment of, 84
 metrics for assessing, 87–88

Inver Hills Community College (Minnesota), 31

Iowa State, 85

J

Jick, T. D., 96

job placement data, as indirect assessment, 94

Johnson, K. E., 97

Johnstone, Robert, 119
Jordan, Tina, 30
Journal of Learning Communities Research, 87

K

Kaffir Boy (Mathanane), 107
Kahn, G., 55, 64
Kallick, B., 72
Kennesaw State University
    assessing program at, 130–131
    FYS/LCs at, xxiii, 35
    implications, 135
    institution and student profile, 127
    metacognition in FYS/LCs at, 31
    program at, 127–130
    results, 131–134, 132*f*, 133*t*, 134*t*
Keup, J. R., xvi, 36
Kezar, A., 49
King, P. M., 70
Kingsborough Community College
    faculty-developed Learning
        Community Agreement of, 49
    testing FYS/LC impact at, xix
knowledge transfer to new situations,
    assessment of, 87
Konstructing Kafka: Radio Theater Proj-
    ect, at Cerritos College (California), 29
Kuh, George D., xviii, xxi, 4, 12, 34, 35, 73,
    83, 84, 86, 151, 180

L

La Verne Experience, at University of La
    Verne (California), 33–34
LaGuardia Community College Connect
    to Learning (C2L), 77
Laitinen, A., 14*n*
Lardner, E., xvi, 19, 34, 45, 75, 87–88, 92,
    94
large institutions, FYS/LCs at small insti-
    tutions vs., 23
Latino students, multiple HIPs and, 11
LCs. *See* learning communities

Leadership and Community Engage-
    ment Living-Learning Community, at
    New Century College, George Mason
    University, 33
LEAP (Liberal Education and America's
    Promise) initiative, xix, 28, 87
LEAP Campus Toolkit website, 87
learning
    disengaged, interrupting cycle of,
        63–71
    by faculty, staff, and students, 57
    Fink on kinds of, 62
    reflective practice and, 70
learning activities, assessment of, 90–91
learning beliefs, controlling, TLC student
    gains at Kennesaw State in, 132, 133*t*
learning communities (LCs). *See also*
    case studies; first-year seminar/learning
    community programs
    assessment approaches in, 85–88
    characteristics of, xv, xvi
    co-enrollment and, 25*f*
    definition of, xvi
    first-year retention, graduation rates
        and, xvii–xviii
    gold standard of, 19
    as high-impact practices, 8–10
    HIP characteristics shared by, 35*f*
    NSFYS 2012–2013 definition of,
        20–21
    powerful, 71–72
    primary role of seminar in, 26–33, 26*f*
    professional development for, 53–54
learning lab, FYS as, 22
learning outcomes
    direct assessment of, 93–94
    for FYS/LCs, 43–44
    multidimensional, 91–92
    variations in, 180
Learning Success Center (LSC), at Mt.
    Hood CC, 177
Leavitt, L. H., 32, 36

lectures
  interactive, for FYS/LCs, 90
  large enrollments and, 7
Legislative Analyst's Office, California
  community college system, 123
Lenning, O. T., 71, 72
letter-grade distribution. *See also* GPAs
  TLC pilot at Kennesaw state and,
    131–132, 132*f*
Lieberman, Devorah, 33–34
Lindsey Wilson College, 27–28
linked courses
  at Cabrini College, 160–161
  and learning communities, 91
  learning communities as, xvi, 21
  at Northern Illinois University, 152,
    153
  at University of South Carolina, 139,
    148
living-learning communities, 21, 24
  at Cabrini College, 159–162
  at New Century College at George
    Mason University, 33
  at University of San Diego, 30
  at University of South Carolina, 140,
    144
location of FYS/LC program, 43, 47
longitudinal studies, on FYS/LCs' effects,
  95–97
Love, A. G., xv
Lueddeke, G. R., 54

M
MacGregor, Jean, 19, 21, 91, 128
Malnarich, G., xvi, 19, 34, 45, 75, 92, 94
MAP-Works Fall Transition Survey, xxiii,
  153–154, 157
Master Academic Plan, at Mt. Hood, 174
Matthews, R. S., 19, 128
McClendon, S., 46
McMorrow, S., 89
McNair, T., 4, 6, 10–11

McTighe, J., 43
metacognition
  FYS as place for, 22
  Kennesaw State University's focus on,
    128, 129
  measuring, by Kennesaw State,
    130–131
  reflection in FYS/LCs and, 31
  TLC students at Kennesaw State and,
    132, 133, 133*t*
Metro College Success Program, xxiii
  assessing program at, 118–119
  cost efficiency of, 121–122, 122*f*
  implications, 123–124
  institution and student profile, 115
  program at, 115–118
  results, 119–122
  student outcomes, 119–120, 120*f*
micro-strategies
  for making learning relevant, 68
  for risk-taking, 76
millennial students, 61
minority students
  at Bronx Community College, 105,
    106–107
  at Kennesaw State University, 127
  Metro College Success Program and,
    115, 124
mission, institutional, 43–44, 54
mixed-method studies, of FYS/LCs,
  96–97
Mosupyoe, Boatomo, 30
Motivated Strategies for Learning Questionnaire (MSLQ), 130–131, 132
Mt. Hood Community College
  assessing program at, 173
  FYS/LCs at, xxiii
  implications, 177–178
  institution and student profile, 171
  program at, 171–174
  results, 174–177, 175*f*, 176*f*, 176*t*

N

National Center for Inquiry and Improvement, 119

National Collegiate Honors Council, 56

National Leadership Council for Liberal Education and America's Promise (LEAP), xix

National Learning Communities Project, Pew Charitable Trusts-funded, 23

national organizations, FYS/LC, 55–56

National Resource Center for The First-Year Experience and Students in Transition
Annual Conference on The First-Year Experience and, 55–56
on first-year seminars, xvii
FYS research by, 8
FYS/LCs studies by, 21–23
national survey, 19–20

National Summer Institute on Learning Communities, 34, 56

National Survey of First-Year Seminars (NSFYS)
2012–2013 definitions, 20–21
on first-year seminars, xv
on FYS combined with LCs, xviii, 26–33
on FYS/LC staffing, 48–49
on learning communities, 19–20

National Survey of Learning Community Programs (NSLCP), 85, 86, 88, 89

National Survey of Student Engagement (NSSE)
assessment using, 86
on Enriching Educational Experiences, 3–4
on high-impact practices, 11
as indirect assessment, 94
on students in learning communities, 10

networking, on FYS/LCs, 56

New Century College, at George Mason University, service-learning and FYS/LCs and, 32–33

new era learning communities, 10

non-tenure-track faculty, 48–49. *See also* faculty

Northern Illinois University
assessing program at, 153–154
FYS/LCs at, xxiii
implications, 156–157, 157*f*
institution and student profile, 151
program at, 151
results, 155–156, 156*t*

novice faculty. *See also* faculty
professional development for, 53–54

Nownes, Nicholas, 31

O

Oates, K. K., 32, 36

O'Donnell, K., 4, 34

Office of Student Engagement and Experiential Learning (OSEEL), Northern Illinois University, 151

online learning portal, student reflection using, 70

online registration, FYS/LCs and, 52

Oort, F. J., 53

open communication and respect, LCs and, 71

organizational theory, collaborative leadership and, FYS/LC administration and, 46

P

Pan African Learning Community, at Sacramento State University, 29–30

part-time faculty. *See also* faculty
FYS/LCs and, 48–49
professional development for, 54

Pascarella, E.T., 123

Patton, Judy, 57

pedagogy
assessment of, 90–91
inquiry-based professional development and, 54
learning communities and, xvi
shift from instruction-centered to learner-centered, 62
traditional, cycle of disengaged teaching and learning and, 63–64
peer preceptors or mentors
at Bronx Community College, 106–107, 108
at Cabrini College, 159
Kennesaw State LC and, 130
learning communities and, 9–10
peers
feedback from, 94
interactions, high-impact practices and, 13
MAP-Works on connections among, 154, 154t, 155, 155t
at University of South Carolina, 139, 146
peer-to-peer reflection protocol, 86
Peetsma, T. T., 53
Pennsylvania Child Welfare Resource Center, 160
Pennsylvania Youth Advisory Board (YAB), 160, 165
Perception and Communication in Meet the Parents, at Chandler-Gilbert Community College, 29
persistence rates. See retention; student persistence
personal gains, high-impact practices and, 5–6, 6t
Pettitt, Maureen, xxii
Pew Charitable Trusts-funded National Learning Communities Project, 23
pilots, for FYS/LCs, 45
plan, environmental scanning, development of, 42–43

PLUS (Progressive Learning in Undergraduate Studies), Northern Illinois University, 151
porous boundaries, of classroom and life experience, 73, 74f
postsemester professional development, 55
powerful learning communities, 71–72
pedagogical methods for, 73, 74f, 75–78
practical gains, high-impact practices and, 5–6, 6t
pre- and post-surveys, for LC students at Mt. Hood, 174, 176, 176t
preprofessional seminars, xvii, 20, 24t, 25, 25t
presemester professional development, 55
private institutions, FYS/LCs at public institutions vs., 23
Pro Forma Model, 119
problem-based learning
FYS/LCs and, 90
lifelong learners and, 94
processes, descriptions of, assessment and, 91
production of learning, shift from teaching to, 61–62
professional development, 53–56, 91, 152, 166, 173
program materials, systematic collection of, 91
propensity score matching, for FYS/LC studies, 96
public demonstration of competence, HIPs and, 13
public institutions, FYS/LCs at private institutions vs., 23

Q

qualitative analysis
of Bronx program, 108–109
of FYS/LCs, 96–97, 183
of Kennesaw State program, 131

on learning outcomes, 92–93
of student success data, 42
quality, HIPs and, 12, 15, 180
quantitative analysis. *See also* First-Year
Initiative Assessment
of Bronx program, 111–112
of FYS/LCs, 96, 183
of Kennesaw State program, 130–131
of student success data, 42

R
random assignment, to FYS/LCs, 95–96
R.E.A.C.H. (Recognize Each Academic
Challenge Head-on) program, Valencia
College, 27
Realizing Dreams (RD) LLC, at Cabrini
College, 159–163, 164, 166
real-world applications, HIPs and, 13
reflection. *See also* site for reflection
by Bronx CC students, 110
cycle of disengaged teaching and learning and, 69–71
by faculty, integrative teaching and, 77
by faculty and staff, 88
high-impact practices and, 13
integrative learning and, 75, 87
Kennesaw State's strategy project
assignment and, 138
metacognition in FYS/LCs and, 31
peer-to-peer protocol for, 86
technology-aided learning tools and, 76
writing assignments, relevance of
learning and, 68
registrar, 48, 51–52. *See also* enrollment
management division
relevance
cycle of disengaged teaching and learning and, 67–69
student persistence and, 92

research on FYS/LCs. *See also* National
Resource Center for The First-Year
Experience and Students in Transition;
specific surveys
longitudinal studies, 95–97
mixed-method, 96–97
national organizations and, 55–56
statistical studies, 95–96
residential environments. *See also*
learning communities; living-learning
communities
Common Courses program and, 140
peer-to-peer learning and, 139, 144
preprofessional or discipline-linked
seminars and, 25, 25*t*
resources, for FYS/LCs, 43, 45–46
retention. *See also* student persistence
at Bronx Community College,
110–111, 112
combining FYSs with LCs and, 12
Common Courses program and, 143,
143*f*, 147
faculty for FYS/LCs and, 78
FYS/LCs and, xvii–xviii
as indirect assessment, 94
learning communities and, 9
MAP-Works survey on, 154, 154*t*, 156,
156*t*
at Mt. Hood Community College, 175,
175*f*
at Northern Illinois University, 152
one-year, at Bronx Community
College, 105, 107–108
student learning outcomes and, 98
term-to-term, assessment of, 85
TLC pilot at Kennesaw state and, 131
return of investment (ROI), students on,
67
risk-taking, in teaching, 64–67, 78
Rodgers, C., 69, 70
role playing, integrative learning and, 75

S

Sacramento State University, Pan African Learning Community at, 29–30

safe environment, learning communities and, 71–72

San Francisco State University, xxiii. *See also* Metro College Success Program

Sandoval, Vanessa, 29

SAT Math scores, TLC pilot at Kennesaw State and, 131

Saunders, K. P., 71

scaffolding
    Kennesaw State LC and, 128
    Mt. Hood Community College and, 173

scheduler. *See also* registrar
    FYS/LCs and, 51–52

science careers, Kennesaw State field trips and interest in, 129

self-assessment, 87, 89, 94

self-authorship
    FLEX at University of La Verne and, 34
    reflective practice and, 70

self-directed learners, dispositions and habits of, 72

self-efficacy for learning and performance, TLC students at Kennesaw State and, 132–134, 133*t*

self-empowerment, 108

self-regulation
    measuring, by Kennesaw State, 130–131
    teaching strategies for, 129
    TLC student gains at Kennesaw State in, 132, 133*t*

self-selection, of FYS/LCs, 95

seminars. *See* first-year seminars

service-learning
    FYS/LCs and, 12, 31–33, 184
    as high-impact practice, 4
    integrative learning and, 75
    learning communities themes and topics as site for, 23

shared vision, for FYS/LCs and its institution, 43–44

sharing common readings, assignments, and projects
    as FYS/LC element, 22
    role of seminar in LC structures and, 27

significant learning experiences
    definition of, 62
    pedagogical methods for, 73, 74*f*, 75–78
    relevance and, 67

significant learning taxonomy, Fink's, 73, 74*f*

Simpson, M. L., 91

site for reflection. *See also* reflection
    FYS as, 22

Skagit Valley College, 86

skills, behaviors, and dispositions and linked-course achievements, 22
    FYS/LCs and, 28

skills seminars. *See* basic study-skills seminars

skills transfer to new situations
    assessment of, 87
    FYS/LCs and, 90

Skipper, Tracy, xxi

Sleegers, P. J., 53

Slippery Rock University, Explore, Discover, Decide Living-Learning Community at, 29

small colleges
    FYS/LCs at large institutions vs., 23
    as learning communities, 9

small group learning, integrative learning and, 75

Smith, B. L., 19, 50, 128

social justice curriculum, at Cabrini College, 159–170

social links to academic concepts, 22, 29
    relevance of learning and, 67

socioemotional support, role of seminar in LC structures and, 27

Solan, A., 71

Spanish-speaking ESL students, 105, 106–107

Spiers, Ruthanna, xxii

staff. *See also* academic affairs administration; student affairs professionals; teaching
assessment of participation and collaboration by, 85
metrics for assessing involvement by, 88

stakeholder roles, in FYS/LCs, 42–43, 47–48

standardized tests, risk-taking and, 65

A Statement on Integrative Learning (AAC&U and Carnegie Foundation), xix–xx

statistical studies, of FYS/LCs, 95–96

Stebleton, M. J., 31

steering committees, environmental scanning and, 42

Stokes, A., 71

strategic plan, institutional, FYS/LCs and, 43

Strategic Program Assessment (SPA), at Mt. Hood Community College, 174

strategy project assignment, Kennesaw State's, 129, 131, 132, 133, 134t, 137–138

structured conversation protocol, for interdisciplinary work, 87

structures. *See also* environmental scanning
assessment of, 90–91
first-year seminar, 8
formal, educational transformation and, 46
of FYS/LC within campus structure, 43
learning community, xvi, 9–10
variations in, 180

student affairs division, FYS/LCs located within, 47, 48

student affairs professionals
bridge-building with FYS/LCs and, 79
core values of integration and community and, 182

FYS/LCs and, 50–51
professional development and, 54
variations in teaching methods by, 180

student engagement
assessment of, 84
FLEX at University of La Verne and, 34
metrics for assessing, 86
participating in high-impact activities and, 4–5, 5t
student survey on perceptions of, 89

student management systems, assessment using, 85

student persistence. *See also* retention
assessment of, 85
Common Courses program and, 143, 143f
high-impact practices and, 6
Metro College Success Program and, 118, 119–120, 120f
at Mt. Hood Community College, 175
at Northern Illinois University, 152
relevance of learning and, 92

student progress and performance
assessment of, 84
metrics for assessing, 85

Student Success and Retention Campus Team, at Mt. Hood CC, 178

student success course, as extended orientation seminar, xvii

Student Success Initiative (SSI), at Mt. Hood CC, 172

Student Success Plan, at Mt. Hood CC, 174

student-centered learning, professional development and, 53

student-faculty engagement, at University of South Carolina, 139

student-faculty research, as high-impact practice, 4

students
of disengaged teaching and learning and, 63–64, 64f

faculty interactions with Common Courses participants and, 142, 143*f*, 144, 145*f*, 146

FYS/LCs and, 48, 52

multidimensional impacts on, 91–92

reflection, and epistemological perspective of, 69–70

surveys, for multilevel assessment of, 89

study abroad, as high-impact practice, 4

success, post-college

FYS/LCs and, xviii, xix–xx, 92

as indirect assessment, 94

Success Coach Advisors, at Bunker Hill CC, 51

Suhr, D., 89

Sult, L., 62–63

Survey of Students' Experiences of Learning in Learning Communities (SSELLC), 86, 94

Suskie, L., 93

sustainability, for FYS/LCs, 46

Swaner, L. E., 4, 11, 12, 90

syllabi

content analysis of, 91

faculty sharing of, 76

T

Tagg, J., 57

tandem bicycle metaphor, 70

target population

for FYS/LCs, 43

identifying, 44–45

Targeted Learning Community (TLC), at Kennesaw State, 127–138

teaching

Common Courses program, 144, 146

conclusion on, 78–79

disengaged, interrupting cycle of, 63–71

in FYS/LCs, introduction to, 61

integrative learning and, xxii

as not limited to faculty, 57

powerful learning communities, 71–72

relevance of learning and, 67–69

risk-taking in, 64–67

significant learning experiences, 61–63, 73, 74*f*, 75–78

variations in, 180

technology, integrative assignments and, 76–77

Terenzini, P. T., 123

term completion

assessment of, 85

student learning outcomes and, 98

test anxiety, 132, 133*t*

Texas A&M University-Corpus Christi, 85

Texas State University, San Marcos, Career Exploration Learning Community at, 28–29

theme-based block-scheduled courses, 9–10, 23, 24

Themed Learning Communities (TLC), Northern Illinois University, 151–153, 154, 155–157, 155*t*, 156*t*, 157*f*

Thoonen, E. E., 53

3Rs

reflection, 69–71

relevance, 67–69

risk-taking, 64–67

traditional vs. revised, 64

time, tracking students over, 88–89

time investment, for HIPs, 13

time-on task, FLEX at University of La Verne and, 34

Tinker, Toni, 30

Tinto, V., 45

transfer preparedness, Metro College Success Program and, 119–120, 120*f*

transparency, learning communities and, 71

Twitter, integrative learning and, 77

two-year institutions

Bronx Community College case study, 105–113

FYS/LCs at four-year institutions vs., 23

implementing FYS/LCs at, xxii–xxiii
Metro College Success Program,
115–126
Mt. Hood Community College case
study, 171–178

U

underserved student populations. *See also*
minority students
access to HIPs for, 15
unions, FYS/LC course loads and, 50
UNIV 101 (The University Experience),
Northern Illinois University, 151–157
University 101, University of South
Carolina, 8, 139, 148
University Housing, University of South
Carolina, 139, 141–142, 148
University of California Los Angeles'
Higher Education Research Institute, 35
University of Chicago, 7
University of La Verne (California), 30,
33–34
University of Missouri, Freshman Interest
Group at, 10
University of Nevada, Reno, Academic and
Career Exploration and FYS/LCs at, 29
University of New Mexico, 85
University of North Texas, 35
University of Northern Colorado, 89
University of Oregon, 9
University of San Diego, 30
University of South Carolina (UofSC)
assessing program at, 142–143, 143*f*
Common Courses program at, xxiii,
139–142
implications, 148
institution and student profile, 139
National Resource Center for The
First-Year Experience and Students in
Transition, 8
results, 144, 145*t*, 146–147
University 101 at, 8, 139, 148
University of Washington, 9

unlearning, risk-taking and, 66
unscripted learning, FYS/LCs and, 62–63

V

Valencia College, R.E.A.C.H. program, 27
Valid Assessment of Learning in Under-
graduate Education (VALUE) project,
87, 93
Velcoff, J., 43
videos, integrative assignments using, 76
Visher, M. G., 35, 36
Vision Learning Community, at Colorado
Northwestern Community College, 32

W

Washington Center for Improving the
Quality of Undergraduate Education
Assessing Learning in Learning
Communities, 87
assessing student engagement and, 86
on creating integrated learning
experiences in FYS/LCs, 34–35
FYS/LC studies by, 21
FYS/LCs program models and, 23
Integrative Learning Library, 29
National Summer Institute on Learning
Communities, 56
National Survey of Learning Commu-
nity Programs (NSLCP), 85
websites, internal, content analysis of, 91
Wellman, Jane, 4, 119
WICOR (writing, inquiry, collaboration,
organization, and reading), at Mt. Hood,
173
Wiggins, G. P., 43
wikis, integrative assignments using, 76
Wilcoxon Signed Rank Test, 132, 133*t*
Williams, D. A., 46
Williams, L. B., 50, 68
within-semester professional development,
55
Worcester State University, 27, 28

write-to-learn assignments, integrative
   learning and, 75
writing assignments
      ECG 100 at Cabrini and, 162–163, 165
      grounded theory for coding of, 109
      reflective, relevance of learning and, 68

Y

year-to-year persistence. *See also* student
   persistence
      assessment of, 85
Young, Dallin, xxi
Young, David, 29

About the Contributors

Lauren Chism Schmidt is director of Programs and Evaluation for the Office of Faculty Affairs and Professional Development (OFAPD) at the Indiana University School of Medicine. Prior to joining OFAPD, she was the director of Themed Learning Communities (TLCs) at Indiana University-Purdue University Indianapolis (IUPUI), where she taught in nearly 30 first-year seminar instructional teams, including online first-year seminars, stand-alone seminars for specific populations, and first-year seminars embedded in learning communities. She has served as resource faculty at the National Summer Institute of Learning Communities, cochair of the 2012 National Learning Communities Conference, and an active member of the National Learning Communities Consortium. Chism Schmidt has served as a reviewer for the *Journal of Scholarship of Teaching and Learning, Innovative Higher Education,* and the *Metropolitan Universities Journal,* in addition to a proposal reviewer for national conferences on learning communities and assessment. She holds degrees in religious studies and higher education and student affairs administration, and is currently pursuing postgraduate work in institutional research.

Lisa Dresdner is the associate academic dean for Liberal Arts/Behavioral and Social Sciences at Naugatuck Valley Community College. Prior to this position, she was director of the Center for Teaching and Learning, professor of English, and former chair of the English Department at Norwalk Community College (NCC). At NCC, she was also part of the Achieve the Dream team and project director for the Developmental Education Initiative grant, which brought learning communities to scale and resulted in increased student pass rates, retention, and persistence. She has presented at national and regional conferences on ePortfolio, integrative learning, reflective practice, and active-teaching strategies. Her interests in women's studies and autobiography resulted in her cofounding the Fairfield County Women's Center at NCC, being co-editor of *(Re)Interpretations: The Shapes of Justice in Women's Experience,* and writing multiple entries in *Encyclopedia of Women's Autobiography, Dictionary of Literary Biography,* and *Encyclopedia of Life Writing.* Dresdner's current research interests grow out of a sabbatical that focused on integrative learning and its application to student success and retention.

Liya Escalera holds an MA in English from Simmons College and an EdM in higher education from the Harvard University Graduate School of Education and is currently a doctoral student in higher education at UMASS Boston. Escalera leads Bunker Hill Community College's (BHCC) nationally recognized Learning Communities and ACE Mentor Programs. In collaboration with a cross-disciplinary faculty team, she also designed and launched BHCC's Innovative Teaching and Learning Series, a comprehensive faculty development program focused on creating a deeper foundation of the study of teaching and learning and reinforcing learner-centered pedagogies and practices.

Ashley Finley is associate vice president of academic affairs and dean of the Dominican Experience at Dominican University of California. She is also national evaluator for the Bringing Theory to Practice project, a national initiative dedicated to understanding the intersection of students' engaged learning, civic development, and well-being. Her recent publications include the edited volume *Civic Learning and Teaching* and also *Assessing Underserved Students' Engagement in High-Impact Practices* with co-author Tia McNair, in addition to several other book chapters and monographs. Prior to joining Dominican University, Finley was senior director of assessment and research at the Association of American Colleges and Universities, where she remains a senior fellow. Her work at Dominican and with colleges and universities nationally focuses on engaging faculty and staff in developing student-centered, sustainable practices that enable the advancement of student success with an emphasis on equity and evidence-based standards for improvement.

Janine Graziano is a professor of English, faculty coordinator of the Integrative Studies Program, and director of the Center for Teaching and Learning at Kingsborough Community College. Her degrees in linguistics and TESOL reflect her interest in language learning, though in the past 10 years that interest has expanded to include learning, in general, and integrative learning, in particular. As a result, much of her current focus is on working with faculty at Kingsborough and across the country to foster and assess students' integrative learning in learning communities. Recent publications include *Sustained Faculty Development in Learning Communities* and *Exploring Voice as Integration: A Direction for Assessing Student Work in Learning Communities With Composition* (both with Gabrielle Kahn), *Integrating Best Practices: Learning Communities and the Writing Center* (with Hope Parisi), and *Assessing Student Writing: The Self-Revised Essay*. Graziano has served as Resource Faculty at the National Summer Institute on Learning

Communities, offered through the Washington Center for the Improvement of Undergraduate Education at Evergreen State College and also serves on the editorial board of *Learning Communities Research and Practice.*

Michele J. Hansen is the executive director of Student Data, Analysis, and Evaluation at Indiana University-Purdue University Indianapolis, where she is responsible for institutional research, planning, and evaluation in the areas of student success, learning, and enrollment management. For the past 15 years, Hansen has also been responsible for conducting outcome assessments and program evaluations of student success initiatives, such as learning communities, first-year seminars, advising services, orientation programs, peer mentoring, success coaching models, and summer bridge programs. Her primary research interests are in the areas of learning outcomes assessment and program evaluation methods, understanding the effectiveness of interventions to enhance retention and academic success of students (applying social psychology theories to higher education), survey research methods, and incremental and fundamental change management. She maintains an active national professional profile that includes participation in national organizations, such as the Association for Institutional Research (AIR); conference presentations; and publications in journals, such as *Research in Higher Education*, *Journal of College Student Retention*, *New Directions in Institutional Research*, and the *Journal of Learning Communities Research*. She has served as external or independent program evaluator for numerous grants including Department of Education (DOE) Title V and III grants, National Science Foundation (NSF), National Institute Health (NIH), and Indiana Commission on Higher Education (ICHE) grants with funding in excess of $8 million. Hansen received her baccalaureate degree in psychology from Michigan State University and master's and doctoral degrees in social psychology from Loyola University Chicago.

Nia Haydel is the director of the Academic Center for Excellence, the Thompson/Cook Honors Program, and assistant professor of Urban Studies and Public Policy at Dillard University. Over the last 18 years, she has worked in academic affairs, enrollment management, intercultural relations, and student affairs. In her current role, she oversees the academic advising, retention, progression, and academic enrichment initiatives for first-year students, as well as the curricular and cocurricular experiences for honors students. Additionally, she has responsibilities related to Dillard University's Quality Enhancement Plan for accreditation by SACSCOC. Her most recent publication (with Steve Buddington) is "Historically Black Universities and Colleges First-Year Students/Freshpersons - Urban Students: Gender, Academic Achievement, Basic Emotional Well-Being, and Educational Outlook" in *The Journal of Education and Social Justice*. Her research interests are the responsibility of higher education to educate the community on social justice, specifically focusing on educational access, power, and privilege. Haydel earned a BS in psychology from the University of New Orleans, an MS in higher education administration from Texas A & M University, and a PhD in educational policy studies from Georgia State University.

Jean M. Henscheid is clinical assistant professor and program cocoordinator in Adult, Organizational Learning and Leadership at the University of Idaho. She has authored and edited books, monographs, and scholarly articles and consulted with campuses throughout the United States and abroad on issues related to the undergraduate experience. For several years, she served as executive editor of *About Campus* magazine and editor of the *Journal of The First-Year Experience & Students in Transition*. From 2011 to 2013, she held a visiting appointment as an associate professor of Educational Leadership and Policy at Portland State University and senior scholar with the PSU Division of Student Affairs. Prior to that appointment, Henscheid was a faculty member and director of general education at the University of Idaho. She had previously led learning community programs and taught undergraduate and graduate courses in leadership and research methods at Washington State University. From 1999 through 2001, she served as associate director for research and publications for the National Resource Center for The First-Year Experience and Students in Transition at the University of South Carolina and has remained a fellow with the Center since 2001.

George D. Kuh is adjunct research professor at the University of Illinois and Chancellor's Professor Emeritus of Higher Education at Indiana University (IU). He directs the National Institute for Learning Outcomes Assessment and was the founding director of IU's Center for Postsecondary Research and the National Survey of Student Engagement (NSSE), as well as related instruments for law students, beginning college students, and faculty. Kuh has about 400 publications and has made several hundred presentations on topics related to institutional improvement, college student engagement, assessment strategies, and campus cultures. He has consulted with more than 375 institutions and organizations in the United States and abroad. His recent books include *Using Evidence of Student Learning to Improve Higher Education* (2015), *Ensuring Quality and Taking High-Impact Practices to Scale* (2013), *High-Impact Practices* (2008), and *Student Success in College: Creating Conditions That Matter* (2005, 2010). Kuh's work has been recognized with awards from the American College Personnel Association, American Educational Research Association, Association for

Institutional Research, Association for the Study of Higher Education, Council for Adult and Experiential Learning, Council of Independent Colleges, National Association of Student Personnel Administrators (NASPA), and National Center on Public Policy in Higher Education as well as 10 honorary degrees.

Maureen A. Pettitt holds a PhD in education from Claremont Graduate University and has been involved in education her entire career. She owned a flight school and air charter business, held a tenured faculty position, and chaired the aviation program at California State University, Los Angeles, and served as a research faculty member for Western Michigan University's aviation program. Pettitt also served as chief scientist for Human Factors at the Federal Aviation Administration in Washington, DC, where she managed the agency's $25 million human factors research and grants program. Since 1998, she has been the director of Institutional Research at Skagit Valley College where she has been responsible for institutional research, planning, and outcomes assessment. She also collaborates with the Washington Center for Improving the Quality of Undergraduate Education on the development and administration of the national Online Survey of Students' Experiences of Learning in Learning Communities. Pettitt has assisted a variety of organizations across the country with their work on strategic planning, institutional effectiveness, curriculum development, integrative learning and assessment, and grant development and evaluation. Her publications and presentations include a variety of topics, such as the development and assessment of learning communities.

Tracy L. Skipper is assistant director for publications for the National Resource Center for The First-Year Experience and Students in Transition at the University of South Carolina. An accomplished editor and writer, Skipper edited (with Roxanne Argo) *Involvement in Campus Activities and the Retention of First-Year College Students* (2003), wrote *Student Development in the First College Year: A Primer for College Educators* (2005), and served as managing editor of the five-volume series, *The First-Year Seminar: Designing, Implementing, and Assessing Courses to Support Student Learning and Success* (2011-2012). Most recently, she co-authored *Writing in the Senior Capstone: Theory & Practice* with Lea Masiello. She holds degrees in psychology, higher education, American literature, and rhetoric and composition. In addition to her writing and editorial work, she has served as a student affairs administrator, taught writing at the college level, and presented writing workshops for higher education professionals. Skipper has presented on the application of student development theory to curricular and cocurricular contexts and what national datasets suggest about the organization and administration of high-impact educational practices. Her research interests include the application of cognitive-structural development to composition pedagogy and the use of writing in first-year seminars and senior capstone courses.

Ruthanna Spiers is an academic counselor for the Academic Counseling and Advising Center at Auburn University. Prior to serving in this role, she coordinated the learning community program on Auburn's campus, growing the program by 200% from its pilot phase. During that time, she also served as a faculty-in-residence and cocoordinator of the peer instructor program for first-year seminars. She has served as an invited presenter on building learning communities for community colleges across the state of Alabama and was cofounder of the Southeast Learning Communities Consortium. She serves on the editorial board for *Learning Communities Research and Practice* and is an active member of the National Academic Advising Association. She holds degrees in psychology, counseling, and higher education administration. Spiers has presented on curriculum integration, learning community development, academic counseling and case management, and parental involvement in college. Her research interests include the use of strategic case management to increase student persistence and retention.

Dallin George Young is the assistant director for research, grants, and assessment at the National Resource Center for The First-Year Experience and Students in Transition. He coordinates all the research and assessment endeavors of the National Resource Center and facilitates and disseminates three national surveys: National Survey of First-Year Seminars, National Survey on Sophomore-Year Initiatives, and the National Survey of Senior Seminars/Capstone Courses. He oversees a number of research collaborations and grant opportunities between the Center and the national and international higher education community as well as across the University of South Carolina (UofSC) campus. He coordinates the distribution of the Paul P. Fidler Research Grant, a competitive national grant that recognizes the development of research investigating the experiences of college students in transition. He is also an active member on the Planning, Assessment, and Innovation Council at UofSC. Before joining the National Resource Center, Young completed doctoral internships in the Office of the Associate Vice President of Student Affairs at Georgia Gwinnett College and in the Department of Student Affairs Assessment at the University of Georgia. He has held professional positions in student housing at Dixie State College of Utah, UofSC, and California College of the Arts. Young's research interests focus on learning outcomes of postsecondary professional preparation, peer leadership, the impact of professional standards in higher education, and assessment. This research agenda has afforded him the opportunity to produce scholarly publications and presentations at numerous national and international conferences.